Everything You E

Not so much from lost to found but rather from perfectly locatable in the Cotswolds to utterly baffled in the American wilderness.

Person Irresponsible

www.mlconaquad.com

If you've a lot on your mind, go for a walk...

To respect the anonymity of my fellows I have changed their names, including trail names, except when to do so would fundamentally destroy the point. I have also altered various personal details so that those individuals may continue to wander along without fear of judgement or identification. Except Jeff. He wanted his name kept.

This story is told from the best of my knowledge and recollection, relying on the diary I typed out each and every night, and from the daydreams that kept my mind active as I mooched along. Any mistakes I make are mine. All mine.

Cover photographs kindly supplied by Jeff Wright.

TABLE OF CONTENTS

Map

CANADA

Washington

Oregon

505.8 miles

455.6 miles

California

The Sierra

Kennedy
Meadows
South

Acton
KOA

Idyllwild

Yosemite

Death
Valley

Paradise

MEXICO

1692.7 miles

Chapter one

Why me?

There's a photograph of me I can just about bear to look at. The concrete monument I stood alongside is five foot-wide pillars of varying heights sufficient to allow people to climb up and strike a pose - often a high-five or a thumbs up with an accompanying beaming grin masking who knows what levels of trepidation. Me, having all the balancing skills of a drunken wombat, sensibly chose to remain firmly attached to the ground, my elbow casually rested on the third lowest of the columns. My photographer, a fellow hiker who called herself Fortitude, took the mandatory starting photograph of me at the commencement of this monumental act of idiocy. Looking at the picture now, I was undeniably fat. My upper abdomen billowed against my top; my upper thighs ballooned out well past my hips. There was a significant number of chins too: a result of an intense training programme which mostly consisted of driving to a nearby cafe and eating cake. Lots and lots of cake. Chocolate preferably. These 'intense' preparations also saw me devouring multiple dinners as if I was already walking twenty-something miles per day, rather than the shlep from the couch to the fridge which was my actual training regime. It wasn't as if I didn't have weight to lose before I began to eat in earnest, but any semblance of willpower vanished now I knew I'd be burning it off come March.

This lunacy was conceived the previous October, a day when I fully committed to hiking from the concrete monument at the Southern Terminus on the Mexican border to the Northern Terminus on the Canadian border. There an identical monument sits, albeit that one is made from wood. Separating them is a tiny path of two thousand, six hundred and fifty miles. I confess it is stretching the truth to say I made the decision to be fully committed. In reality it was more like a series of happenstances that swept me into this utterly insane adventure. But before I explain the why and the how, there are a few things one might find useful to know.

I have sometimes heard people, like myself, refer to the trail that links Canada to Mexico as the Pacific *Coast* Trail. They are, quite frankly, ill-informed and plain wrong. It is patently not a quick hop, skip and a jump along California's golden beaches, picking up a

1

deep bronzed tan in Santa Barbara, before heading home a short while after. It is, *I learned*, located several hundred miles inland, deep within the wilderness, on the crests of the highest ranges of the Sierra Nevada and Cascade mountains. If it was not arduous enough being that bloody long, they also made it that bloody high as well: a fact that I remained livid about almost every time I ran out of steam on a steep uphill.

Ordinarily, if such a thing existed for me, I was acclimatised to living at four-hundred feet above sea level. Arriving at a tiny dot of a town named Campo, near the Mexican border, idling at around three-thousand feet above the nearest beach, practically induced the headiness of altitude sickness there and then. The nearby southern monument is where the vast majority of thru-hikers begin walking the Pacific *Crest* Trail. All heading in a good northerly direction that seemingly causes one to spend a considerable amount of time going west or east. I could only assume this was to elongate the trip as much as possible. Either that or it is to avoid Death Valley, I'm not quite certain. Probably both.

This route is now infamous because of its association with the book, *Wild*, and the eponymous Hollywood film. It is Cheryl Strayed's coming of age story of a wild-but-technically-no-longer-a-child adult who lost her way following the death of her mother four years prior. It involved a lot of sex, some heroin, and a divorce. To come to terms with it all, she found herself walking one thousand miles of the PCT, stopping to sniff desert sage here and there. It was the archetypal journey from lost to found, whilst following a well-mapped track and avoiding some of the truly horrible bits of the PCT like the Sierra mountains, which the ill-informed and plain wrong call the *Sierras*. I learnt that along the way too.

These kinds of expeditions, I assumed, were for the young and the fit, of which I was neither. Being two decades older, at forty-six, I figured I'd need at least twice the distance in order to find whatever it was I was looking for, although I hadn't got the faintest idea what that could be. I really couldn't even tell you why I was doing it in the first place. Enough people had asked me that I'd had ample opportunity to come up with a pithy reason but sadly that reason eluded me.

Most people who know me suspected it was another one of my geographicals: an act of up-sticking and off-sodding whimsically in the futile hope of finding everlasting happiness elsewhere. But this didn't feel like a geographical: for one, I was too plump to be running away from my problems; for two, I loved living where I was, and for three, I really couldn't be bothered moving once again. I had friends and everything, responsibilities, duties and a cat. I also had a bank account that really didn't need me to bugger off for six months.

And yet, there was a compulsion, a pull or seemingly unquellable urge, to follow in her footsteps - perhaps if only to find the promised peace at the end of the rainbow. An urge I'd ultimately succumbed to and which now culminated in this very photograph of me standing bewildered alongside the concrete monolith marking the commencement of a trail I had never heard of seven months previously. The story has no true beginning, but the blame I can lay at the door of an incredibly good friend called Bex. She had lost her driving licence following the acquisition of a brain tumour, and so along with others, I became one of her unofficial taxi drivers, ferrying her between hospital appointments and coffee shops. When our conversations ran dry, we'd resort to recommending recent films and books that had filled our time. The standing joke between us was anything she deemed riveting was a cast iron guarantee I would despise it.

I pooh-poohed Bex's entreaties to watch *Wild*. Watching other people exercise is traumatic and yet Bex persisted. In the end, I conceded with the threat of cooking dinner for her and her fiancé, for whom I was 'best-manning' at their forthcoming wedding. And that is what happened. The food, a buffet of hot and cold salads, was, *of course*, ample and delicious. I think most people know not to argue with the chef. Salsa, though, probably wasn't the best choice of accompaniments as the opening scenes introduced us to Cheryl's ketchup-covered de-socked foot, raw with infected blisters and abdicated toenails.

My innate curiosity bought me the book. Thank God they rewrote the horse scene for the film. Alas, Cheryl's exit at the Bridge of the Gods led me to purchase six more books on the PCT in rapid succession. I then added *A Walk in the Woods* and *The Way* to my 'Recently watched' category on Sky and that was that: I had already begun manically hiking back and forth to the refrigerator to replenish my snacks. The longing would not dissipate. Lounging in the bath watching YouTube videos of the Insta-wannabe-famous chart their own thru-hikes probably did not assist in the slightest.

That I am also an alcoholic who made this decision sober is quite possibly the proof that one can be more insane after getting into recovery than before, or at least, remain every bit as obsessional. By that I mean, if I had been asked why I was doing it and I'd answered, "Well, it seemed like a good idea at the time," and that time had been with two bottles of wine in me, then all of this would make a great deal more sense, but I haven't had a drink for several years. Perhaps because I am one of *those,* I seek out podcasts of other alcoholics to listen to as I go about my business, many of them I locate on YouTube. That is why on a wet, windy October lunchtime, I found myself soaking in my bath casually scrolling through videos looking for something to distract my inner turbulence. As I battled past the stream of adverts for rehabs and whisky, a consequence of YouTube's warped algorithms, I found myself staring at a thumbnail entitled 'How to apply for a PCT permit'.

Now like many alkies, I am a 'ready, fire, *aim*' type person. Spontaneity is something I do so well. Likewise, I am adroit at demolishing my best laid plans without any due diligence whatsoever. Fortunately, the application process is more of a pot-luck lottery and takes place around six months prior to the overall trail conditions becoming accessible. This delay ensures one is left with an excess of time to dwell on the proposal. Moreover, hiking the PCT takes a considerable amount of preparation. It is simply not that easy to abdicate from life for half a year, quitting jobs, houses, social-life, and giving one's children up for adoption if need be, and so on. Despite all that, there is quite a large sub-section of society who want to do exactly that, whether it is to do a thru-hike or travel around the world in a dinghy. We can't all be certifiable.

That said, *Wild* is held up as the single biggest reason that attempts to hike America's third longest path, although officially the world's longest continuous trail, have reached burgeoning levels in recent years. This popularity means that permits are now formally issued and there are far more disappointed applicants than successful ones. Interestingly though, I learnt amongst the thru-hiking community, I appear to be the only one who has watched the film. It is simply just not *de rigueur* to admit it. That faux pas outed me as being different from the rest from the get-go. The perennial oddball on the side feigning indifference, desperate to fit in, yet always seeming to find myself standing adrift. I am, and have always been, a bit of a psychedelic wallflower: a head girl type who keeps getting caught smoking behind the bike shed. There are times I like this about myself and other times when I loathe it.

But back at this point in the proceedings, soaking away in my bath, I knew none of the bureaucratic requirements of just getting onto the PCT. Undeniably though, that particular YouTube star's video had inadvertently alerted me to the fact that permit-issuing day is held just two days a year. For Northbounders, or NOBOs to use the lingo, the best chance of getting a permit is on the October application date. It was just really peculiar timing that the process would commence at six o'clock, UK time, that very evening and last only for a couple of hours. I exited the bath at wet-neck-speed and found myself completing a number of different on-line courses in record time and naked. The first about leaving no trace when visiting the wilderness, merely footprints. Mine were still drying on the carpet stairs. The second on how to make and put out a fire safely. This was demonstrated by a ranger with a long-handled shovel, something I didn't think most hikers, long-distance or otherwise, carried with them.

Serendipity had thrown her final dice and I had my permit within the hour. I had a start date of March 24th, not too bad, and not too far off the ideal starting date of April 15th. I celebrated this by joining various PCT Facebook groups because I was now *one of them* before reading the multitude of posts from people who weren't going to be *one of us*. About three and a half thousand people have a crack at the PCT each year, with around twenty percent getting to the antithetical terminus - although actual statistics vary. With that level of drop-out, voluntary or involuntary, there is much debate around whether the system is fair, or indeed, safe. But that is all part of the politics of such a venture, none of which I cared for at that moment in time. I declared myself an asylum seeker of the trail and now all I required was refugee status from the US Embassy in the form of a visitor visa.

The following day, I popped over to see the betrothing friends, letting them in on the bad news: I wasn't going to be best-manning at their wedding after all; instead, I was off to walk the Pacific *Coast* Trail. I did say I was horribly sorry about that. Two

5

days later, they said I was going to be best-manning after all, and they were horribly sorry about that too. They'd brought the wedding forward from late March to November, so it was best if I focused on writing my speech. With that, we all threw ourselves into wedding plans. Or rather, they did, I romped on with my trail preparations, which as I have already outlined, involved a lot of eating, a bit of tent buying, as well as the purchasing of a rucksack, a sleeping mat and sleeping bag. These are the so-called 'big four', of which weight seems to be the major criteria: a factor that seemingly passed me by as I opted instead for the 'bargain' consideration. In my excitement, I purchased various other items I thought would be just wonderful to go long-distance hiking with, such as a flask, an umbrella, and a cushion for sitting on. I envisaged myself lounging around drinking coffee and inhaling the breath-taking views, being all wistful and suchlike.

Indeed, many coffees were imbibed as I plotted and researched all things PCT. Once or twice a week Bex and I shared our notes of the latest developments in our respective adventures: her wedding and my paper trailing. Within a few months I had a new passport; a US visa and a permit to trek into Canada, which after many failed attempts was issued, complete with a blue-pen correcting the spelling of my name - I'd got it absurdly wrong. Bex would tell me nothing of her wedding dress, but I'd bore her senseless with my choice of clothing. I had something to keep the sun out, the ticks off and the warmth in at night, plus a change just in case it rained. I anticipated I'd be wearing the same attire throughout the entirety so I needed something that could cope with desert, mountains and forests as well as spring, summer and autumn. After Bex returned from her honeymoon, she presented me with a sleeping bag liner, a pair of calf-high gaiters and three carabiners. I had to ask her what the gaiters were.

Bex died in early February, sixty-eight days after the best day of her life. We had both lived our lives fast and hard, and she departed at the happiest time of hers. I cannot say her passing inspired me to seek out memes to post on Facebook of life being too short. Nor did it birth any urge to tattoo YOLO on a body part, the modern day 'carpe diem' that has somehow morphed into persuading one to be the biggest idiot possible and damned be the consequences. It is, after all, the raison d'etre of many a heavy drinker on their way

6

to full-blown alcoholism. These aren't always my sentiments; although I swore many times along the way that if Bex wasn't already dead, I'd probably have killed her for being the person who planted the seed in my head. All the same, I remain ever grateful to her for encouraging me to proceed when doubts bubbled within, both before I left England, and very much when on the trail. As Bex discovered her imminent demise was on the horizon, never once did she ask, 'why me?' Only, 'why not me?'

In the end, it all comes down to 'why not me?' Mine, however, is much less of a story from lost to found, but rather one of previously locatable and now utterly baffled. This is not just about a hike between Mexico and Canada, but rather a recognition of everything you ever taught me as I listened to podcasts from my fellow alcoholics day after laborious day.

****

The walk of shame

I accepted I was the insane one until the rest of the world started going to hell in a handbag. I also wondered if I was the only one who had to ask Google what the difference was between a pandemic and an epidemic. The former, it transpires, is the latter with a passport. For a while, I was just glad that we had something to conjugate that wasn't bloody *Brexit*.

A day previously, President Trump had announced a ban on visitors from Europe, apparently oblivious to the fact that the UK hadn't actually *brexited* yet. More to the point, even if we had, this would not be changing our geographical location. For now, though, Britons could still travel to the US. Less than twenty-four hours later someone must have mentioned that we too had the Corona Virus, as they were calling it, and inevitably we were given a thorough banning as well. In that time, I had slipped through immigration, oddly finding myself queuing up behind the YouTube star whose video had alerted me to getting a PCT permit. The immigration officer asked if we were together but just in case he was masquerading as a drug mule, or had a temperature, I said no. That it was also the truth is also a valid point.

There is a moment in one's life when one realises one is careering out of control, and I have had many such moments. When I first got sober, people told me, very oddly, that the path narrows and life was now about going in a good orderly direction. This observation conjured up the notion of queuing lemmings. I resigned to nod and smile at their prophecy, but I particularly welcomed the idea of launching myself off into an eternal abyss as I reached the top of the queue. I felt it was something that could not come soon enough. Sobriety, I supposed, was to tame the unpredictable firecracker that I was, someone who never knew what was going to happen next, nor indeed how I was going to react to it. I was someone who never really had a life's purpose beyond: 'the plan is: there is no plan.'

I most definitely didn't rush onto the road of recovery screeching, "Woo-hoo! What a ride!" Rather I toppled in despising myself just as much as everyone around me, feeling pretty hopeless and helpless. Now I was a few years down the road, the path had truly narrowed. Up until the point I found myself standing before the monument, I believed people were talking metaphorically. As I took my first tentative steps around the trailhead, life had become infinitely literal: there is indeed a noticeably clear and distinct path to follow as one embarks on a trip into the wilderness. Moreover, when going knowingly into the unknown, woe betide anyone who goes off-piste because it is simply not following the *Leave No Trace* principles. Besides which, one gets lost very quickly and no one wants to do pointless miles when Canada is such a long way away.

I had expected to see crowds. At least fifty people have a permit to start each day, and others might have shorter distance permits too, but there was just me and my fellow hiker, Fortitude, and our driver, a volunteer 'trail angel' who had picked us up from a hotel in San Diego. Fortitude had lunged into the vehicle, physically bagging the passenger seat, leaving me to lie in the back of the small delivery van on a single thin mattress. Our trail angel, when not doing random acts of kindness, was a 'van lifer', her well-used vehicle also doubled as her home. As we headed out of the megalopolis, it was apparent our driver relied on the engine running to re-charge her phone each day. Now with uncurtailed power, her eyes darted between her smartphone transmitting *Family Fortunes* and the asphalt. She swerved with hysteria when the contestant answered, "September" to the question, "Which month are babies born?" I gripped the edges of her mattress and tried not to judge, or comment, or have any opinion whatsoever. Rather, I told myself to focus on things to be grateful for and be in the moment and appreciate the power of now and all I have survived, such as every junction, traffic light system, highway and overtake.

An hour and a bit later, relief mixed with fear coursed through my system. Standing at the front of the terminus I could quietly admit, "Woo-hoo! What a ride!" and be thrilled the worst was over. I thanked the angel, and the Gods of road safety, for my safe arrival at the beginning of my journey. With that I passed the first of probably hundreds, and regrettably not thousands, of trail markers: small triangular signs with rounded tips affixed to a post or tree trunk. A single fir tree stands as the centrepiece afore a teal backdrop of snow-capped mountains, all framed within a white border. These, the span of a hand, would be an enormous source of comfort along the way, when I could spot them. In this covid-era I knew not to touch it, even though for the most part, I still privately dismissed the covid-worriers as people who needed to get out more and get a life and all that. But if signs could talk, I imagined this one would rate each hiker's chances of seeing the last of the trail markers up in Washington, giving less than one in five of us the nod. I have no doubt it would have visibly shook itself into smithereens on the sight of me.

I glanced back at the infamous wall that keeps the marauding Americans out of Mexico. It was then nothing more than flimsy sheets of rusty metal spray-painted with yellow numbers and topped with two rows of tangled barbed wire that went on for as far as the eye could see. I once lived in a house with a chain-link fence that looked more robust. It was a cool day, not a burning furnace as I feared the desert would be. There was a trickle of breeze, although the place was otherwise quiet bar the helicopters overhead purring back and forth trying to spot the deluge of illegal immigrants that Trump believed swamped these parts. The area was empty save for the sandy metre-wide trail forging a path through the desert scrub. Unlike how one might imagine a desert, this one had a substantial amount of dull green foliage. Largely spiky brush, interspersed with aloe, spindly cacti and the fatter prickly pear, as well as of course the jumping cholla - a cactus that likes to attach itself to any passerby. The place is a haven for the paranoid: everything is truly out to get you.

Fortitude, confident about completing twenty miles and getting to a comfortable camping spot, charged off. Alone, I completed the first mile, denoted by a sign predictably graffitied with the pithy quip: only 2,652 miles to go! I tiptoed in her footsteps, already providing a comfort that I was indeed going in a forward trajectory, albeit not matching her considerable stride. I was mostly staggering - a veritable walk of shame revealing my lack of finesse as a hiker. My body was spectacularly failing to absorb this sudden addition of a large hump. I had never before carried a rucksack as heavy as this: at least the weight of a four-year-old child, although significantly less wiggly. It impaired my ability to walk in a straight line. Already I was learning I didn't need a drink to walk like a drunk.

Nor had I ever been hiking with a backpack containing overnight requirements such as a tent. I'd always presumed a hike to be something one does before returning to a cottage, a hot chocolate, and an even hotter bath. It wasn't too late to go back. Embarrassing, yes, having to explain to people that really it wasn't for me, but I could move towns, cut my hair, change my name, re-fashion my clothing and pretend to be someone with some sense. I could confirm it by telling myself, "this time I'll be different," which is what I've told myself at every fresh start that I have ever had. I've had many and too many passports to prove it.

Perhaps that's how I perfected the art of comparing my insides to your outsides: you seem to live your life purposefully; you have a sense of belonging; you don't need to go on long walks to find yourself; you already know what you're doing. I don't know who 'you' are; but the demons that lurk within me seem to know you all the better if I've never met you. I began the second mile berating myself for not taking the time to actually wonder what a thru-hike would really be like. The snakes, the bears, droughts and snow, the living in a tent, the pooping in the woods, or rather rocky outcrops, and the isolation from the world at large. All these things make for marvellous TV, but they are also the reason why living in a solid-brick house with high-speed broadband is the far more popular option.

The last time I was this bewildered and terrified, I was navigating a cobbled street as I slunk towards a small chapel which hosted a meeting of *Alcoholics Anonymous*, swamped with shame and humiliation. No one wants to be one of *those*, and I wasn't. I just had a drinking problem that wasn't so terrible that I couldn't stop but I needed just a little bit of support and encouragement to have a break from the stuff. That is what I told myself after my second successive failure at *Dry January*. I'd opted to do it in February on account of it only having twenty-eight days. In 2016, I conceded that I could stop, but couldn't stay stopped even for an entire seven days. At least, not seven consecutive days in any case. Although I was certain I could manage seven days out of the entire thirty-one days of January definitely, absolutely, unquestionably. Slowly, I had come to a vague realisation that something always happened that had me reaching for a bottle. Like the mailman delivering a parking ticket. That was bad enough, but I was too fretful to face the post for much of the time, so much so, that I had left it to fester in the corner for so long the fine had trebled. I feared suffocating in agoraphobia almost as much as I feared people. Sometimes I drank because there was nothing on TV to dovetail my mood: indifferent. If I was in a rare jolly mood, I needed enlightenment. Sometimes I'd justify having a drink because I tripped over the cat, but most of the time I had to find the little sod in order to trip over him. I never drank before six in the evening but many a time I wished my afternoons would evaporate.

In truth, my biggest reason for going to AA was fear. Fear that I'd end up homeless; with nothing to my name other than a sleeping bag and a few token possessions. I started to introduce myself with just my first name like they did, rapidly followed with a cough to avoid saying *that bit.* Then soon enough I started saying *that bit* too, not because I wanted to fit in, although I did, but it was more to spare hurting their feelings. Eventually, I conceded that I was indeed one of those. In return they welcomed me, and told me my path would narrow, that I'd learn to go in a good orderly direction. Some even promised I'd live a life beyond my wildest dreams. As I embarked on my third mile, I realised I was now walking my nightmare. I was truly homeless having given up my house. Worse, what few possessions I did have weighed a bleeding ton.

****

Sticks and stones won't break my bones, but names hurt

My name is Person Irresponsible, and you can call me a Cov-idiot. In real life I have a real name - one of those that comes into fashion every second generation or so, which pretty much guarantees a thorough teasing in the playground if, like me, you are of the wrong generation. In my case, there were accompanying hand gestures and intonation that came with my moniker, but currently it is one that the current crop of childrearers seem to adore.

Thru-hikers don't use their real names, not after the first few weeks ordinarily, as trail names have been bestowed. Usually, they are a result of some quirk or behavioural defect, and that's why there's quite a few Kitchen Sinks, Wrong Ways and No Sporks knocking around. Others self-select their names, avoiding the embarrassment of having to introduce oneself as, "Hello, I'm Humongous Smorgasbord," which makes for a wonderful ice-breaker but ultimately reduces one to "HS" as one tires of explaining how that came to be.

At mile three, I introduced myself as Person Irresponsible to a tall, lanky and incredibly delicious-looking Australian who'd bounded up to me. *"Personally Responsible?"* He chimed back. It was the first of a gazillion times I had to enunciate my irresponsibility less personally. I had met my second thru-hiker, something we already called ourselves, even though neither of us had thru-hiked anything in our lives before.

Perspiration leached through my long-sleeved top despite my putting on deodorant first thing, binning the remainder in my quest to reduce the pack's weight. Sweltering under the midday sun, little trickles of underarm sweat began their quest south. "I'm bloody freezing," said the Aussie in his shorts, t-shirt, fleece and puffy jacket. We walked together another couple of miles, I say walk, it was more he sauntered along with his long legs and athletic demeanour, and I staggered, sweated and swore before announcing at the fifth mile that I needed to collect water. I didn't, but the nearby stream came with some very fetching flat-topped boulders to sit on. I didn't want to admit that I was already beaten by the trail, my hip blazing in agony. The yet unnamed Australian strode off with ease.

I remembered now, somewhat inconveniently, that I had scoffed at the young Cheryl Strayed's measly first-day outing of six miles through the desert. Now my very own backpack, notably lighter and smaller, was shaming me to a standstill. Removing it, my limbs moonwalked me to the smooth-topped boulder, as if I was bouncing around in slow motion. Despite opting for the most popular-sized rucksack, holding nearly sixty litres, and forking out a fortune for its ultralight properties, I had negated it all by not packing more discernibly. A man filtering water from the creek mentioned it was due to rain later, and if it came earlier, did I really want my sleeping bag to be attached to the outside of the rucksack? "Only novices do that," he said, and that's how I discovered I was a walking billboard of idiocy.

Ultimately, I made it to the eighth mile. At least, I thought that's where I was, but I couldn't be certain. I was using Guthook, a navigational aid which indicates mileage, water sources, good spots to camp, and best of all: places of interest. These are very often 'gate' or 'fence', but sometimes one gets lucky with 'cliff'. I had no idea where I was exactly. Most people have a blue dot to depict their location, but I had no such thing, because in the two days I'd had to get myself organised before hitting the trail, not only did I spectacularly fail to obtain a US sim card, but I had also acquired a couple of blisters trying to do so. It was a salutary lesson that there are many differences between shopping in the US and the UK. Adamant I had to buy a mobile phone for a pay-as-you-go sim, the store manager informed me that I must set up myself back at my hotel, then ring their customer helpline if I had any problems. The helpline informed me that the manager should have set it up. Back to the Verizon shop I went, where he then extracted a further sixty dollars to bring it to life. Still, it didn't work. He then regrettably informed me it was store policy they would refund less than fifty percent of the purchase, which was now around four hundred dollars. I rang my bank, using Verizon's landline, to cancel all the transactions. This wasn't actually possible, but the agent suggested I say frighteningly big words like Financial Ombudsman and Fraudulent Recovery Unit out loud. I made it sound as if she was in the process of whacking an exceptionally large red button to alert someone, somewhere, that a substantial crime was underway in a remote corner of San Diego, and we should expect the SWAT team to descend forthwith. The manager fell for it and shortly after I got all my money back. Duly reversing all the charges, the manager whined that I needn't have rung the bank to report him. Still, I like gullible people, largely because I can be one myself. But the day's shopping had still left me phoneless, vulnerable and with two holes in my right foot. Nonetheless, I was grateful because the experience gave me plenty to bond with hikers, as we shared calamitous Verizon stories to while away miles in the coming months.

To complicate matters further, several weeks prior to my departure, my UK mobile phone had taken to teleporting my location: only a street or so in the wrong place, but occasionally an entire village. Nonetheless, I was never where I was supposed to be. Momentarily, I switched off Airplane Mode and restarted the phone to see if moving to America had fixed the problem. I was inundated with texts from people reckoning I must be gutted about the travel ban that had just been imposed. My failure to obtain my location cost me a small fortune.

Whether or not I had made eight miles or eighteen, my legs buckled. By eating some of my supplies, I reasoned I could lighten my pack by a few hundred grams at the very least. I set up my tent, the Belisha Beacon, for only the second time. The first time had been in my former garden, an acid test to detect any latent hiking talents. I had dubbed it the Belisha Beacon on account it was a very striking luminous orange. I'd been drawn to its novel pyramid shape, convincing myself the colour alone would frighten away the wildlife, with the added benefit that I'd never knowingly lose it when I'd have to toddle off for a pee. Once erected, which proved relatively straightforward, using just one of my hiking poles, and all of my tent stakes, I pulled out the heaviest of my dinner meals: the 'suitable for vegetarians', and most popular freeze-dried hiker ready-meal of 2019 - Pad Thai. I'd bought three of them. I poured in the hot water, waited for the necessary rehydrating period before diving in.

Whoever named it Pad Thai was a jeffing liar.

****

It doesn't rain in the desert

As dusk emerged, dimming out the day, I sat forlornly inside my tent silently willing someone to set theirs nearby. One by one I'd

14

pick out the sounds of footprints coming closer. On occasion, they'd pause to inspect the Belisha Beacon then mutter something about an incoming storm before pottering off as if the light wasn't fading at all.

I had always secretly been afraid of sleeping solo until I got to my early thirties. By then, I'd learnt booze could knock me out at night. I've always presumed my nervous insomnia to be a legacy of boarding schools, where we'd been packed to the rafters in bunk beds in freezing cold stately homes. They are places where parents pay a fortune for other people to terrify us into submission, run as they are by matrons and sirs barking and barracking us into responsible adulthood. I had detested it. For several years, I begged to change to a nicer one: one that was less prissy 'all-girls school', a place more suitable for the wilder, restless little person that I was rather than the ladylike, wifely material the school, and my parents, aspired for me to be.

Five years later my parents relented, and I moved schools ready to start my GCSE years. The new one still had bunk beds and an absence of privacy, but the dorms were considerably smaller. I suppose I got used to never being alone, although that feeling of being lonely was all-pervading even then. I had friends but I had never truly connected with another human being, not even the man I'd go on to marry. Thrilled when this lover insisted on moving in quickly, any doubts I had over-ridden by the clinical advantages of having someone there. It meant I could sleep in the dark, not having to leave a hall light on so I could spy whatever non-existent intruder had filtered through the three-inch steel door that kept me apart from the staircase on the third floor of the apartment block. I married him under the delusion that never again would I need to worry about someone abseiling through the high-rise window to raid my home. I always suspected the *Milk Tray* man wasn't actually bringing chocolates. At least, not for the likes of people like me.

The morning after the night before saw me delighted to find sleep had eluded me not one jot on my first full night in the wilderness. I had gone out like the proverbial light just as the proverbial light went on to illuminate another part of the globe. My mid-life bladder waking me twice to pee, I presumed like the Pad Thai, I had over-rehydrated my body. Without street lighting, the night sky glowed all of its own accord making the incursions into a nearby bush relatively straightforward. The predicted rain splattering across the nylon fabric woke me at two-ish and I dozed on and off until dawn. I lay there relieved that the ominous storm had gathered but then passed by without a roar or a strike to its name.

The good news ended at daybreak. The Belisha Beacon had manifested its very own climate - drenching my sleeping bag. If I thought my pack heavy the previous day, a soggy sleeping system, and three-quarters of a no-longer-dehydrated Pad Thai meal were training me today to be the *World's Strongest Woman*. The only way I could reduce the weight of the pack was to eat more of the Pad Thai for breakfast. Two mouthfuls washed down with a cup of coffee and I was beaten for a second count. Compounding my problems, I'd made porridge too. For the first time in my life, I found the porridge equally as repulsive, despite it once being a boarding school staple. All those years of being coerced into eating whatever we were given because of starving orphans in Africa, and the moment I most needed that much-honed skill, it had vanished. Discarding inedible meals for the wildlife is strongly discouraged, lest we habituate them. No one needs a coyote knocking on their tent demanding breakfast at sunrise. I packed them up to tackle later.

My ample arse would have to just eat itself. Already stiffened from the previous day, I old-lady groaned bending down to dismantle the tent, stuffing the whole swampy mess into its bag, which had mysteriously shrunk overnight. I gathered up my plastic poncho, which doubled as a ground sheet, and fought my way into it. Next, I hauled the sodden rucksack onto my back and unsuccessfully attempted to place it underneath the sand-encrusted poncho. Like furniture from Ikea, plastic sheets that cover both one's front, down to one's knees and hibernate the pack, are a two-man job. Predictably, there was a dearth of suitable men. I set off instead with my poncho rucked at the top of my pack, leaving the rucksack exposed to the gentle drizzle. The front flapped away in the gentle desert mist, occasionally rearing up over my head. Occasionally being every ten minutes or so.

I was less than an hour further down the trail when lumbering towards me was the first human contact since daybreak. Squinting through my befogged glasses, I recognised Fortitude. I presumed I was going the wrong way until she announced she was going home. She'd slept less than a mile from me, already

16

disillusioned to be twelve miles short of her intended target of Lake Morena. "This storm is unpassable," she wailed, indicating the thick fog obliterating our surroundings. "And there are more storms coming, it's going to be a very wet spring." If you'd asked me, I would have told you it was a bit damp but a bit far-fetched to call it a storm, but then I have lived in Scotland, a place where they have a hundred different types of rain and at least seven levels of wet weather.

My biggest fear of the desert, aside from the rattlesnakes, the cold nights, the axe-murderers, and the scorpions, was running out of water. Subsequently I carried a ton of extra, keeping my head demons liquidated. At a kilo per litre, or two point two pounds as the Americans would say, desert water is an atrocious but necessary commodity to carry. This winter had been unusually dry with barely any precipitation. Then March arrived and Mother Nature got busy rectifying matters. This year, hikers would have ample water: seasonal springs would still be pumping long into the summer; creeks would still ebb and flow, and random tanks would be filled to the brim with stagnant water and dead mammals. I was clueless about how much liquid your average woman drinks: all I knew was that I drank way too much coffee and, coincidentally, I peed a lot. I also knew that my first encounter with water today was some eight miles away at Hauser Creek. I figured at my current rate of progress I would arrive there sometime near midnight so I was rather glad that I still had an abundance, at least three litres, which I hoped would be plenty.

Unless, of course, one meets a couple of fellow hikers enjoying a spliff. In their nirvana, they will tell you with an emphatic degree of absolute confidence that the trail goes 'that way'. Like me, you might opt to believe them. I'd gone a mile downhill before the elder of the two could holler loudly enough for me to turn around. Hands on his knees, panting heavily, he gasped out his correction. I can routinely get lost in my own living room, and yet I was irked at him for his mistake in the wilderness. Still, I thanked him for chasing after me and stumbled onwards back in the direction of the trail.

I ground out another eight miles, meeting no one until late afternoon where I was chased down by Scott, still on his first day out. Loud and enthusiastic, he strode past at a cracking pace, only to overshoot the trail each time it intersected with a dusty road, or cross-trail. Several times, he reintroduced himself with a sheepish 'me again!' With his speed, I had no doubt he'd be in Canada within the month, although I supposed a few detours to neighbouring states may well delay the actual arrival date. As I gingerly stepped my way down the path, carefully placing each aching foot, I could hear him in the valley below, chatting away at full volume, guiding me and the Belisha Beacon into our camp spot for the night. The second fellow introduced himself as Mike. He had already acquired a sprained ankle so had resigned himself to staying at the creek for a few days until he was ready to limp out. Shortly after the YouTuber of my bath and airport ventures turned up, before departing at great speed having shown off his very pristine branded shoes. Four more arrivals pitched up. Then four more.

It was a relief to build the tent, letting it dry whilst I shovelled in the remainder of the inedible Pad Thai, spooning it in between slurps of hot coffee and handfuls of M&Ms. Finally, after four sittings, there was no more of the pocket vomit. Four more arrivals joined us, but all declined my unwanted spare packets of Pad Thai. Most lingered in their tents, a few chit-chatted about hiking food and different trails, then the camp quickly settled. As the sun set, the bullfrogs ramped up, and my fellow campers composed a chorus of farts and groans to a backdrop of creaky sleeping pads and, of course, coughs and snores. I felt awake for long tranches of time, yet perplexingly, I had an abundance of dreams. Neither pleasant nor unpleasant, just factual in an odd way. Eventually light came and the sounds of people heating up water then packing down their tents gnawed away at my innate laziness.

My pack was again heavy with overnight condensation stuck fast to the tent, Worse still, the dampness had also been ingested by the sleeping bag. I had staggered mere feet when the deluge descended. The storm I'd previously scoffed about fell torrentially, an accompanying wind whipping up into a frenzy at the point the coast-like terrain commenced its crest-like reality. My new normal began with a gigantic one thousand, two-hundred-foot surge uphill spread across two and a half miles, lifting me away from Hauser Creek. The trail would then drop back down by four hundred or so feet back to three thousand feet above sea level. I believed I greeted just about every single one of the day's newcomer hikers as they overtook me in the race to get to Lake Morena campgrounds: a place offering hot snacks and a smattering of log cabins. Most aimed for the concrete toilet blocks where they could enjoy temporary refuge from the unrelenting weather.

****

Where fools fear to tread, angels rush in

"I wouldn't even mind fishing right now, and that's quite possibly the most boring thing to do ever," said Daniel as we stood on our veranda admiring Lake Morena. We were waiting to move from our cabin, numbered eight, to number four which was identical in every conceivable way except its precise location. For reasons I couldn't fathom, the computer system at Lake Morena was incapable of transferring bookings from one hut to another and so the three of us: Aleta, Daniel and I, could take our stuff over after lunch, and simultaneously the people in Cabin Three could move into our old cabin, and that way the incoming people who'd initially been allocated Cabin Three, identical to Cabins Four and Eight, would not be impeded in anyway. I think that would make more sense if I was drunk.

I had already decided the previous day that a second night of sitting out the storm was in order and the cabin, bare of bedding and indeed mattresses, let alone any form of entertainment, still offered wonderful respite with its gas heater. Daniel, who originally had the wooden hut to himself, had taken pity on me and Aleta, sporting as we were the drowned rat look. He'd opted for a third dry, warm night. Aleta figured she'd decide what to do the following morning, and it turned out to be a quick decision. As the only one with any internet reception, she'd read out the weather forecast from the bunk above, "for today and tonight in the direction we're heading, it is rain and snow for seventy percent of the time. Below thirty degrees." We both looked towards Daniel, a US citizen, to explain what that meant, which turned out to be below freezing in European speak. "Wow, that's unheard of for this area," said Daniel, ordinarily a resident of nearby San Diego.

As each day yawned on, the most volatile storms were gathering elsewhere. The PCT Facebook pages, of which there were a plethora, had gone into meltdown as those preparing to embark on the trail, and those already on it, became the subject of consternation:

19

selfish, inconsiderate, and reckless are some of the more polite terms bandied around. Aleta became our hut teleprompter on all matters insulting. This had all erupted in a matter of twenty-four hours, after the PCTA, the association which manages the trail, sent out an email asking everyone to go home. Overnight we were no longer being revered for our bravery but dissected as contaminants and plagued rats, the carriers of a virus named after a beer, memes of which prompted much hilarity but little else did. The PCTA stated we risked spreading it from town to town, putting pressure on sparse health care resources. At the bottom of the email, in the tiniest of font, they admitted they had no legal powers to enforce our removal from the trail. They couldn't ban us, but they would if they could. Nearby groups of people converged with chatter of lockdowns and martial law, and then more murmurings of rebellions and anarchy. The world suddenly felt a much more frightening place off the trail than on it.

Outside more PCT thru-hikers gathered. A Georgian had generously purchased a few bottles of wine, pouring it into cooking pots, as we all stood the mandatory six feet apart in an ever-growing circle as people mulled over their options. Soon there were over twenty of us. The Georgian mimed pouring me a glass but I declined with a simple, "no, thanks." It had taken over a year before I learnt I could just say that without constant fretting. People rarely bat an eyelid at my refusal to partake. When they do, I simply reply that I'm allergic to alcohol. It usually gets me a ton of sympathy and it amuses me enormously when people say they are deeply sorry about that.

I have come to learn, unusually for the human race at large, that I have no mechanism within me that declares I've had enough. The more I drink booze, the thirstier I get. My mother always called alkies 'weak', which was rather hypocritical of her, I realised a few years ago given her weakness barely ever coped beyond lunchtime. I held onto the notion that it was a willpower problem for some time after I joined AA with its famous twelve-step programme. I can still recall the first time I heard someone call alcoholism an allergy. In my head, I scorned the concept with a less polite term than poppycock. But I was taught that the word *allergy* simply means 'unusual reaction'. I simply can't have just one. I've never wanted just one. I don't get the point of just one. I would rather not drink at all than have just one. In fact, if I fear there won't be enough to quench my insatiable need for drink, I find it easier to not have one at all. That is what makes me a typical alcoholic, rather than being a park bench drunk complete with a brown paper bag hiding a bottle of vodka, as I'd presumed.

I don't know if alcoholism is physiological or psychological, or, most likely, a toxic combination of the two. I am no more an authority on addiction than I am a virologist, but I've noticed many people consider themselves foremost experts on both. For me, these days, I think of it just as much as an 'illness' as diabetes. With the correct treatment, with proper, healthy practices like avoiding some things and partaking in others, there's no reason for me to ever again get myself comatose in compromising situations.

There is, however, the inescapable reality that learning to be sober is a horribly uncomfortable process. At its most basic, it is learning *to adult* long after one's peers have seemingly got their stuff together, all the while facing the wreckage of one's present. My own drinking career had begun aged seven, my mother's rationale being if you expose children to adult privileges, they won't go wild with it in their teenage years. She was right: I didn't. My teenage rebellion, true to all teenage rebellions, was to be as little like my parents as I could feasibly be, so I was as teetotal as she was over the limit. If I could have adopted myself out, I would have. My drinking to pass out really began in my mid-twenties when I was a proper grown up, with a proper job, and proper career aspirations. It was a weekend thing, except when it wasn't and when it wasn't I told people I had the flu. I was quite a sickly twenty-something looking back.

Sometimes, very facetiously, when people ask why I don't drink, I boldly tell them I'm an alcoholic. I can always elicit a laugh, especially if I say it with a smile, a head tilt and a very challenging direct look in their eyes. They don't take me seriously. The first step is about honesty, learning how to tell the truth after years of lying, cheating, manipulating and deceiving. When I tell you, sarcastically, I'm an alcoholic, I'm not lying, but you'd never know, because I don't look like one nor do I sound like one. I do, however, think like one. That's why there is more to being in recovery than learning how to say 'no, thanks' when offered booze. It's about learning how to do the right thing, about trusting instincts, about being responsible. It's about growing up and taking healthy risks. It's about self-esteem and self-respect. It's about courage, wisdom and faith. And for the most part, I don't have a clue about any of those things. That's why being in recovery is about continuously and consciously acquiring those practices. It's a slow process which begins long after one has already become deeply entrenched in faulty thinking.

At most AA meetings, the first chunk of 'Chapter Five' entitled *'How it works'* is often read aloud from the *Big Book*, the guiding literature of the twelve-step programme. I like it when speakers include the bits of blurb before and after the actual lists of steps. A later paragraph includes the line, "We are not saints," and I am the embodiment of that fact. I am not perfect. I don't make great decisions. I am not a great representative of Alcoholics Anonymous. I am sober though, so that's progress.

It was in those rooms I learnt the real first step, the one that begins a thousand journeys, is always the biggest and the hardest. There really is no difference between bravery and stupidity until the benefit of hindsight is applied. And even then, you, I and the rest of the world will filter that through different lenses. This is my lens. If the names you call me won't break my bones, don't think they won't hurt. They do. But I genuinely believe that calling someone derogatory names only entrenches their viewpoint. It's no accident most alcoholics only call themselves alkies once they have ceased to drink. Yet so many of us are quick to tell other people what to think, what to do, and what to say, yet slow to apply our very own advice to ourselves. Learning to tread my own path is the freedom of being sober and the reality of being a fool. It is often said in the rooms of AA: it really is none of my business what anyone thinks of me. The problem, of course, is that we live in an era where people make it their business to let one know their innermost thoughts.

And so, the recently christened 'Vulture of Humanity' and I, amongst several others, opted to plod on when so many, for their very own perfectly reasonable reasons, chose not to.

****

Chapter two

Powers greater than myself

I nearly wept with joy as I picked up my repacked rucksack without screeching "Jesus Wept!" The total obliteration of anything deemed 'almost essential' having made all the difference. Eating a gigantic packet of M&Ms for breakfast helped too. With all the time on my hands at Lake Morena, I had tried to better estimate my actual eating needs until I got to Julian, the first town I intended to visit. I could certainly live without sweets and chocolate. I opted to keep the porridge for breakfast with added dried fruit, cereal bars for lunch, and one hot Knorr meal such as Pasta Alfredo or Spanish Rice in the evening. These I could supplement with some dried vegetables, like edamame beans. Carrying three empty water bottles was probably the single biggest difference. Jesus was to weep yet again, but not so urgently now the unrelenting downpour hammering down had ensured plentiful supplies of streams from which we could refill our water bottles more often.

All campgrounds up and down California were to cease operating with immediate effect. Campgrounds are distinct from campsites. The former are managed, and often come with picnic tables, sometimes grills for barbecues, trash cans and latrines. Truly plush were those offering amenities such as showers and cabins. The latter are vague patches of bare ground, sometimes flat enough to hold a tent or ten. Leaving the campground at Lake Morena I said hello to people who were continuing, and goodbye as 'tramilies', established cohorts of hikers, broke up, parting ways permanently.

More laughter and confusion reigned as we swapped stories of what we'd read or heard about America and the rest of the world in relation to Corona. All towns in California were shutting down. It was going to be difficult to hitch-hike, something hikers depend upon in more typical times in order to get to towns for resupply. The local ranger had warned earlier that hikers were facing discrimination amongst the local townsfolk. I learned from the Canadians that the border between there and here was to be shut. People were racing to get back to their country of origin fearing that planes were to stop flying altogether. Perhaps our travel insurance would be revoked, some had been already.

I dithered, then figured I would see how I got on before making a final decision whether to carry on or not. Anxiety is a subtext to my life, throwing up all sorts of nervous reactions. Making decisions rarely has to be done promptly, I've learnt. I can ponder, I can mull over things. I can listen to your views. I can break open my mind, and that's the hardest part. But it's about coming to believe, the process of getting to a point of finality, rather than holding on to an instant compulsion or snap decision, then digging in with dogmatic determination. The final decision will always be mine.

I wandered on. I selected an AA podcast I'd previously downloaded. The speaker was once asked if there were three birds in a bush, one decided to fly away, how many were left? Three, of course. It simply made a decision; it didn't do a damned bit of flapping. I have a tendency to do a lot of flapping, and very little flying. The second step is not about believing one way or another, just about reflecting and considering, and taking the time to do that. Just trying to put 'Ready, Fire, Aim' in the right order, because consequences were things to be lived with.

I'd promised myself I would listen to an AA 'share', a recording of a speaker at a meeting, every day in lieu of attending face-to-face meetings. Going to physical meetings meant I didn't have to live with my thoughts in isolation ever again unless I chose to. After a while I also came to believe that I could never have become sober on my own volition: there was an undeniable power being with similarly afflicted people that got me drink-free and kept me there. The day's speaker reminded me it's the third step that uses the God word, not the second or the first. How we don't need to fear something that's over there, until it's over here, but often it's the God word that stops so many from taking the first step. I find it hard just admitting I don't know what to do, but I get an undeniable thrill when things are chaotic, unfathomable, and scary. And when that happens, I've been told to pause to wait for a sign to proceed. The day's speaker had intimated newcomers should "Take the cotton wool out of our ears and shove it in our mouths." Hostile advice but he has a point. Often there is so much inane chatter in my head, it tramples away any reasonable voice trying to make itself known.

I decided to keep walking just for today, to see how things went. I also asked the universe for a sign that I should carry on. Getting comfortable with being certainly uncertain, and relinquishing the need for control, to just learn to take it one step at a time. That's the stuff I've been inculcated into in recent years. Five minutes later, I tripped over a non-existent stone on an otherwise gloriously smooth part of the sandy trail, landing with a thud, which then reverberated up my spine as my rucksack rapidly propelled itself forward, coming to a sudden halt on impact with the back of my head. My involuntary yelp on landing only served to add dirt to my diet. Ten minutes later, my phone, already a barely useful navigation tool, packed up completely: it simply wouldn't power on.

An hour later, a bonny and energetic woman introduced herself as Half Missing, on account of a mishap combining a cabin heater and some polyester shorts. As a result, her leg wear now had a wider selection of leg holes than is typically found in such attire. She too had a snail's pace, albeit one who limped. Her presence certainly helped me overcome my worries that I had no navigation whatsoever, no way of knowing where water was, as if it wasn't patently bloody obvious as we splashed through stream after stream.

I heard about the latest goings on on Facebook courtesy of Half Missing. "Cookpot said *this*, but Heavensent is a bitch for saying *that*. These people just couldn't hack it, but they're blaming the virus. Anyway, Quadrangle said *this* and he's always right." Half Missing was a yapper, which made a wonderful change from the pesky voices rampaging around my inner cortex. The world's views conjugated; I was then thoroughly updated on all matters modern-day marijuana.

Long gone are the days of stuffing a bit of brown sludge into some tobacco, rolling it up and igniting it, which is what I'd done in my student years. These days, it comes in vape form and in a variety of different strains. Some enhance your sex, others reduce pain, mellow you out, make you hungry, alleviate *hanger*, reduce constipation, bung you up, wake you up, make you go to sleep. You name it, there is a non-addictive, non-habit-forming puff for every conceivable human behaviour and emotion, and, like the ever-promising alcohol, in California it is perfectly legal. If vaping isn't one's thing, it's also available in liquid form, as well as sweets and sherbets, all wrapped up in colourful, childish packaging. It still gets her "veeeery high," Half Missing sang at me. A while back she'd taken herself into a recovery programme but then she was diagnosed as bi-polar, and that's how she realised she wasn't an addict after all.

She just had big highs and great lows, and it wasn't her fault. Besides, she informed me, "most of the time I fall asleep when I get high, so it doesn't count." Her company made for a fascinating perambulation as we snaked between Lake Morena and Mount Laguna. This two-day, twenty-mile trek rose up hundreds of feet gradually, offering the false promise that this was finally going to be a wonderful walk in the wilderness despite it pissing down for much of the time.

I stopped regularly to give my legs some respite and I'd lose Half Missing in a cloud of vape fug as she too caught some breath. In so many ways, I admired her, hobbling around determined to keep going despite visibly snagging at times. I'd wince in sympathy watching her trying to overcome a large step, sometimes crawling up on her hands and knees. I understood her need to realise this burning ambition, a decade in the holding, to complete the PCT. It wasn't her first attempt; injury had befallen her before. Alas, history was starting to repeat itself and I watched on as she regularly halted to stretch out her patella. No matter how much pain she was in, she would never pause to take breath with her rapid-fire commentary on all matters PCT, drugs and other people's reaction to the virus as we wobbled along. I really didn't know how she did it. Actually, on second thoughts, I definitely did.

The desert finally started to look like a desert should with sandy bowls punctuated with gnarly shrubs. I surged ahead of Half Missing after she'd stopped to change shoes to wade a river. I figured wet feet were the least of my problems. At the thirtieth mile, I conversed with a smiley woman who initially I hadn't recognised, then remembered I had met her as I traversed, painfully slowly, up the first hideous climb at Hauser Creek. Mind you, I'd practically met everyone that day. Her tramily, people she was travelling with, had bailed on her. She was happy to mosey along with me for the time being but had yet to acquire a trail name. A few days later a bush emitted a low-slung growl as she ambled by. Given her penchant for all things leopard print, including gaiters, we could only assume that the residential mountain lion, or cougar if one prefers, or puma or painter or panther or catamount, one can take one's pick, took umbrage to her interloping. That is why she was christened Wildcat because that way we covered all the bases.

26

Crossing over a dirt road, we were spellbound by 'trail magic'. Random PCT supporters, in this instance a man with a typically American oversized truck and several bulky coolers crammed full of beer, soda, snacks and cake, have a confounding desire to stand there and watch hikers devour the lot like starving hyenas. Hijacking one of the deckchairs, I demolished a Tangelo, a tangerine orange hybrid, downed a full-fat coke, and, having scored some 'healthy points', I proceeded to inhale a large slice of cake, delighted by the opportunity to indulge in two of my favourite pastimes.

Half Missing caught us up mid-feast, still as chipper as she'd been a few hours before, and the three of us began hiking together, overcoming my initial fears of being so novice and without adequate navigation. That evening we collapsed on the side of a hill, near two German hikers and Daniel. I fell asleep to the sounds of Daniel's guttural snoring on the other side of some shrubbery. He'd left the cabin after me and brought news that Aleta had opted to go home.

****

When the going gets tough, the tough check into hotels

Life on the trail remained as chaotic and unpredictable as ever. Each night seemed to be a variation of the haphazard approach to setting up camp as the previous one. It began with trying to find a spot that was reasonably flat and one that could contain all three of us. I'd then start the process of building the Belisha Beacon, pegging down the four corners of the gauzy inner, before attaching the centre hook to my hiking pole, and setting that as high as it would go. After that, I'd throw over the bright orange flysheet, pinning it down into its hexagon-shape. I'd hoped that in time, I'd be able to sleep just under the inner; using it as a fly-net but it was still much too cold and damp for that. But I couldn't escape the sides of my tent. My sleeping pad, whilst very comfortable, was much too long, and the fly collapsed in. So much so my feet and my head were in constant contact with the condensation clinging to the inner lining. Someone recommended keeping a small opening towards the top of my tent for the moisture to escape, it had made little to no difference. I still woke up every morning a soggy burrito.

In American parlance, it was still sub-thirty most nights, or below freezing in my language, rendering it necessary to sleep with the water purification kits, battery pack, and my still useless mobile phone inside my mummy sleeping bag. A practice which ensured that every time I rolled around, my already battered feet were given an additional clattering.

I marked my sixth day on the trail by ascending to six thousand feet via a climb of nearly two thousand feet, in just seven miles. I found my own pace, sloth-like naturally, and just staggered along as best I could. A hobble rather than anything smooth or gainly. As the path rose, I was taken aback by small spots of snow hugging some of the cacti. Not a single Geography teacher had ever mentioned these co-existed in lessons. These smaller patches became larger patches. The climb turned most arduous in the third mile when the entire trail whited out. Were it not for footprints to slip my own feet into, I'd be utterly directionless. The miles, which were long anyway, lengthened further as I slipped and slid my way up the mountain, glad of hiking poles to keep me upright. It felt more like cross-country skiing than hiking, and prior experience had taught me I am absolutely hopeless at cross-country skiing.

Mid-afternoon saw me stop for lunch. I *say* lunch, I meant a handful of raisins and two cereal bars, washed down by a micro-cup of instant coffee, a treat whilst I hung the Belisha Beacon, my sleeping bag and sleeping mat to dry on a sunny spot just off the trail. As I contemplated my aching self, an older hiker swept past, bellowing out, "That's a Douglas fir tree - first I've seen on the trail." No less than five minutes later, a similarly aged gentleman waltzed by, pointing to the same tree, with a loud, "That's a Jefferson Pine - first one on the trail I've seen." As botany lessons went, this one proved very confusing. Either way, I realised I knew nothing about the differences between firs, pines and conifers, given they all look like Christmas trees to me. Further entertainment arrived in the form of another man who pointed to the pine cones, easily the size of rugby balls, haphazardly lying about the place. He casually mentioned it might be best if I didn't sit under these trees lest one of the ginormous cones bounce off my exposed head. I added 'dropping pine cones' as something else to stress about.

I rejoined the trail, squelching through more snow, then slush, then heavy mud, then more snow until eventually I popped out into a proper campground, complete with proper marked picnic spots, and proper RVs and proper people. I noticed a sign saying, 'Mount Laguna, one mile'. That one mile was far longer than any other mile I had completed in nearly a week on trail, and I'd now completed over forty of them. If that was a mile, I suspected I'd make it to Canada sometime around 2022. Hopefully by then there'd be enough herd immunity, we'd reference the virus like Smallpox, in the past tense. For now, though, it was all anyone ever talked about.

I celebrated nearly a week on trail by spending a third night in a hotel. This thru-hiking was proving to be a far more salubrious affair than I'd expected. Although salubrious was not an adequate description for this particular hotel room, with its aged brown carpets, and brown wallpaper that could possibly have been a different colour back sometime in the last century, like the 1970s or feasibly the 1950s. It came with a bucket in which we could soak our dust-fettered clothing. I'd opted to share a room with Half Missing, so we took it in turns to shower, then whacked the air heater to full blast, stringing out our dripping gear on anything suitable. The room soon became a sweaty sauna rendering our ablutions pointless.

I divested even more stuff that I'd previously classified essential. This time my machine-washable sanitary pads. I'd figured they'd be useful to keep my knickers clean and fresh, given I'm of that age that laughing and sneezing come with unintended urinary consequences. What I'd discovered was these bamboo monstrosities, although environmentally-friendly, swelled up with sweat. They were hardly thin and discreet to begin with, more akin to the cheap pads of yonder year, forcing a straddled walk. To my horror, the one I'd worn today had produced a large blood blister in the nether-region. It exploded as I gave myself a less than vigorous post-shower towelling. I'd expected blisters, but not there. Half missing, thankfully, was fully missing, on what looked like the beginnings of a very bloody birth.

This was readily forgotten when I discovered my phone had suddenly, of its own accord, switched on, and although there was no internet in the room, the nearby shop had free wi-fi. I grabbed my sleeping bag, bundled myself up on the cold concrete ground outside the local store and surfed away in the freezing temperatures. I had reached hobo status level two.

****

Travel narrows the mind

On I trudged. Thrilled finally to make five miles in three hours despite regular pauses for water. With my phone, always a power greater than myself, now working again, I could carry so much less, confident about the location of permanent sources, although I remained cautious of making life a burden for myself. Wildcat had pushed on, and Half Missing had lingered back at the hotel to do some shopping. Solo now, I felt every inch of my vulnerability. There were no signs that anyone had gone before me, no fresh puncture marks alongside the trail from hiking poles, no new footprints, and no voices carried by the wind. I had already adopted the hiker deportment: head down, hands gripping trekking poles for dear life, focusing only on the uneven, rocky ground ahead of me. I was really not cut out for this level of exertion.

I was gone three hours when I first happened upon another human being: a couple out walking with their dog, a huge but amiable beast appropriately called Bear. I was about to greet them, unsure where the trail had disappeared to, as I turned toward them, my eyes struck behind them. Vast open lands, hundreds of miles wide, or so it seemed, the floor of the world deep below was a stark emerald lawn, with a central mass of small hills in striking contrast to the dry, beige, rubbly terrain with which I was already intensely familiar. Beyond our elevated cliff, the land lay lush and cosy, snugly protected by an encampment of rugged mountains, many of them snow-peaked. Of course, it was into those I was heading. They were exceptionally pretty from a distance, but far from warm and enticing. Like the scene opening in a panoramic movie, no mobile phone camera, certainly not one I could afford, could do this justice. But I knew then why I was doing it: for those moments when I looked up, my brain frazzled, and I'd forget how to exhale. I was aware, less of how much everything damned well hurt, but more of how privileged I was. That I should savour the moment, because tomorrow it would all still be there, but I would be gone, unlikely to ever see it again, and even if I did, its mind-blowing qualities could not be reignited. It was just like early sobriety, the wonder of waking up without a hangover, having strung together the first few days of refreshingly clean living.

I sat a while, the literary part of me wanted to say to intoxicate myself with the view, but my more pragmatic reality was it proved opportune to take the strain off my back and feet. I listened to the couple as they lavished love all over Bear. The internet access at Mount Laguna, as intermittent as it was, had stirred up an avalanche of homesickness in me. I couldn't recall ever suffering from homesickness in all my years of travelling. I had put the '*I*'*s* in itinerant - never really stopping anywhere for more than two or three years. I'd been living in the Cotswolds now for nearly four years, the longest I'd stayed in one place. I realised it was the longest I have ever stayed in one place since I was a young child, boarding school imprisonment discounted.

I thought by travelling so extensively, I could claim I had the broadest of minds. When I look back, I can see things I was blind to at the time. Hindsight being the only twenty-twenty vision I will ever have, and even then, every memory is just a recollection of another memory, and therefore not necessarily real or accurate. The past shape-shifts at each recollection, but I still had fond memories of the Cotswolds and I yearned to return there. I hesitated to call it home though because I lose homes like other people lose gloves. I have only ever known how to run away, to quit and start again someplace else with the pledge of 'this time it will be different', and it always was different. At least the scenery was, and the people, but whatever I was looking for never quite materialised. It seemed to me that having homesickness was an admission of needing to belong somewhere, and to be a part of something. To admit I couldn't go it alone anymore.

Now with the virus, everything was being disbanded. Yet I still imagined my fellow alcoholics trooping off to their regular meetings. I visualised each one depending on the day of the week, even if I didn't regularly attend that day's meeting, I'd know people who did. The last meeting I'd been to, on the eve of my flying out, I'd made the mistake of asking Old Marjorie how she was doing and getting the usual cantankerous retort of, "I wish I was dead," which was how she greeted most people. Young Marjorie had died several years previously. "I'm not in a box, what more do you want?" was the more typically chipper reply from the ailing Lightning Jack, on account of a scar that runs down his right cheek. I wondered how Faye was doing with her new baby. Whether Drunk John was sober

31

this week. A more hotch-potch, mismatched group of people you could never hope to meet.

It was at one of these meetings that I heard someone say that they were looking for God at the bottom of a pint glass and that made sense. I had made an entire career of escapology. When I joined AA, it was never with the intention of sticking around. I certainly didn't want religion. I don't think many people do. And thank God, I still don't have religion. In part because when I was trying to find a 'power greater than myself' I took myself off to church for Christmas Mass. There the vicar gave a surly speech about only seeing his parishioners once a year. I decided that was a message from God in itself and have stayed clear of churches except for marriages and funerals ever since. Being in AA means there can be a lot of the latter to attend.

Instead, a belief system found me. I simply decided one day that I would no longer believe in coincidences. I don't know why I had previously been so convinced there was no such thing, just that I knew that it was most likely because someone had told me that. So, I decided, there and then, I would no longer be convinced no such thing existed. If I was a switch, I had just flicked myself from off to on. It also helped that when I was coming up to the first anniversary of my last drink, I stood on my porch, smoking a cigarette. I was reasoning that surely now after such a time period had elapsed, I could restart my drinking career. My body had had a good break after all, and of course, it would be different this time. The war within my conscience was palpable, and I, the innocent bystander, observed myself wrestling with the notion of 'going out again' to use the AA parlance, or staying put with the endless attendance of meetings to talk about the thing we don't do anymore. And that's when my phone rang and a woman's voice said, "You don't know me, but months ago someone gave me your phone number." That's what we do in AA, we give our phone numbers out to strangers and this one had given it to someone else, and that someone else had, in true alkie style, rushed out to call me four months later, long after I had forgotten giving it away. I had never taken a random call from a drunk before. I've never taken one since for that matter. I didn't tell her I was planning to move on, but I listened as she told me how she wasn't an alcoholic but...

Later that day I went for a long drive to a meeting two hours away for no other reason than I could. I took my place on a church pew and glanced up to where a laminated sign had been stuck crookedly on the wall. It exclaimed, "there is no such thing as a coincidence in AA." I flicked the switch and decided from now on, whatever happened, it would be best to accidentally find myself in a meeting, telling strangers my most embarrassing secrets than accidentally finding myself drinking again, acquiring more. Now because of that moment, here I was feeling sick with 'home', and desperately wanting to be there. Yet even if I wanted to go back, I had nowhere to go. The UK was now in a severe lockdown. AA was no longer to be found in musty church halls or village community centres, or hospital wings or schools, or through chance encounters. Not that anyone would know we were there anyway, unless, of course, one knew we were there. We are probably the most well-known stealth organisation going, and we are everywhere.

That's what I thought about as I sat on a large boulder resting my aching back, listening to the couple talking, soaking up the view, my head looking up and out for a change, not on my feet below. The man with the dog picked up a stone and underneath an inscription for a website awarding him a cash prize. That damned rock had been beside my foot the entire time.

****

The crash and bang of the wilderness

When the storm hit, a full twenty-four hours ahead of anticipated, it absolutely wiped us out. We'd stopped early, four-ish as the mountain became engulfed in a white mist racing above and below us. The wind ratcheted up, driving down sheets of rain, keeping us huddled in our individual tents, unable to hold conversations with one another through the din. I heard Wildcat's tent collapse and a spontaneous yelp shortly followed. Soon I was battling to keep my own tent together, it had now taken to leaking all over my possessions. By three in the morning, my tent was toast, as was Daniel's, which stopped him snoring. It was about the only thing that could.

I roused myself at dawn. Looking about me, it was carnage. I had two substantial pools of water in the tent, everything in the vestibule sodden. Nothing survived the storm unscathed. Wildcat and Daniel elected to wait out the morning. Drenched from head to toe by the time I'd dismantled the Belisha Beacon and packed it away, I set off with a brisk walk. Freezing didn't come close to describing it, miserable would be more accurate. Mist swirled around each hill obliterating any views and the wind fierce. Worst of all, as I snaked around each curve of the mountain, I was stuck with the earworm, *"She'll be coming round the mountain, when she comes,"* a particularly irritating folk song, and one I simply couldn't shake no matter how much I shook.

Late morning, I was overtaken by a couple from the UK, whose names escaped me, and whom I'd assumed would have made many miles by now. They dodged past. "We should have gone to Scotland," boomed the lass before vanishing into the future. The rain pelted down until early afternoon, and then 'puff' the sun poked out. I happened upon a sandy piece of flat ground, with a small stream flowing through it, joining in with another who had hung his entire belongings on the few weedy desert oaks. It took an hour to get everything dry. As the man vacated, a Danish woman arrived. She was plagued with phenomenal blisters on her hands, a result of sunburn, surprising given the last few days. I learnt she'd been part of a trio, but two of them scooting along more strenuously than she found comfortable. She let me know that Wildcat had left the trail as her sleeping pad had deflated and her tent had also been damaged in the storm of last night. Daniel arrived and told me Half Missing had pressed her SOS button fearing hypothermia. A ranger had picked her up in the morning. I'd been surprised to see her tent on the adjacent mountain the night before as she'd reckoned on only doing five miles because of her knee. I hoped she would return; it would be hell to have only completed eleven more miles than her previous attempt.

The following night, I camped down with Daniel and the Dane, who I learnt was called Insane Shopper a consequence of panic buying four packets of plain noodles. When the rest of the world at large was obsessed with obtaining as much toilet paper and hand sanitizer as feasible, Insane Shopper clearly didn't want to get caught short with an insufficient amount of plain pasta. They weren't even the hiking staple of Knorr's three-minute noodles, but the sort that contain four servings per packet, and take an age to cook. The very type of foodstuff that hikers shun on account it consumes too much propane. She was still carrying sixteen servings in her backpack.

That evening, the wind having blown itself away, we could finally enjoy the true sounds of the wilderness. Somewhere in the far distance, the crack of gun fire reverberated around the valleys. Then later, as dusk descended, a coyote pack howled, sounding not unlike when people sing in a Zoom meeting: out of tune and out of pace with one another. In the dark it was hard to know how far away they were. And, of course, there was always Daniel's snoring, it haunted me everywhere, even in Mount Laguna through the hotel room wall.

Daniel by day is a likeable enough chap, although one inclined to transmit every observation or occurrence generated within. He has a naturally slow articulation and a tendency to repeat himself frequently. As we lumbered down the trail towards crossroads that would ultimately take us to the lower lying town of Julian, I tired of listening to his never-ending utterances. I slowly cooked as we neared the floor of the desert. At the bottom of the descent, my knees on fire, I'd managed to pull away from him a little, but he'd caught me when I rested at a dry riverbed for a sip from my ever-dwindling supply of water. I'd miscalculated, not expecting the temperatures to fly up the thermometer as quickly as they had. Praying I could manage without too much discomfort, I knew there to be a water cache within a few miles: gallons of bottled water supplied by mysterious trail angels. They take the time to deposit huge vats of the stuff near the trail and retrieve the empties in order to keep supplies topped up on a near-constant basis.

From the Guthook navigation system, I could see the trail was largely linear now to the junction, probably about three miles in total. I followed Daniel as he walked through the riverbed and carried on in a south-east direction. Quite the opposite to what I thought we were supposed to be doing. Given I can get lost in a straight line, like a sheep, I simply tottered after him. A while later, it felt all kinds of wrong. A gnawing feeling of displacement. There were no telltale signs of the trail yet the path sandy. I raced to catch up to Daniel, sandbagged by the exhausting heat. "Oh," he said when I suggested we were going in the wrong way before slowly drawling, "But I'm from San Diego, I know these parts because I grew up here. Used to ride a bike, and we relied on a dinosaur bone to find our way," and off he strode. Now completely disoriented, I couldn't figure whether to leave him to it and retrace my steps or give in to his certainty as he marched off. I was even more perplexed as to why no one has previously mentioned dinosaurs lounging about the desert.

Catching up to him once again I pointed out that the trail seemed 'over there' to my mind. Daniel again was adamant he had a great sense of direction. Eventually, I persuaded him to get his phone out - it had the all-important little blue dot indicating our proximity to the trail. When he'd finally located his glasses, he agreed he was well off beam. "That happened when I left Lake Morena as well," he giggled, "I got me so lost."

Nearly an hour later, we located the trail and then for another hour we stuck fastidiously to it, shuffling through a carpet of tiny yellow blossoms which smothered the desert floor. With all the rain, we could expect a treat soon, at least florally-speaking.

Unexpectedly, we managed to get a hitch pretty quickly. I say 'we', I meant me. Daniel, now keeling himself, had plonked himself in the shade away from the road, confused as to why there was no cache. It left me to hang my thumb out at every passing car. I struck lucky at my third attempt.

I bagsied the front seat, leaving Daniel to occupy the soundproof rear of the food delivery truck. It had been nearly two decades since I last hitch-hiked. The last time was around Siberian Russia with its sub-zero temperatures, when I was young, reckless and free. Now I could tick off hitch-hiking in the desert too as a grumpy middle-aged woman. Clearly age does not necessarily bring wisdom. That night I settled down post-shower in a strangely comfortable bed, with pristine white sheets, in one of Julian's hotels. I fell asleep once again to the dulcet tones of Daniel's snoring seeping through the walls.

****

The restoration of insanity

Julian is the first true pitstop for many a thru-hiker. Famed for its apple pie, it was originally a town built entirely of tents, until sanity was restored when someone suggested housing may be the better alternative. Ordinarily, the town would be thronging with tourists and hikers making use of its ample hospitality, overwhelming the usual one and a half-thousand populace. This year word had filtered through, contrary to official notification from the PCTA and the rumour-mongering on Facebook, we would be welcome here after all. Others maintained we were not, and that we risked arrest, or worse, harassment from vigilantes. Julian claimed its own jobsworth sheriff, something that struck me as American as apple pie. That alone made me feel wonderfully renegade.

It is, undoubtedly, a town for which the word 'quaint' was invented, shops adorned with wild-west facades and boutique verandahs, now shut up save for a few rebellious coffee shops and restaurants doing take-outs. Out of necessity, the supermarket was open. All I aspired to do was lie in a hotel bed and not move for the entire duration of my stay. I yearned for a full day free of walking the trail, to give my feet some reprieve from the non-stop pounding. It is a level of brutality they had never experienced before. I was surprised my toenails hadn't shaken themselves off already.

Alas, I learnt there was no such thing as a day off on the trail. Town chores are numerous. First up: shopping. Scrutinising each nearly-bare shelf, panic-buying had decimated many of the dry goods, was a chore made more discombobulating as I was foreign to the brands. I couldn't just grab and go my usual comforts. This was coupled with the fact that I hadn't got the hang of hiker food yet. It was all revolting. As a vegetarian the tuna in oil and dehydrated chicken offerings weren't for me. I also have an intense aversion to powdered potato meals, similar to 'Smash', the rescue remedy for parents and boarding school kitchen workers alike, who couldn't or wouldn't cook in the 1980s. Forcing that repulsion into me, under the threat of no pudding or worse, has left an indelible scar on my psyche. Dehydrated potatoes can be branded any which way, my insides could rest assured, the encounter was not to be re-lived. As a wise fellow on a podcast had suggested: Insanity is not doing the same thing over and over again, expecting different results; it is doing the same thing over and over again, knowing full well what the results will be. I did my best to restrict my shopping decisions based on the weight to calorific value, so porridge oats, cereal bars, Knorr instant pasta packs, and dried fruit to appease my internal critic, were frittered into my trolley, or cart as the locals would say. Nonetheless,

I still overshopped, and I hadn't even factored in the excess from last week. It is said one packs for their fears, well apparently, I feared becoming a skinny bitch.

The other fixation is obtaining gear. I made a decision to jettison the Belisha Beacon and replace it with a two-person, lightweight tent, popular amongst long-distance hikers. I ordered online for delivery at Warner Springs, a mere thirty miles away figuring it would likely take me more than a couple of days to get there. Delivery driving, no matter what they were carrying, was deemed to be essential work, and on-line shops had yet to succumb to the deluge of bored home-bound shoppers. I also ordered an American sim card in the hope of finally rectifying my location problems with the navigation app, Guthook.

Then there was laundry. I opted to hand-wash using the dregs of the hotel shampoo, in the absence of a laundromat. If there was one, it was a well-kept secret from me. Until now, I hadn't realised that laundromats in America were still a thing.

Then, of course, there was the eating of proper food, the ultimate in a balanced diet: The vegetable pizza, washed down with fresh strawberry milkshakes and iced tea. Getting the biggest ones available made pizza and milkshake the ideal serving for all three main meals of the day, plus the crusts had snacking value when dipped in the wonderfully garlicky ranch dressing that almost everything American is served with.

There was also the cleaning of me, dirt-caked fingernails, dirt-caked toenails for that matter, and dirt-caked eyebrows. It was increasingly difficult to touch my feet at all without flinching or wincing. Their hypersensitivity changed my gait. When I divested my backpack, I could only gingerly limp around. It is known within the hiking community somewhat predictably as the 'hiker hobble'. In short, one takes on the comportment of an arthritic octogenarian having discarded his walking frame.

Tending to my long hair consumed the most time. When walking I kept it plaited, Pocahontas-style. It didn't make me look at all cute or alluring. After a week on the trail it was matted to hell, giving me the full savage look, and it took over an hour to brush through. I supposed I could have tried to detangle it after I'd finished hiking each day, but another significant discovery I'd made about myself was that I had an incredibly short attention span.

On the trail, I didn't seem to be able to complete one task, without distracting myself with another, usually before I'd even got to the halfway point of the first. Rarely did I get my tent up swiftly, before I felt it necessary to go and converse with someone building their tent. Then I'd return to start blowing up my sleeping pad, before realising I'd got nowhere to put it. I'd leave it half inflated and attend once again to the tent, before it would occur to me that I needed to scour my surroundings for large rocks. Then I'd figure I might as well start boiling water for dinner whilst I was at it. Then, the pot would boil before I'd finish bashing in all the stakes, prompting me to start on dinner duties, which would then kick-start a discussion on 'what's for dinner?' with others around me. Before bed, I'd still have to recharge the mobile, write my diary, unpack my rucksack, ready the next day's snacks, get breakfast on hand, re-bandage my blisters, filter water and God knows what else. I would half attempt them all before acknowledging I still needed to properly stake in the bleeding tent, and dinner was now overcooked and over cold. I had absolutely no reliable system for settling myself in at night. I was a randomator, and my lack of efficiency, lack of anything close to organisation, was irksome, and part of that problem, I determined, was the structure of my rucksack - with no discernible system to it.

After a 'zero', or a full day's rest, notwithstanding all the washing, shopping, checking in with friends in the UK, reading emails, ordering stuff, and paying bills, one's final act before checking out is the complication of repacking a rucksack now that everything was clean or dry, and an abundance of new supplies had been acquired. It involved the portioning out of meals, stamping down my dried-out sleeping bag, slotting in bits here and there, then pulling stuff out and re-starting, only to culminate in me beseeching God, the Lord Jesus, and the entire cast of the Muppets as soon as I put it on my back. What I wanted to avoid was having to retrieve my tent stakes from the bottom of my rucksack, a place they would end up inexplicably every evening when I needed them first and foremost. Today, I positioned them more handily, even though all I was doing was walking to a different hotel room to share a room with Insane Shopper on the other side of town, where I'd unpack the lot once again.

On the way, I grabbed some of the famous Apple Pie at Mom's cafe, making my order six feet away from the server, having sanitised my hands on the way in. It was then an odd practice and the vodka-scented lotion had my stomach convulse. I hadn't had to smell alcohol for several years and although I'd been in pubs to eat occasionally, I didn't really spend much time in them. I don't have booze at home and although I have friends who drink, I tended in the first year or two to leave early so they could enhance their time with prosecco, cocktails or whatever plonk they'd bought that was a bargain that week. It sort of remained a habit. These days I don't hang around when people start getting drunk, I've no need to. In many ways, I'd lived in an AA bubble socialising within the fellowship, staying clean and staying dry. It'd been a very safe harbour, but my favourite saying, not that I've ever heard it in AA, is that a ship is safest at shore, but it is not what it was built for. If AA claimed to be a bridge to normal living, I still had no idea what that looked like. I just knew normal terrified me.

As I waited for the pie to warm, a father and son duo wearing masks entered as they went about their everyday. I even asked to take their photograph, I was so astonished by *their* presentation. It seemed so hypervigilant. Despite watching the news, despite the angst-ridden insults flying back and forth across Facebook within the PCT community; the name-calling, the strangers going onto our social media telling us to stop, or to jeff off, living in the hiking community, kept me inured to the growing pandemonium spreading across the world. I found the mask-obscured faces startling.

Several hikers I'd previously met on the trail were now homeward bound, their parents had convinced them for the most part. Others had wanted more of a social scene, although I thought that was what we were all trying to escape from. The world can be terribly *peopley* at times in my humble opinion. There were a lot of tears, a lot of sadness as Julian, the first or last town on the PCT, became their first and last town stay. Perhaps for some the virus was a convenient excuse. The YouTuber at the airport, who I'd last seen at Hauser Creek, uploaded a video entitled 'I did the right thing' which momentarily united both sides of the debate to mutually condemn him. He pissed off the continuers by quitting in the first place on moral grounds, only then to reveal in his vlog that his sponsors had threatened to cease supporting him. The 'go home now' lot then vilified him because he didn't quit promptly enough!

40

Elsewhere, back in my so-called 'normal world', the disease continued its insidious and inevitable progress: isolating people, creating tensions, splintering friends and families, raising anxieties and generating fear. Within the confinements come elevated levels of domestic violence, increased alcohol and drug taking, children starting to miss schools, workmates failing to show up for work. People dying or acquiring substantial long-term health afflictions. Others stop bothering to dress properly or create conspiracy theories. Some cry for help, some are heard, most are not. These matters are everyday stories in AA. Meetings can be a carousel of tragedies outlining the reality of living with an incurable disease. Our stories, of course, end with explaining how we've all found ways to live with it: of finding a new normal. Recovery is hard work sometimes, with big compromises, and even bigger consequences. It's about not knowing what the future holds but being certain that one way or another it is going to be okay: different, but okay. I suspect few believe that when they commence the second step, the point when we have to start the process of *coming to believe that a power greater than ourselves can restore us to sanity.* It's the taking of the third step where we temporarily put our cynicism aside and just try to do something different, that we make a decision to stop trying to control everything and everyone, and to hand it over and live within the moment, come what may.

And perhaps that's why I carried on regardless. Pandemonium was no longer my comfort zone. I wanted peace and order, and I badly wanted to resume this very real journey. For all of the physical pain it was causing me, I was willing to plod on. It was my new normal, and somehow sleeping under the stars in a damp tent, surrounded by wildlife felt safer than being isolated but homeless back in the UK. No doubt someone could help me out somewhere if I'd asked, but I didn't. I picked up my rucksack which I'd left outside Mom's, as I cursed out loud, I was distracted by a woman driving by, yelled out of her car window, "Are you hiking the PCT?" I nodded vigorously. "You're a fucking maniac," she laughed before accelerating off with a salute.

****

Chapter three

Forces to be reckoned with

Half Missing, Insane Shopper and I trudged up the steep climb out of Julian. Unfortunately for them I headed the pack, enabling me to make the executive decision of when to stop to relieve the lactic acid ripping through our calves. Naturally, stoppage was frequent, and almost always abrupt, causing Insane Shopper to bounce off my rucksack, and Half Missing to bounce off hers.

As ever, Half Missing brought up the rear, espousing us with her incredible knowledge of what was going to happen next in terms of trail and terrain. In between pants, I enquired of her what the holes on the trail were. They were abundant, and without mindfulness, likely to catch a pole or a shoe. "Tarantulas," she replied. To my horror, we were sleeping amongst them. Turns out they are not remotely harmful to humans, although they have a painful bite, it's not much worse than a bee sting. In fact, what I needed to worry about, Half Missing informed me, was the brown recluse, the black widow and the yellow sac spiders, amongst several others. Ordinarily as long as I am armed with a vacuum cleaner, I can handle most spider infestations in my home but out in the desert I was infesting theirs, and their venom is hospital-inducing.

Then there's the poop. Some animal or other, having devoured something fluffy, often followed it up with berries for dessert. It then toilets a hairy mess, peppered with half-digested fruit, on a rock casually minding its own business. It was a constant reminder that foxes and coyotes weren't far away, and Half Missing reassured me, they were terribly territorial about their space. Thankfully, I learned it was too cool at present for the rattlesnakes to be out, but clearly it was not going to remain that way forever. After all, the desert section was no less than seven-hundred miles long, and with our current speed, we were likely to still be in it by the time the US elections swung around in November. Further down the path, I was charged by a tortoise, anxious to nip my toes as I tried to photograph it. Momentarily, I despaired I might not outrun it.

We lost Half Missing early in the afternoon as her leg was causing her more pain than her stamina could manage. Insane Shopper and I tramped onwards, experiencing for the first time 'a no-room at the inn' moment when a small flat-spot in the crook of the mountain was already inhabited with three tents. I could only imagine the competition for space in a normal year meant one couldn't be fussy about assembling a tent over a dubious hole, or perhaps nearby some very human-esque poop. We're supposed to go two-hundred feet away from the trail or from camp spots, but in the middle of the night, if nature calls, then I very much doubted everyone obliged. Certainly not for all matters liquid, and certainly not with my bladder and current temperatures. This year everything was so much quieter, it was rare to come across anyone else at one's target destination. We'd ended up staggering on another mile, worth it for finding a patch with a view. High up, lying in our tents, we could overlook a sprawling mountain range, naturally snow-crusted and picture-perfect.

The following morning, we awoke to our tents snow-crusted and picture worthy too. Oodles of the stuff splayed across our hill following an unexpected overnight dumping. I'd had the bright idea of wrapping the end of my sleeping bag in a bin-liner to protect it from the damp walls that caved in, and in my wisdom, I had recommended it to Insane Shopper. In the morning, my lack of intelligence bore out: I learned one doesn't have to be menopausal to produce sufficient sweat in the night. Trapped by the plastic wrapping, our individual perspiration was simply absorbed by the footwells for us to squelch out in the morning.

As I lay there waiting for the day to warm up, as well as my hands and feet, Insane Shopper relayed the news that a PCT hiker had gone missing. The unknown hiker was thought to have exhausted her phone battery and had no personal locator beacon. It didn't bode well for her. Packing up, I realised my own battery recharging pack had also met its demise. Moreover, this was warning enough I needed my own SOS button. I'd planned on getting one before I set off, but the initial carnage of it all meant it had been overlooked. I fully intended on putting that right as soon as I arrived at a place with wi-fi.

It was not long before we bumped into Half Missing again. She reckoned the woman had become lost around Mount San Jacinto, over a hundred miles ahead. The worst place to get lost given the huge snow blizzard of last night. The range was still ice bound from the late spring weather. "It's all Mother Nature reminding us who is in charge," Half Missing espoused as we discussed the latest with Corona, atypical weather systems and the superbloom that was about to hit the desert. Superblooms are a rare phenomenon: only occurring after unusually wet winters. This year, it had been remarkably dry until the latter part of February and now March, when matters had been rectified with some for the road thrown in for good measure. Now it was expected that the wildflowers would burst into life spectacularly, igniting seeds that had laid dormant for years. This would only happen if the clouds continued to shield the desert floor, preventing it from getting too hot too quickly, and kept the winds abated until the delicate shoots had successfully embedded. We were already seeing evidence of orange poppies and the bright yellow brittlebush smothering hills in the distance. The prickly pear was starting to bud, some revealing gaudy pink flowers, but mostly for now they remained tightly bound in their liminal state.

The following day, as we embarked on what was my thirteenth day out in the wilderness, including those nights spent in the wilds of towns, news filtered through there were three more SOS buttons pressed overnight. Immediately Facebook lit up once again, with all the tactlessness of the keyboard warriors, castigating us for putting search and rescue teams at risk unnecessarily, diverting their services from the truly in need. One poster took the time to write out to his adoring audience a screenplay of a PCT hiker being rescued with a cough. It was obnoxious but it served its purpose to rile people up into frenzied indignation. They insisted their way was right, and they abhorred dissent no matter how reasoned it was. What was once a popular place to share information and bring together strangers along the trail to form a transient community was now decimated into 'them' and 'us.' The 'us' part began to establish ourselves elsewhere on Facebook with any trouble-makers booted out, leaving two separate echo chambers.

In truth we knew scant details about any of these emergencies, just that they were all in the region of the San Jacinto Wilderness. A detour was advisable because of its snowpack. Like many who start on any mission, there was a purist element to me. I had a plan of how things should be, how I wanted to do things in a linear, logical fashion, and that to deviate from it, was somehow wrong, or cheating, or ironically put me at risk of being judged inadequate. I supposed it was a unique choice for any hiker to make, and I decided to go into my own liminal state and defer making any decision once again. At the same time the PCTA announced they would not be checking permit start dates and for some that meant many would take this as a free pass to begin when it suited them best, which would be after these storms had passed.

Our little trio began our meander towards Warner Springs, a tiny hamlet of a town. Joy arrived in the form of meadows: a sweeping basin between two mountain ranges, covered in tall grass and short flowers. A truly flat oasis holding just a few mellow dunes to cross. It was all too short before we were back on to the next mountain range to staggered up at our own pace, lost in our own injurious pains and thoughts. I'd acquired blisters, and the deep muscle ache known only to those idiots who go straight from the couch to '5K' twice a day, day after day. Somehow, I was leading the way again. I remained consistent in the afternoons, neither fast nor slow, so it was me who happened upon two burly uniformed men first.

With hideous bright yellow suits, carrying long-handled shovels, I assumed they were something *enforcement*. The narrow trail with its jungly sides offered nowhere pertinent to hide. For a moment, I believed my days on the run, or rather lollop, were over. "Where are you going?" the taller of the two giants asked, blocking my way. I answered cagily, "As far as I can!" "Canada?" he specified. "Yes," I couldn't lie. "Well, well done you!" he beamed. I didn't tell him that I was on day thirteen and I was yet to pass the one-hundred-mile mark. Behind me, I saw Insane Shopper, like me a foreigner, with her less than camouflaging blue and white speckled shirt lurking behind a shrub. Five minutes later, Half Missing, being American, instantly recognised the fireman's clothing, and true to form, it induced that caving sigh in a woman who had just fallen into infinite lust.

We bedded down at mile 105, having covered what for us was a substantial eleven miles. Insane was limping on a tender knee and Half Missing was similarly struck too. I probably could have done another two miles or so but once I saw the little stream with its sandy sides cutting through a shaded spot, I knew we were going no further. Better to have a few miles tomorrow to Warner Springs, than a day doing nothing, was our mutual reasoning. We'd be arriving in the hamlet on a Sunday, and the Post Office, where our deliveries awaited, would be closed. We plonked our battered feet into the icy cold ditch to admire our chaffing. The tops of my normally alabaster legs were red and raw, Insane's were dry and flakey, but Half Missing, despite her elfin size, had bloody wounds in lieu of lily-white inner thighs.

Our feet were soon joined by those of NoNameFromTheUK as we watched squirrels and crows lark around. Overhead two hawks had a bitter aerial fight. There was only one thing we could really talk about, though: the presumed death of Microsoft, a twenty-two-year-old PCT hiker who had slipped off the trail, plunging down an icy ravine on San Jacinto earlier that day. We assumed, rightly, the initial accounts of a missing woman were mis-reported early doors. Later we were to learn his name was Trevor Laher, an experienced hiker who was living his dream. Despite his father imploring him to quit, he had opted to carry on. He'd been navigating a particularly treacherous icy section in the San Jacinto Wilderness without the aid of crampons or microspikes. Like all of us, he'd not brought with him any winter equipment, something typically only necessary in the Sierra. May he rest in peace. I would also like to thank his father for his tireless efforts to make the PCT a safer place for everyone.

****

Whose will is it anyway?

As we continued northwards, the middle of the day happened, and thus the desert heat cranked up, making hiking more burdensome, socks more sweaty and blisters more engorged. It was a relief to arrive at the anthropomorphic Eagle's Rock. Exposed to the harsh noon sun, the unusual rock formation offered little by way of respite beyond what was acquired from dropping our packs. Insane and I took our time to scramble around it, posing for photographs, as we waited for Half Missing to catch up, something that took well over an hour. A ton of day hikers and horse-riders, all clean and fresh-looking, joined us. It was already peculiar seeing people with small packs, if any. I took this as a sign I was adjusting to life as a hump-backed snail.

Overwhelmingly everyone we met was enthusiastic, wishing us luck with our endeavours to get to Canada. There was no animosity here. We asked for updates on Corona, and all replied with 'pfffft' at the madness of it all. Many indicated they felt it was no more than a sniffle, a hoo-hah that was to pass by soon enough. I hoped they were right. We live in a drama-filled, catastrophising world and perhaps that has worn its course, or perhaps civilisation's mettle was really being tested. Amongst the din it was hard to know. The pandemic, with all of its accompanying frothy outbursts on social media, just seemed to encourage the three of us to hunker down and get on with it.

I once read somewhere that something like five percent of the population simply cannot do what they are told and perhaps I was only ever meeting those five percenters. I slotted on my daily AA podcast. The speaker reckoned, dismally, only about five percent of alcoholics get into recovery, the process of succumbing, or surrendering to use the more popularist term, to doing what is suggested. It's what stops us getting well for the most part. For most drunks there's a persistent belief that Recovery is another country, and it won't work for us. Besides, who needs twelve stupid rules to live by? Although in AA the steps are called 'suggestions', the running joke is, of course, that when you've got to jump out of a crashing plane, it is *suggested* you wear a parachute.

The speaker talked about grasping the fatal nature of the disease of alcoholism, how once a person has understood that their natural state is inebriated or wishing they were, they are trapped in a mindset, condemned by a body with no off-switch. The lift, the train, the crashing plane, call it what you will, the juggernaut of the disease only goes one way. A drunk, though, can be an eternal optimist about their future drinking career, and yet perplexingly a stubborn pessimist when it comes to all other matters. It is little wonder I live in a permanent state of bafflement. The truth is, of course, most drunks are plain wrong about the future most of the time. In reality, the order of events, the happenings, sometimes called the 'yets' or the 'agains' vary from person to person, but these are the stories we listen to at meetings. In essence it involves jails, institutions and finally, and rarely quickly, death. Or in our case, avoiding it.

Death is usually recorded as something else: suicide, cirrhosis, liver failure, heart disease, fell down the stairs, got into a fight, hit by a train, cancer and so on. All our stories in essence revive hope in the listener but only if they are listening. Hope was the first positive feeling I acquired when I arrived, a respite from boredom and despair. And all too often I see people leave in their droves in the faint hope that willpower alone will overcome their drinking difficulties. On that matter, I remain pessimistic. AA is said to be a spiritual solution to a problem that persistently refuses to arrest by other means.

My own view is that I simply don't know if recovering alcoholics are the chosen few or the few that chose. It was a phrase Bex's sponsor had said, her sponsor felt it was a choice, but Bex felt like it hadn't been a choice that drink had just stopped working, and she found herself in the rooms one day pushed or pulled, but certainly not of her own volition. I also felt compelled, I'd rung the helpline after reading a book about a lass going into rehab. It was a chick-lit thing, not something I'd read ordinarily, I'd just had a sudden urge to reread a book last perused in my early twenties. In this modern era, it was a click away on my Kindle. I'd read it in one night, then rang AA just before midnight to talk about my drinking in the expectation that they'd tell me I was just overdoing it because, you know, life... No one was more astonished than me when someone actually answered the phone.

She said she was a 'grateful alcoholic'. I realised I had no idea what an 'oxy' was, but sure recognised a moron when I heard one. But after a few years, I now see recovery is a privilege and not a right. I've been shown that it's not a punishment but a reward. The twelve steps offer a way out of a hellish existence. Of course, there are other ways; I've not tried them because I'm sticking with what works for me.

For many of us the biggest stumbling block to the twelve steps is the *God* word, which appears for the first time in the third step, when we agree to stop fighting and hand our will over to a God we cannot see, touch, feel or understand. It is a divisive word and whenever someone puts up an objection, I liked how the day's podcast speaker had replied with "I don't believe in the God you don't believe in either, but I do feel the presence of something in my life." What cannot be disputed, however, is AA's origins in Bible Belt America running through its literature. Often we are told to get on our knees and pray, to "hit the floor". This is particularly problematic for a thru-hiker of my type because getting up again is bloody agony and not guaranteed.

48

There is no universally agreed definition of God, nor any AA-approved method on how to revere one. For me, it isn't even a deity but a force, a sensation I can tap into deep inside me. What I really like about AA is one can stand on one's head singing *Kumbaya My Lord* wearing a *Burka* every lunchtime surrounded by joss sticks should one wish, no one would bat an eyelid. I use the God word because I am fundamentally an efficient, some would say lazy, person. It has one syllable, contrasted against 'higher power', which has four, and don't expect me to say 'God as I understand him' because I have a problem with the pronoun, more so than how waffly it is. I do not classify myself as a Christian. As a child I had asked to go to church. My mother, an evangelical atheist, sneery of all religions and spiritual practices, laughed out loud, refused, and a few weeks later told me to say I was 'Methodist' if anyone asked at the new school I was attending. Months later, I was sent to a Church of England boarding school. Then, if not now, they were legally obliged to force boarders into a Sunday Service. Mine took place in an adjacent church and it was a dreary, cold, and dull experience, nothing other than a weekly routine to be endured and definitely not enjoyed. Aside from weddings and funerals, I still don't venture into churches, but I do now have enormous respect for anyone with faith.

Today, I just have a belief in *something* and that's enough for me. I reminded myself daily that I choose to be a member of AA and not just an attender. Now that I couldn't get to meetings in person, I was making do with recordings of speakers and could only hope they offered the same magic that in-person meetings had. I wondered about Zoom meetings too, whether they'd work for us in the same way, and whether newcomers could inhale the hope, feel the warmth from a collection of people with a common problem. Meetings were firing up online all over the globe, giving access to recovery twenty-four hours a day, seven days a week, as long as one didn't live in the wilderness. I was sticking with my daily dose of AA, turning on my phone when going downhill or at flatter stretches. My gasping on the ascents drowned out my listening capabilities.

I opted to take my daily third step after I'd listened to the podcast, waiting until I found a time that I was alone. I'd recite aloud all the things I was grateful for at that moment. It countered my head demons that like to tell me it's all shite. Sometimes I did this mechanically but more often than not, I was finding I did it with a corresponding deep feeling. *Thank you for keeping me safe last night. Thank you for the fact that I've not seen a rattlesnake today. Thank you for the food I ate, even though I still think it's disgusting. Thank you for the company I'm keeping. Thank you for keeping me sober. Thank you for the painkillers I've taken,* and on and on I would blather. I never ceased to amuse myself by saying out loud "Thank you for the sanity I have," to the mountain walls. I tended to list at least ten things each day, if not more, to be grateful for. Then I'd recite my third step prayer: *God, I offer myself to you, to build with me and to do with me as you will. Relieve me of the bondage of self, that I may better do your will. Take away my difficulties, that victory over them may bear witness to those I would help of your power, your love and your way of life. Your will, not mine be done.* Adherents of the third step prayer will note the lack of Shakespearean 'thee' and 'thou' because I deeply loathe Shakespeare, the god of literature.

It's hard to know what God's will or my will is much of the time. I can only put it down to a feeling that I have sometimes, not even all the time, in a space just above my stomach. I know when I'm doing the right thing, and when I'm not. Sometimes I don't know why I'm doing something, I've no explicit reason for doing it, but it feels okay. 'Feelings are meant to be felt,' is another common refrain of the sponsor to the newcomer, but this alcoholic had made it a lifetime's occupation to not feel. The best thing about getting into recovery, they say, is that your feelings come back, and the worst thing about getting into recovery, of course, is that your feelings come back. It had taken me my entire first year in sobriety to identify what all the different feelings were, mostly they were a churned-up mess of despair and terror, anger and resentment.

As we settled into Warner Springs, pitching our tents with great difficulty in the beachy spot on the outskirts of the blink-and-you-miss-it village, we were joined by two Germans: HeadGirl and Dr. Doolittle, a swiss man called Photo, and an American called Beetroot. He was flush with stark sunburn. They'd been delayed waiting for shipments to arrive. We discussed this 'selfishness' that we all felt. It was easy to suggest that everyone was to some extent, and after all, we were in America the epitome of 'all for one, one for all' individualistic culture. But perhaps 'selfishness' meant we are all unattached - to homes, families and jobs, that we could just run for the hills and make merry whenever finances and time permitted.

We had anticipated hostility in the towns but our experiences in the desert section of the PCT were the precise opposite. Reports left, right and centre on Facebook were of being warmly welcomed. Local's malevolence was reserved for the city-dwelling Californians who were jumping into their RVs to vacation in these small towns and hamlets, doing their furloughs that way. It seemed those with the money could easily bugger off during this downtime, bringing with them the city air, and possibly the virus. In AA we often say alcoholics sit in gutters looking down on people and it felt akin to that. The pandemic was creating a need for one group to bully another. This wasn't helped by the political leaders of our time, each vying to strike a course different to their opponent.

I knew then I'd be carrying on as far as I could go. It felt like the best way forward but that didn't mean I was not conflicted. I think that's human. I knew Insane Shopper hadn't got enough funds to get her to Canada, and that Half Missing might not have the physical robustness, but for now I had both. With the high attrition rate already, I did wonder how lonely this endeavour may end up being. It was a bit like being in early recovery, I started with a handful of fellow bewildered newcomers and within a few months I'd already forgotten their names. It left me the perennial neophyte being the last one in and all. I did not know then the local government had rolled out an attractive alternative initiative to enable drinkers to learn how to control their drinking. I remain grateful for that ignorance.

The following day we headed over to the community centre, which sold basic rations and held hiker's supply boxes which they had pre-prepared and forwarded on. Ostensibly it was closed, but the indefatigable Patrice, who ran it, was willing to charge battery packs, mobile phones and other paraphernalia. One could also purchase basics listed on a laminated sheet attached to the link fencing. Insisting we sanitised everything before we dropped it into a box, we would then stand back six feet, so she could collect it. She drove the two-hundred metres or so to the centre, assembled our orders, then drove back, dropping our wares into a different box. Then pacing behind a haphazardly drawn line, she'd make sunny conversation. We would then approach to pick up our ice-creams, ramen noodles and crisps to keep us preoccupied as we sat in the baking sun waiting for our electronics to recharge. She repeated this hour after hour, quietly asking for a small donation, all to try to keep the cash flowing so the centre would remain afloat for its usual patrons to use, hopefully, the following year. At this rate of to-ing and fro-ing, she'd have covered the distance to Canada long before I would.

As I basked in the sun, we were joined by Mr. Bojangles, older, perhaps in his sixties suffering with considerable hip pain. He left his pack with us to head up to the post office, demonstrating the remarkable trust that was assumed between strangers that look, and in our cases smelt, alike. I'd never heard of Mr. Bojangles until Bex's funeral. It's a song covered by Robbie Williams, originally by Neil Diamond. She'd chosen it for the moment her coffin was to be carried out from the church to the hearse then on to crematoria. I felt her presence then, fighting the anguish I felt about her demise for the first time since that day. It was a comforting cry, but I know then I felt a form of reassurance about continuing being the right thing for me.

I've learnt that giving into fear is never the easier, softer way but more importantly, I reminded myself that as an alcoholic, I would always have difficulty following a project from beginning to end. It is a common trait. I have a tendency to not join in, to not participate and to give up as soon as things don't go my way. I suspect that's why people who undertake expeditions, whether it's the trepidatious twelve step adventure, or a more physical one like this, end up having a spiritual experience. As an alcoholic, I've learnt I can all too readily focus on the result and quickly become demoralised. Quite often, it is my expectations that are too high, and so my resentments expand to bridge the gap. In order to find a new space, a new place to exist and thrive, one has to do the hard yards. And that's why, it meant venturing on for me. I didn't know if I could do this. I'd been taught over and over that every day is about making a start, and not concentrating on the finish. And that I could start my day again and again, even on the same day. If the morning hadn't gone well, then there was still the afternoon. If the last hour was hard, then the next one might be easier, it might be harder, but I couldn't decide until after I'd completed it. Bex's husband was fond of reminding me that it won't happen this way, and it won't happen that way either. My angst, though, threatens to be all consuming. I would just have to hang on to my hat and find out how it would happen, and that if I was meant to finish I would, and if I wasn't, I wouldn't, but I could accept that it was mostly out of my hands.

A driver stopped by and dropped off a box of tangerines, oranges and tangelos, another reminder that all is not what people tell you, but what you discover for yourself. The kindness of strangers remained unabated. After I had finished my ice-creams, I'd had two, plus some chocolate and some crisps, I strolled tentatively uphill to the Post Office to collect my new tent. In yonder year we'd pick up any necessary kit along the way but now with all the gear shops closed due to California's draconian lockdown, everything had to be ordered ahead of time and sent on to the next stop. If one got there before expected, or if there was a delay in the kit being delivered, it knocked on to the schedule. Of course, one could only send things to the post office if the supplier used the US Postal Service. Anything else, like FedEx or UPS, then one required a private address, like that of Warner Springs Community Centre. This year we needed to check in advance if they were active, many of them weren't, or were, then weren't, then were again. California was the first state to go into lockdown, and as a consequence there was a sudden surge in people ordering online. Things that were expected to ship within three to five working days, were now taking weeks. I was delighted to find my tent had arrived on time, but my US sim card hadn't. The postal worker informed me he hadn't sorted the cart yet. He showed me to a picnic table behind the building, out of sight of any passing police, and told me he'd probably take an hour or two. I drank coffee after coffee obtained from the nearby petrol station, 'a buy one, get as many top-ups as you can' deal. Eventually he located a small thin envelope addressed to me and I was good to go.

Half Missing and NoNameFromTheUK decided to stay on another day. Half Missing's drug supplier had let her know he was hiking up his prices, business was booming, and consequently he was a man in high demand. Half Missing wasn't willing or able to pay the excess, so she'd opted to wait out another day for another supplier. I was keen to make moves and thankfully so was Insane Shopper. "This place is covered in poo," she observed as we packed up. I felt more hobo than hiker camping in a town, and with the sanitation facilities decommissioned because of Corona we all had to go somewhere. So do all the dog walker's dogs, as well as the free-roaming cows, and some random turkeys. The entire place seemed to be encircled in shite.

****

Submitting to sleeplessness

Insane and I stumbled into Mike's place just past five o'clock. A scrappy sign claimed the homestead open to hikers. A quarter of a mile or so later, we pushed open a creaking gate decorated with the skulls of a ram and a boar, probably, although my knowledge of skeletal matter is a little disappointing. At least one of the horns had been transplanted from another unfortunate creature. Historically, this was a must-do destination for hikers, who descended in their scores to hang out for a day or so, smoke some weed and generally rock and roll. Now it was a ghost town although remnants of its past remained: laundry buckets strewn about the yard; paintings celebrating each 'class of'; the infamous old pizza oven, and ashtrays dotted all over the veranda. We studied the visitor's trail register book entitled the 'Rebellious Class of 2020'. Two people had visited yesterday, Insane recognised the name of one entry, me none.

The place was desolate and ramshackle now, although still maintained by Ghost, himself a former PCT hiker as well as a surf-boarding, republican hippy with a devout belief in God. He showed us where to charge our devices, and the latrine system - a choice of two toilet seats both nailed onto the one large wooden box. It is probably the most redeeming part of staying at Mike's place, offering as it does a shit with a substantial view. One can do one's morning ablutions and mindfulness meditations simultaneously without fear of being interrupted. Ghost informed us we could sleep in the old mobile home, leased out for free on a first-come, first-served basis. It should be last in, definitely condemned. One could fight not to sleep in there.

So far, I'd only spent one night in my new tent, which looked exactly like one a child would draw. It was a single-walled triangular prism which could be accessed from either side. Incredibly lightweight, the lightest on the market, it could theoretically house two people. I thought it was best occupied by me plus my ample arse and rucksack. I dubbed it the Clingfilm Castle because it is practically see-through, although tinged with blue colouring. It was so spacious; I found my sleeping pad and I tobogganing to the bottom corner for much of my first night within it.

Sleeping on a blow up-mat takes a lot of adjusting to. I am a sprawler ordinarily, taking over an entire bed, moulding around myself a foot-long cat, who stretches like a slinky to at least three feet during the wee hours. I was particularly not enjoying sleeping on a foot-wide strip of lumpy air. If I laid on my back, it was so peculiar, I could do little but doze. On my side was better, but within a few minutes I got terrible hip pain and then an ache in my back emerged shortly after. The only way to alleviate this was to sleep on my front, depositing each boob in one of the mattress' many depressions, rather than on a comfy pillow as I would normally do. The issue remained as to what to do with my legs. They were confined by the sleeping bag, limiting my sprawl, but even if I allowed one leg to break free by lowering the zip, my knee chilled against the tent floor. I had this endless scrap until eventually somehow my brain powered into sleep mode.

Being zipped up made temperature control practically impossible. At home, a solitary foot can jut out from under the duvet, and equilibrium is soon restored to my inner thermostat. Not so when sleeping in the ever-warming desert. I'd been sleeping fully clothed, with all three top layers on, including a puffer jacket. I would reach boiling point sometime around ten o'clock, but then by four a.m., I would be sufficiently disturbed to put my puffer back on. The desert temperatures truly plummet when the night sky is clear. It's not just darkest before dawn, it is also bloody freezing.

Being the only visitors at Mike's Place, Insane and I were so bone-tired the option to not erect tents appealed greatly, and thus we risked the flea-pit. We mitigated that menace by placing our sleeping mats over the heavily stained mattresses and used our own sleeping bags in lieu of the blankets available; all in the vain hope our own stuff might offer some protection against its lurgies. Being inside offered, perhaps, a better night's sleep.

On trail I was also plagued by random itchiness throughout the night. I suspected it was menopausal: my skin having neither rash nor bites. Perhaps, though, it was the absence of thorough cleaning. I was used to showering, or rather wallowing in a bath, every day. My hair had become a grease-fest slapped against the dome of my head, but mostly it was hidden under a cap with side-panels for extra protection against the desert sunshine. I'd smother myself in sun cream daily but still I was burning red hot by the end of each day. Insane Shopper was a delectable fuchsia so I could only assume I was too.

I'd attributed some of my sleeplessness to something primordial activated within me. I was forever keeping one ear open just in case a saber-toothed tiger escaped from a nearby zoo or something. I still woke up early no matter what. In contrast, Insane had absolutely no problem staying asleep all bloody morning. She also loved, and definitely needed, a cooked breakfast to get some oomph into her before she could depart for the day. Typically, hiking life for her was as flat as an ice rink. In fact, a sleeping policeman could be considered a substantial hill in Denmark, a country whose highest point is around one hundred and seventy-one metres above sea level. That's a mere five hundred and sixty-one feet. We ascended and descended that five or six times a day, and we hadn't even got to the Sierra yet.

Insane was also questioning whether her circulatory system was a hindrance. She'd had problems before. Although I wasn't fast myself, and I stopped frequently, I was able to pull away from her at each climb. I'd say with ease, but it was more of a case that I'd pause ten percent less often. It was painful to watch her even as she was getting fitter. It was sinking in that not only could I do more mileage, but I needed to. I was getting fractious; we didn't seem to be able to get to double digits before talk of erecting tents commenced. Usually, by four in the afternoon, when it seemed the unrelenting heat was never going to dwindle, we'd be calling time on the day.

Now with March shifting into April, the heat began to scream by ten in the morning, and yet it was rare we got going until nine-thirty. As we'd packed up at Mike's Place that morning, very early for once, I was optimistic for a good pre-seven am commencement, making best use of the chilly morning. Then Insane announced she was to wash her knickers. Already raring to go with my pack on, I was astonished she hadn't thought to do it the night before. With no navigation, I'd be a fool to go my own way. Once again, I mentioned getting up earlier, like a metronome going back and forth, so as to maximise hiking in cooler temperatures. Insane said very little on the matter.

Later that day, we again discussed putting up our tents, at four-thirty, exhausted and sore. We'd been pummelled by a heavy wind for much of the day. As was typical, I'd inched ahead on the ascents, her catching me on the descents. By the time we'd linked up after ten miles on the trail, Insane's phone's battery was kaput, a consequence of checking it every few hundred metres as she laboured uphill to see if she was nearly there yet. We'd to-ed and fro-ed debating to camp next to the water, a quarter mile downhill, then having found the spots less than comfortable, hiked back up again

"Let's get your phone working," Insane shouted over the fierce gusts battering our tents, now she'd been able to recharge her phone. I managed to get the sim card out of my UK phone only to discover that until Insane had phone reception, we couldn't activate it. We were still two days, possibly more, from our next pitstop.

****

Letting shit happen

Letting go was a terrifying prospect for me in early recovery. "I have a fear of becoming the hole in the doughnut," said no one until they read it in AA literature, and even then, I think quite a lot of people go 'eh?' In essence, it is at Step Three when the choice to change is made and we relinquish the ideas and the plans we had and quit trying to run the show. Rather, we try doing things as they are suggested to us, and to learn to live in the moment, and do the next right thing and all that jazz. For me, it meant stopping the endless bargaining and negotiating. I'm a great negotiator: if you don't do it my way, I'll do my utmost to make you see it my way, and if you're in charge, I'll bargain and bargain even if I don't care what the outcome is. And if it's just me (versus the world in my head), then I'll set my expectations so high, that failure is practically guaranteed, and that way I can justify getting drunk, or pissed off, or feel sorry for myself.

The day's podcast speaker had talked about one's choice being narrowed down so significantly, that in essence there was not much left to negotiate by the time he took the third step. Still, he'd rushed out and taken his third a full three years after getting into recovery. It's hard to admit defeat and harder still to let something else take charge. That can be as simple as just listening to someone else's experience. Not their opinion, but their actual lived experience. Then, and only, then one can incorporate those ways of thinking and doing.

As I set off that morning, I planned to finally do my first fifteen-mile day. I'd had enough of the part-time walking, the slow starts, and early finishes. I'd informed Insane of my intended stopping point that day, a spot near the highway that led to Paradise. Paradise Valley Cafe, in actual fact. There it was rumoured we might be able to have a proper breakfast, served all day. Only I hadn't expected to be afflicted by that great leveller of all people: diarrhoea. I'd hoped it was a one-off bout, but I discovered I was full of shit, and it, not me and my plans, was going to be running the show that day.

I'd seen YouTube instruction videos on how to do your business in a bush, but I'd argue it's one of the advantages women hikers have over men: great squatting muscles, given we've all had those 'Annie' moments. Insane had a peeing aid so she stood upright to pee. I'd tried one of those many years ago for another adventure, practising as suggested in the shower beforehand. When it came to the real deal, I was forced to concede it wasn't for me as the pee maintained a steady flow down the inside of my leg right down into my shoe. I still have no idea if this is because I have a wonky vulva that defies engineering, or whether the tool was engineered by men for women. The latter is more likely I suppose. I think I'd know with my sexual history, no more of later, that some bloke might have just mentioned that mine doesn't look like *the ones on 't 'telly*.

But no peeing aid was going to come to my assistance today. The back-end stuff, be it solid or liquid, requires more careful depositing than the front end. In particular, it is suggested very strongly, and very repeatedly by every US Forestry Worker I happened upon along the way, to dig a cat hole of six or seven inches with a very small trowel, a hiking pole or a stick and then do the 'ready, aim, fire' sequence. Unfortunately, this is less successful when you have an upset stomach. As my sponsor is apt to tell me, "Person, if there's a stick to be picked up, I guarantee you'll pick it up with the wrong end." And that's why on this day, I decided it was high time to buy one of those lightweight trowels everyone raves about. There is a substantial dearth of good shitty sticks in the desert.

58

The other thing about learning to *Let Go, Let God* (as you understand <insert your own pronoun here>) is that very quickly one can find delights which one might not otherwise experience. Today's salvation came quickly enough in the shape of Mary's Place. It is a dedicated PCT rest area for thru-hikers, complete with a random library, a latrine, a shower and a picnic table. Fascinatingly, the table is watched over by cardboard cutouts of three transcendentalists: Henry David Thoreau, John Muir and Walt Whitman.

Mary, who I nominate for sainthood, had also supplied a covered tank full of clear water. Earlier in the day I'd refilled my bottles with a hideously green pungent liquid from a cistern which was rumoured to have decomposing animals floating around in it. It was little wonder the plants at Mary's place were so lush, I was sure I was not the only one who watered them with the remaining liquid compost I'd been carrying. The latrine came with reading literature, a first-aid kit and a wealth of 2020's rarest commodity: toilet paper. I was nearing the end of my own supplies with nether-region conditions being what they were, I feared I'd have to make do with a prickly pear. In the first-aid kit, I'd hoped to find some Imodium or similar but that was not to be. I did, however, lavish my over-wiped anus with Benadryl, an antihistamine lotion which boasts anti-itch properties. Whether this is its intended use I cared little, but it not half alleviated matters.

Shortly after, Insane arrived. Amazed she'd been so close, we dined together and then I pushed on to complete the remaining six miles to Paradise Valley Cafe, or rather the point the PCT intersects a tarmacked highway; the cafe itself is situated a mile west of the trail. A small campervan picked me up straightaway, and just like Pavlov's beloved dogs, I was salivating to the point of drooling at the idea of decent sustenance, more so than the enormous Labrador with whom I shared the back seat.

I'd already planned to sample as much of the cafe's menu as I feasibly could: drowning a fresh, crisp side-salad with a delightful ranch dressing, wolfing down a cheesy omelette or a Beyond Burger, the vegetarian alternative, or a pizza or whatever was hot, fatty and moreish. I could practically smell the iced tea, cooling my rasping tongue, followed by an energising percolated coffee that the Americans do in a way that is unfathomable to the UK. There is a chocolatey loveliness to it, especially when laced abundantly with 'half and half', a deliciously creamy milk favoured in America.

More than miffed to find the cafe closed, even though it was not long after three, the kindly hitch-givers gave me a half a litre of water, which tasted terribly chemical, and a ride straight back to the trailhead where I stalked off sulking. I opted not to stay at the previously designated tent spot, but to use my frustration to push on. This lasted an entire mile when I realised there was also a dearth of any decent flat spots for another five miles beyond the one already occupied just to the right of me. I put up my tent and made polite conversation with the resident PCT hiker, whom I'd been leap-frogging for days. Each time he'd passed me, or I him, he'd said there was no point rushing through the desert section because the Sierra wouldn't be passable until June the fifteenth. But I was timebound by my six-month visa, and I figured getting an extension would be almost impossible this year. My campmate for the night was permanently leaving the trail the following day, this adventure not panning out as he'd hoped. I had no way of telling Insane that I'd carried on.

As dusk fell, I finished yet another gag-invoking rice and pasta Mexican mix, washed down with a tiny cup of instant decaf mixed with coffee-mate flavoured with sickly vanilla essence. I studied the next few days' hiking which was to take me to mile 179, the next junction to a town, this one called Idyllwild. I read the notes supplied by other hikers, which I'd last updated in Julian. They all remarked on the immense snow levels. There was also a trail marker eighteen miles ahead, a red warning sign, indicating the approximate spot that Trevor "Microsoft" Laher had perished. Ice axes and microspikes were strongly encouraged and I had neither. All posts indicated that going to Idyllwild via the Devil's Slide Trail rather than hitching from Paradise Cafe was lunacy in action. The Devil's Slide Trail is ordinarily a two-and-a-half mile, one and a half thousand-foot descent of misery, but this year hell had also frozen over.

Decision made: I was going to skip this bit and rejoin the trail slightly ahead of Idyllwild where it would be safer, beyond the Mount San Jacinto wilderness. In the morning, I'd walk back the way I'd come, then to Paradise for breakfast, hopefully access some wi-fi and then head into Idyllwild. There I'd figure out how to get back on the trail, well beyond the dangerous section after a day's rest. That was *my* plan, anyway.

****

Crowded in a lonely place

Life is what happens to you while you're busy making proper plans preventing piss poor performance, and life at this moment brought an earthquake; an outlaw AA meeting; a four-day layover in Idyllwild; quite a lot of drink and some drugs, as well as a ton of new gear.

Arriving at Paradise well in time to be its first customer, I was astonished to find myself in second place. Half Missing, after three days of hiking on her own, had decided to terminate but then heard that Insane and I would be shortly arriving, so she'd jumped ahead to regroup with us. Of course, I then had to tell her that I'd misplaced Insane yesterday evening in my moment of impetuousness. Half Missing then informed me that Insane had actually managed the fifteen miles. She was due to head down to the cafe for breakfast herself. Indeed, she arrived a few hours later. And with that we booked an entire log cabin for the three of us in nearby Idyllwild.

We spilled out from our ride's car in plenty of time to check-in. We could then enjoy the remaining daylight hours browsing the windows of shops not likely to be opened anytime soon. Idyllwild is aptly named, a southern Californian mountain resort popular with outdoor recreational types who have a curious penchant for going to high places, ostensibly to climb *Suicide Rock* but often just to escape the unrelenting desert heat even if only for a day or two. I presume not for nothing is the town known as 'mile-high Idyllwild' which may also provide a perfectly reasonable explanation as to why its town mayor is a dog called Maximus Mighty-Dog Mueller II, or Max for those on paw-shaking terms. Alas, in these Covid-fearing times, even the dog was furloughed.

We made a beeline for the food outlets for a take-out lunch, and then set about eating, unpacking and washing back at our cabin. I contacted my UK mobile phone supplier to send the unlock codes for my phone so I could use my US Sim. I was subsequently astonished to learn it would take ten days. I ordered a small SOS beacon, some puffer pants for the icy nights, more KT - a magic kinesthetic tape for relieving sports injuries, but now deemed useful for patching up holes in clothes and preventing blisters on hands and feet. It is far better and lighter than Duct Tape. I selected new shoes and a new battery pack. Anything that could be fast-tracked delivery. As box after box arrived for me at the chalet, the deliverer said, "Careful of that one, it came from China," with reference to the conspiracy theories popularised by the incumbent president. Even while shopping I noticed I was buying foodstuffs from far-flung places. The world's capillaries still moved around even when its veins were clamped shut.

That night the earth certainly moved for us all as the town was struck by an earthquake and several subsequent aftershocks. Memes circulated: Corona Virus: Everyone stay inside; Earthquake: everyone run outside; God sings: *You put the scared people in, you put the scared people out, you put the scared people in, and you shake them all about.* Unfazed, dealers arrived selling their wares, and cans of beer popped open left, right and centre as people congregated at picnic tables. I had never thought about the fact that drinking and pill-popping would be compatible with long-distance hiking, but it is, and I've noticed it's rarely discussed in literature.

Sometimes, I find it little wonder that I stayed in a state of oblivion about my own drinking, when even shops sell amusing punny signs and trinkets about gin or prosecco to decorate kitchens and living rooms with. I'm so hard-wired around alcohol that I can spot a glass of wine in the fuzzy background of a film, but not notice a blatant continuity error. It's only when one sets themselves apart and stands off to the side, one can truly decipher how every day and unnoticed the whole drinking culture is. Now with lockdown it seemed to be exploding to new levels. An abundance of jokey memes circulated on social media about the joys of homeschooling young children whilst under the influence; how at the end of this, half the population will be expert bread-makers, the rest seeking help for alcoholism. That, *thank God,* off-licences, or liquor stores as they say in the US, were deemed essential, whereas churches had now been locked up.

Within weeks, AA phone lines were reportedly over-run. Like everywhere else, AA could no longer hold in-person meetings. People on both sides of the pond were suddenly forbidden from meeting face-to-face to share experiences and offer support to break the interminable isolation of the secret drinker. It is that support which is the blood flow of AA's system: helping one another get or stay well. Entire volunteer armies for a wide range of charities nationwide were also disbanded in both countries. I got my first inkling of what living in pandemonium was like: who matters and who doesn't.

The pandemic moved closer to home when a friend's sponsor died after forty-odd years of continuous sobriety. "From Covid, or with it?" another friend asked when I spoke to her, an intelligent health-care professional on the front lines. That evening I watched a small gathering of PCT hikers congregate in various states of inebriation and I got a glimpse of our recklessness. I stayed away, not because of the virus, but because I hate being around drunk people.

I picked up a message on Facebook from a local AA. He had a coffee pot if I had a resentment: those being the essential ingredients of all AA meetings. The next day, he and I shared recovery stories, outside, socially-distanced and against the rules. The coffee was divine. Then a finger-whistle attracted our attention and a location yelled out. We jumped in his car to go out of town to a parking lot. There people sat in the boot of their stationary cars set six feet or so apart in a large circle. Others arrived on foot or bike. The opening lines were read, '*We are a fellowship of men and women, who share their experience, strength and hope with one another...*" Immediately, I felt at home and safe with people who have a disease, just like me, that wants us dead.

Somewhere in all of this melee, Half Missing and Insane Shopper hatched a plan for us to jump ahead to Acton at the 444th mile. From there we could head north to pass the seven-hundred-mile mark, then head back later to Idyllwild to do the near three-hundred miles in the middle. It was a good plan, one that would piss off the purists and the dogmatists, but the adage, "Hike your own hike" came into its own here. I likened it to AA's 'stick to your own side of the street,' a more polite way of saying mind your own business and stop your bleedin' curtain twitching whilst you're at it.

Two days later, we arrived at Acton KOA, a section hiker and fan of the PCT giving us a free ride the entire way, stopping only to pick up coffees and doughnuts from fast-food outlets. The KOA campsite remained defiantly open but like everywhere else it had closed all of its amenities. There were no bathrooms. We did the 'shop dance', one in at a time, roped it to remain in a tightly confined area. We yelled our requirements to the shop-keeper, in this case a tent space for one for the night.

We put up tents early-afternoon. I was baffled as to why, given all the respite of four days of zero mileage, we weren't at least putting away a couple of miles whilst we could. Rather we had paid to stay in a campground next to train tracks, where foghorns announced the passage of impossibly long locomotives ferrying container after container, hour after hour. For all my acute abilities to notice booze in the moment, it was weeks before it dawned on me the two of them were nursing a four-day hangover. "Get yourself out of the gutter, and stop looking down on people," I know that's what a good sponsor would have told me.

****

Chapter four

Taking a feminist inventory of myself

I suppose any transformation must commence with a thorough understanding of who you were to begin with, and it turned out I used to be quite repressed. As we neared the end of the fourth week, Insane Shopper and I were now on burping and farting terms with one another, a first for me. Worse, I had become inclined to announce to my fellow hikers that I needed to poo and off I went. Sometimes, I heard bushes yelling at me that they too were having a poo. The process of becoming a thru-hiker, I could only conclude, was learning how to become the most revolting version of oneself, and then discovering there are new lows to attain. I was reaching levels of grossness that I would normally never admit to. I'd learnt how to snot rocket, footballer-style. If I was itchy in the nether-regions, a thorough scratching was absolutely fine whether or not there were bystanders: just like there had been in the tiny town of Agua Dulce where I treated myself to a coffee then lay legs akimbo on a park bench as I slurped up the dregs of it noisily, and all without a modicum of self-consciousness.

My morning rituals now included self-diagnosing whether or not I had Corona. Reports indicated one of the earliest symptoms being a loss of smell. As I'd long since dispensed with deodorant, my inner quack assured me I was negative as I unzipped my sleeping bag and unleashed the trappings of the night. The miasma worsened by the abundance of underarm hair. This is ordinarily frowned upon: hair and women have traditionally been so taboo that it took me decades to notice that television adverts always show beautiful models shaving already hairless parts of their body. That I had hair sprouting haphazardly in random places was testament to the fact that as a woman, I was clearly sub-par. I also had a bikini line emerging: my underwear had worn away a strip of pubic hair on either side of my pelvic region. As I traipsed through Vasquez Rocks, a region famous as the settings for Planet of the Apes and the Flintstones, I determined I'd make a suitably hirsute extra. My hair was now so greasy, I could feasibly arrange it *Thelma* style, without requiring a single bobby pin to keep it in place.

The trail through Vasquez Rocks was utterly breath-taking not for its effluvium, but rather its enchanting natural architecture.

The area is littered with compacted sandstone striations protruding out at sharp angles out from the bronzed sand: the wreckage of a bygone era known for epic earthquakes emanating from the San Andreas Fault. The rock glows a burnt orange at times, but with the day's drizzle, it was mostly grey and pockmarked. Rainfall dripped onto the pebbly trail, trapping the water into a stream. By the time I'd got to the upper part of the hill, gasping for air, I was as damp and soggy as my surroundings, my trousers clamped to my legs. Still, I was glad of the milder undulation, coming as it did with soft, but squelchy, sandy ground.

I'd put on some oversized wet-weather trousers and a see-through plastic anorak first thing even though the outfit was way too big for me. The two-piece had been the only size available at the outdoors shop, and like the long-since discarded poncho, they had promised much, but being pocketless and too long, they had delivered little. Catching my foot in the excess trouser leg, I thundered forward, landing sharply on my right hand and whacking my left knee on a half-buried stone. I'd lain there for a while, quashing my tears, waiting with dread to see if the pain would be permanent. From the sloppy floor, I opened one eye, then the other to notice a rubbish bin less than fifty feet away. It was quite the random piece of civilised furniture. I hauled myself up, nurturing my hand gingerly and with a great flourish, a few loud curses and final 'feck you', I ripped off the plastic overclothes and deposited all the rain-proof gear into the trash can.

One of the vastly underappreciated luxuries of living a sober life is that when I get a bruise these days, I know exactly how I got it. The downside, of course, is that I feel the moment of impact too. Hiking had returned me to the days of clueless and careless; my legs were a veritable collection of blue, black and green splodges, each day's walking only adding to the tally. This day finally concluded with the surprise of discovering an entire toenail in the bottom of my sock. The '*piggy that had none*' was now a literal interpretation of the '*This Little Piggy*' poem. It left me with a toe that looked like it belonged to a large plastic doll. It had the slot for a nail to fit into but there was absolutely nothing but flesh there. My stomach somersaulted. Trench foot can readily be a problem, but I anticipated that to occur in the Sierra, not in the desert. In any case, I had always loathed my feet. I've had bunions without even once stepping into a stiletto. I can't take heels of any kind whatsoever because my feet are so mangled. In my early teens, I used to think my hideous feet would make me unmarriable, in my late thirties, I wished they had. Now I realised they were a vital part of me, and I came to marvel at what they were achieving.

I was also losing weight. I'd learned this was unusual for women hikers early on, but then I had all that cake to shift. Women thru-hikers tended to change shape within the first few months but gain pounds initially as we built muscle mass. Men, of course, lost weight much more readily. It was anticipated that both genders would have suppressed appetites for the first few weeks of a thru-hike, and I was certainly experiencing that. My inner skinny bitch was delighted. As a teen, I'd been very controlling around food portions, caring less about nutrition, and more about calories. I'd been overweight in my mid-teens, picking up quite a bit of so-called 'puppy fat' just when I changed schools. Looking back now at photos I wasn't anything close to obese as I believed myself to be. But jibes are cruel, and any woman I'm sure that isn't picture perfect, or movie-star ready, gets their fair share of comments from boys probably just as insecure. I learned early on to compare myself to others and it is a habit I've never lost.

I've carried that 'fat girl syndrome' my entire life. Perhaps this mindset is pretty common, especially amongst alcoholic women. Oddly when I was drinking, I'd batter and abuse my body seemingly without care. Alcohol is terribly aging. Abstinence and AA are said to be the best anti-aging agents women can get - whether or not we think we are worth it! Early recovery can be particularly brutal for women: as many of us suddenly put on a ton of weight after a few weeks or months of being sober. For me, it added to the despair and frustration of coming to the reality of recent years. We're told, though, to eat chocolate and sweet things to ward off the alcohol cravings. A lot of women shun that advice, taking up all sorts of diets and exercise routines to counter their suddenly-burgeoning bodies. In those precious early months, I've witnessed many become obsessed with their appearance and shape once again, only to then find themselves over-doing it, become demoralised and put themselves at the jeopardy of a relapse. 'Keep it simple,' I was told. Deal with the things in the order they are going to kill you, and fat thighs have never killed anyone.

I was looking at my body with a new curiosity. At Idyllwild there'd been a huge mirror in the bathroom, and I'd been astonished by just how much loathsome cellulite I had. It had been the first time in years I had truly observed myself naked, safe in the knowledge that there was nothing more that I could be doing about my physique. As I tented up that night, I surveyed the wreckage that was my skin, and I was quite in awe of my list:

One infected blister, back of right foot,
Five nearly healed blisters across the top of both sets of toes
One wound on top of left foot
A mahoosive graze on wobbly bits at bottom of back - from rucksack
Bruises from my rucksack straps across shoulders
Large bruise from corner of sofa Mike's Place mobile home still on left thigh
About six smaller bruises on left knee - from today
Deep scratch on bottom left leg
Three healing wounds on hands - no longer infected - one a self-inflicted knife wound
Swollen wrist - today
Bruises on left arm - no idea
Bloody bogeys. No idea why
A scorched bikini line (both sides)
A very sore anus - I'm starting to wonder if I have giardia
One missing toenail
One broken fingernail

Nothing healed swiftly on the trail, but I had a new admiration for what I was actually doing, and how much my body was able to tolerate, notwithstanding the cramps, the repetitive strains, and the bizarre shooting pains surging up through the soles of my feet as I pounded away metre after metre of the trail. As a teen, I was frequently told by doctors, school nurses and teachers that I made too much of a fuss when I had period pain; that I needed to learn to get on with it like all the other girls did. "Women's issues" they called them, implying they were second-rate, and not particularly interesting. And now here I was, with my fibroids and unsighted endometriosis scars, only discovered when I'd had an oophorectomy, getting on with it. As I always imagined, life was so much easier now that period pain was no longer bedeviling me on a monthly basis.

When I did my first fourth step, my womanhood was one of the many resentments I had never truly understood. When talking about it, it dawned on me that all too often I had allowed others to tell me what was wrong with me, rather than trusting my body to tell me that something was not altogether right with it. It was a medical form of gaslighting, being told I was imagining it, when in reality either the science wasn't there, or my needs were invisible. Today, I know period pain is not just 'one of those things.' I'm learning and getting better at trusting my gut and myself. That it's okay to speak up and speak out. Demure, for me, was becoming so last century.

****

The underlying causes, conditions and calamities

With the jump ahead, the overall scenery had changed quite remarkably. At times I could imagine myself in Wales with its low-slung rolling hills, overgrown with dense creosote bush. These ones, though, were devoid of sheep and other non-threatening inhabitants. In Wales, one would not see a coyote fleeing around the nub of a mountain or a giant yucca with its protruding dead stem towering over me. The weather, however, was tremendously Welsh: overcast and gloomy, dark clouds coming and going, sometimes spraying out their contents all over me.

The day before, I'd announced I wanted to start extending my daily mileage, news which was not greeted well. "We're a tramily, we stick together," Half Missing retorted, but it didn't sway my feelings that I was underperforming. We had only managed two-hundred miles, and that was in twenty-four days. I was getting irked by it all: the late starts, the early finishes, the long hotel stays. Half Missing was adamant we shouldn't worry about it, that usually people do it in five and a half months. She reasoned we had plenty of time, equally adamant that for the first month or six weeks, we needed to wait for the arrival of our trail legs. This is a much-touted phenomena when everything supposedly magically snaps into place, and longer daily distances become easier to acquire, rather than the daily relentless slogs they currently were. Half Missing name dropped some well-known long-distance YouTubers urging hikers to

69

limit themselves to ten or so miles a day. "But not for an entire month, just the first few days - to warm up, and get used to things." I countered. Besides, we were averaging eight miles a day when I factored in all the time we'd spent off trail.

"If I'd known you'd be pushing out long mileage, I'd have stayed in Idyllwild," Half Missing spat back at me. If you could slam a tent door, she would have. Zipping up the side panels to vent her spleen didn't have quite the same impact. Insane Shopper was pondering whether to go home too as her aging father had just been hospitalised with an infection. She was worried about her mother getting Corona. I felt very snared, beholden to do the right thing by others once again. But the fact remained that my objective was to get to Canada and lying around in hotels and campgrounds wasn't making the distance for me. I was restless, irritable and discontent to use a familiar AA cliché.

As I was already up early, typical for me, my tent was packed, and I was ready to go. Naturally, they weren't. I'd suffered my entire life being told, "I'm not a team player," only I got into AA and learnt I was a people-pleaser. That one baffled me. How could I be so selfless, prioritising others' needs above my own, and yet simultaneously be incredibly selfish, focused only on my own goals and wants? Family for me was also a dirty word. It isn't essential to come from a dysfunctional background to become an addict, but it certainly provided many excuses to drink.

That's why the much dreaded fourth step proved infinitely helpful when I finally succumbed to its charms. A podcast speaker had observed something similar, stating it was "the most feared step of them all, which was odd because it's the ninth that is the real pain the arse." I don't suppose I was alone about my reticence to plunge forward and take a very hard, long look at my pasts, at the things that made me angry; events that had irrevocably wounded me or entrenched within me a lifetime of defences and self-sabotaging behaviours. I started and stopped with the blame game. I felt, and still do, that it really didn't help that the authors of the twelve steps deigned to call the fourth step, "a searching and moral inventory of ourselves," because the moral word really does put the fear of God even into the most atheist of us.

The easiest way out of living with myself was to point the finger at everyone or everything else. I wanted to do anything other than give myself a fair and thorough appraisal. No one likes the truth, but I've learnt there's my truth, your truth and the truth. Usually, I'm in denial on the latter two and bullshitting on the former. Like everyone, there's stuff I thought I'd take to the grave, degrading stuff, that would tarnish my image of being the wronged party, or rather remove my delusions of sainthood. It's the step where I faced the guilt, the shame and the remorse.

Of all the steps, though, it is the loneliest step, I think. It's the one that only you can do. No one can tell your story for you, no one can minimise your tragedies nor force you to take a judgemental or forgiving approach to it. That said, for me it is the step that triggered a new way of thinking. Unfortunately, thru-hiking brings huge chunks of time alone lost only in one's own fantasies and laments. The podcast speaker said our minds were dangerous neighbourhoods, so it was best we didn't go there unaccompanied. With other illnesses, especially serious ones, there's sympathy and understanding, but not so much with addiction, not unless you're in a fellowship.

I left Insane and Half Missing to their own decisions. Later that morning, I could hear Half Missing talking to, or perhaps at, Insane across the valley behind me but not the details so I knew they were making good progress. I kept pottering on. The day's descent was unbelievably serene with, for once, soft sand underfoot rather than ankle-twisting craggy rocks. I managed to get a nice head of steam as the trail rolled down and down. At times, I felt like I floated, especially as I glided through gorgeous woodland. This was what I imagined walking the PCT would be like and I loved it until I didn't. Then I was beside myself. Utterly bereft that it came to an abrupt end at a road. I wanted it to last all the way to Canada. Now I was faced with yet another five-hundred-foot climb, steadily ascending the next two miles. I passed two women, who'd been overtaking us daily, and us them. They were already camped up, tents rammed together, very snuggly. I didn't want to see if there was more space because it was still only half past two in the afternoon. I drew an arrow straight on in the ground and added a 'PI' underneath so the other two would know I was still on trail and forging ahead.

Unexpected heavy weather was billowing in once more obscuring the crests of the mountains. Sloppy drops of rain splattered around, and it was bitter cold. I contemplated stopping and retrieving my puffy jacket, but then remembered I'd stuffed it to the bottom of my pack that morning. Unusual practice for me but I'd wanted it dry to wear later, not wet as it normally was so I just moved on, breaking off only to collect then filter water quickly at a nearby stream. Now though, teeth chattering, fingers numb, feet agonising and back breaking, I was nearing defeat.

I gave up with my hiking day three miles before I had intended to, managing a mere fourteen miles, exhausted by the day, my head a frenzied mess. I was annoyed with them, annoyed at me and pissed at the weather. Terrified that I really couldn't do this trail, that it was too vast, too high, too hard, too jeffing everything. Going home wasn't a viable option either. I had no home to go to. I'd given my place up, my stuff was in storage, the rental market shut down. Everyone was in lockdown and isolated. How would I even quarantine?

It's only once one has gone through the steps for the first time, that one realises that they are the easier, softer way. The alternative is to remain a dry drunk, or worse, a drunk, but of course, like many, I had believed there must be another way. That was why I had dilly-dallied for a long time before I embarked on them properly. Years earlier, I'd lost my true home in Wales, and with it all my aspirations, when my husband walked out. I staggered around for years after, half-heartedly trying to put my life back together. When I was frightened, I could still get mad at him for leaving, when I was happy, I was glad he was gone. Our love affair had been a simple story of two incapable drunks trying to function in a marital unit, and we'd both failed abjectly. It ended in the usual recriminations of, "he's a twat, and I'm the virgin Mary." I stopped drinking exactly one year after the divorce was pronounced. I say stopped, I paused for ten weeks. Then I had a bad day, so I drank again. A one night special that I told no one about. I carried on counting sober days, pretending that one day had ever happened. But it had and it tormented me.

I wouldn't get a sponsor for a long time. The day's speaker had listed what a sponsor wasn't - they weren't a parent, or a boss, nor a bank or a taxi-driver, just someone who had learnt how to work the steps into their lives and was willing to give up some time showing a newcomer how to do the same. I had an inherent fear of authority and perennial hatred of being told what to do but I found someone who was guiding and not overly didactic. Looking objectively at my life had been an adventure into unfamiliar territory and one I desperately needed to explore without collapsing into a morass of self-pity. I had thought the steps would be all about not drinking. I was wrong. It was about learning how to thrive and not just survive. Addicts of any type are often bound in a need for instant gratification, and I was no exception. The podcast speaker was keen to remind us that the long-term results are typically so much better than quick wins. Naturally, I hate the slow burn, the working hard for obscure and unguaranteed results in the future; the constant endeavouring to not succumb to my impetuous nature.

I pitched my tent, emptied the contents of my rucksack inside, then arranged them neatly into different piles of utility. The spare clothes were annoyingly sodden from the day, so I left them in the pack and set about pumping up my sleeping pad before collapsing onto it. I had a system now, so my evenings and mornings had an efficient routine to them. As I set up my cooking pot, my right foot erupted into waves of torture and I noiselessly screamed and writhed around the confines of my tent. It appeared to be the toenail-less toe but not the actual toenail part, rather the bone. I fished out two painkillers and cursed and moaned a lot, although silently so as not to disturb the wildlife.

"Oh, my God," Insane announced, each coming out between pants. "I've had an ordeal with Half Missing, I'm so glad you're here, I couldn't have climbed much further." She went on to say that when they got to the road, Half Missing abruptly hailed a car and left the PCT, mentioning something about needing medication for her bipolar disorder. For reasons which escaped me, she'd stopped taking her prescribed medicine. I recalled she'd had several meltdowns in Idyllwild, which I'd put down to her using so much marijuana on top of booze. On top of that she'd accidentally also left her vape in the trail angel's car. Now she was taking some pretty intense marijuana edibles. I presumed these would mess further with her bipolar moods.

I had been on antidepressants for two years, and I'd stockpiled up enough to get me through the six months I was in America. I realised early on I wanted to feel again: every damned thing. I was on such a low dose anyway that I didn't suffer particularly from withdrawals, at least not that I recognised but Half

Missing had been on high numbers. I'd also just thrown away my anti-anxiety meds. Not that I'd taken any of them for well over two years, but I'd brought them just in case I got scared. Not because I needed them, but to abuse them, to use them to change how I felt when perhaps it was most appropriate to be frightened. I hadn't yet taken one, but I'd had them close to hand, "just in case". Undoubtedly, I was still behaving like an addict. It was a reminder that I will never be cured and, for addicts like me, the slope can be especially slippery, and often unsighted.

I also know that medication has been a contentious issue for some in AA. The extremely dogmatic argue that if you take psychiatric medicines, you aren't sober. This was certainly a view promulgated in the 1980s by a specific enclave within AA known as the *Pacific Group*, who spawned several off-shoots identifiable by their much more emphatic, overt recovery practices. The Pacific Group had produced a large number of the podcasts that I was listening to. The origins of the speaker can sometimes be distinguished by whether or not one refers to themselves as 'Recovering' or 'Recovered'. The latter group are more likely to advocate against psychiatric medicine. More liberal AAs, and I include myself in that, remind me to quit playing doctors and nurses: unless, of course, one is a doctor or a nurse in the specialism of psychiatry, and even some of them might want to mention their drug taking to a colleague. I know that I am most certainly not qualified to have an opinion on anyone else's need for pharmaceuticals.

The next day saw the weather become one torrent of abysmal deluge after deluge. Insane touted the idea that we holed up in our respective tents for the day, or at least until mid-afternoon. I vetoed it, wanting to start making real inroads into this journey, to stop procrastinating as I saw it. I agreed to a lazy start but then set off with a vengeance first thing. Nine miles later, both of us near hypothermic, everything we owned was wringing wet. I stopped roadside and assembled my tent for respite, waiting for Insane to arrive. From there, we hobbled down a two-mile tarmacked road, trying to thumb a lift. Understandably even protected by their cars, drivers gave us a wide berth. It took us an age to get to Green Valley's small convenience store, with hot coffee and warm air coursing through its aisles. There, by chance, a warm-hearted gentleman tried his best to find us a bed for the night but without success, so he took us off to Palmdale. It's a heaving city on the outskirts of Los Angeles County. We sat out the rest of the rainstorm there. I had been wrong to carry on that day, and I said so to Insane when we added two more zero days to the tally.

We lounged around our drab motel room until eventually we reluctantly began the process of planning the next full day's walking. Our driver opted to pick us up early in the morning, disappointing Insane who'd rather prefer a long hotel lie-in. Insane had already announced she was limiting her ambitions to fourteen miles because she just didn't have the ability to do two hills in a day. I felt that I no longer wanted to know what was coming up, that I'd just handle it. I'd decided that's how I was going to approach my trekking from now on: to just do what was in front of me and put my expectations of mileage to one side. That said, I would be pushing on as much as possible, and I realised that could mean continuing alone.

I decided in the end to wait for her at the fork between the PCT and the Upper Shake Campground where she'd aimed to stay that night. I had wanted to say thanks and farewell properly. However, I'd presumed a sign would point out the detour, but I never saw one until I was two miles beyond the campground, and it was pointing back the way I'd come. I was in the flow, my trail legs emerging in the mid-afternoon when suddenly the pain would momentarily evaporate, and then I'd surge. I would keep 'camelling up' each time I happened upon a good flow of water, getting as much fluid into me as bearable, then hiking onwards. I only just found the side trail to Sawmill Campground as dusk became night, staggering up the final half-mile uphill, breaking through abominable knee-deep snow. I was to be alone for the first time since my virgin night on the PCT.

Having finally reached the heady numbers of twenty miles that day, my legs now roared hot and beaten, groaning as I extended them down to peg the lightweight aluminium stakes into the ground. A most god-awful wind blew in and I feared the Castle would end up on top of the mountain, and me at the bottom of it. It had taken some time in the dark to pitch securely, cajoling frosted fingers to co-operate. Only then could I cook one of those 'delicious', so *they* say, mountaineering dried meals that claim to be two portions. A mushroom risotto, with its enticing 'ready in a few minutes' advert on the front that turns out to be ready in half an hour when one reads the 'how to make' instructions on the back. It was, however, palatable, but not that palatable. Worse, with my suppressed appetite, I knew I'd be having the remainder for breakfast, lunch and afternoon snack, thus discovering like all ready meals, it had worsening palatability at each innings.

I settled down to bed with the canvas rattling all around me. My bladder started gnawing at my psyche even though I'd gone before dinner. It was now too blustery and bracing to venture out again, and I tossed and turned fruitlessly. At midnight I distracted myself by reading about my location on Guthook. Several hikers from the previous year mentioned a resident bear that had become notorious for beating on the metal rubbish bin adjacent to the camping area. The bear was not unduly perturbed by humans, separate authors noted. They recommended tying one's food up a tree, a bear hang as it's called, far from one's sleeping place. Lacking the ability to tie my food anywhere, and my daily fare currently adjacent to my right foot, I felt like I was trying to sleep next to a ticking time bomb. From then on, every god-damned rustle sounded like a bear's paw crunching on the snow enveloping my tent. The wind hammered on and eventually it blew the bloody doors off, taking the guideline with it. My hiking pole then collapsed over me bringing the rest of the tent down. I managed to secure it in a fashion, but then my bladder really started agitating. I dug around and found an old Ziploc and figured I'd try that trick. Alas, soon after, I had a wet sleeping bag, wet puffy pants, and my newly-clean-on-knickers were also quite sodden. The Ziploc was full to capacity so I sealed it and threw it into the vestibule area.

An hour later, the bloody tent doors blew off again. I wrestled to get them back into position to protect me from the full wintry flurry of the rainless storm, but as I did so, I accidentally rested my arm on the inflated Ziploc. My puffy jacket, essential for protection against hyperthermia, took the brunt of the near-frozen pee. Suffice to say, my night was not remarkably successful, but I certainly learnt a lot. I think I finally fell asleep around dawn. Shortly after, I then dragged my sorry, very sorry and very soggy arse out of the tent, which was now again partially collapsed. Only then it was for me to find, or rather not find, my glasses. I put on my prescription sunglasses, packed up, moved to the camper's picnic table before thoroughly unpacking every pocket, bag and Ziploc I could until I found them at the bottom of my sleeping bag. I had no idea how they ended up there. Once I put them on, I realised I'd been sleeping next to the bear's favourite trash can all night. Or rather, not sleeping.

****

Fear of people and equipment insecurity will arrive

Nearing the end of my fourth week on trail, and in just one day the snow, previously whitening out the terrain, had given way to the heat of lower lying land. This section of the trail circumvented the bulk of the Mojave, America's driest and smallest desert. The vista had become all-absorbing with its promised superbloom erupting across the hills, smothering the basins with the competing yellows of desert sunflowers, popcorn flowers, and sand verbenas. The mass was occasionally speckled with white lilies and primrose. Elsewhere, rolling mounds were swamped with bright orange poppies, so delicate they quickly lost the fight against the surging desert breezes. It was the purples of the knee-tall lupins that really struck, amassing for miles at a time, wowing the gaze. Seemingly, I had traversed from snow-bound winter to the peak of summer in the course of one day, boggling my mind and the senses of my body.

Of course, this change required a laborious descent of two thousand feet, threatening permanent erosion of knee cartilage. As the afternoon wore on, the heat rose to barely tolerable levels. I gulped down a quarter of a litre of water only to be taken by surprise by two men, the first people I'd seen all day. They blocked my path forward as I attempted to rejoin the trail. Tall, with their heads sun-capped and eyes obscured by mirrored sunglasses, the remainder of their faces were covered by shrilly-coloured bandanas. They were very questioning: whether I was doing this alone, and where I was from, and did I know Lucy Sutton, who apparently walked the PCT last year and was also from the UK? She'd stayed with them, they told me, and all I could think was that I'd definitely watched far too many episodes of *Criminal Minds*. They told me to go to their truck and wait for them. White, they described, and when they returned, they'd give me a drink and possibly some snacks.

Being alienated from the wider world, I hadn't realised America was masking up even outdoors. It was like I'd been teleported back to the Middle East, to yet another childhood home. I'd spent my formative years in a place where women shielded their faces in public, rendering them visibly invisible. These two men's attire obscured their smiles and eyes which disabled my unreliable ability to ascertain whether they were friend or foe. I can sometimes fear men, in part because it has been ingrained in me from childhood, the stranger dangers, and those age-old legacies that somehow made Eve responsible for everything that Adam did, thought or said. Of course, life experiences are infinitely educational, leaving so many of us wary that we accidentally punish the innocent. I declined their entreaties over and over, adamant I wanted to keep my day flowing in my own steady but cumbersome way.

As I continued the path downwards to Pine Canyon road, they caught up and overtook me as the trail levelled out, insisting once again I went with them. As I crossed the tarmac, they waved a bottle of Jack Daniels in my direction, and yelled, "Are you sure you don't want some?" I smiled and waved my "no thanks!" If they'd had kittens this would be a very different story. As they walked away, they murmured they were trail angels for the section. They were there to leave gallons of water on an otherwise dry patch for us hikers. I'd misjudged them and felt dreadful given I'd been the first thru-hiker they'd met in this unusual season. I wondered for the rest of the day whether I had demoralised them, and that my behaviour would condemn all future thru-hikers to an arid day's hiking. The guilt was tremendous until I reminded myself that I am, in all likelihood, a terribly inaccurate clairvoyant, with an overzealous and often inappropriate sense of responsibility.

Later, as I gathered rocks to help pin my tent into the dusty ground, I was thrilled to have counted away another twenty miles, and not been distracted by them. Did I really need to hyper-analyse every interaction I have with individuals who have the misfortune, as I see it, to interact with me? It's none of my business what they think of me, and they've probably already forgotten me. AA promises fear of people will leave us, and it does to some degree, a lot of degrees, in fact. Paradoxically, if I know a person is in recovery, I am significantly more comfortable around them, especially after they've told their tales of drunken violations, exploitation and serial cheating.

The next day saw me swamped in more superbloom. As I rounded the crest of a gentle hill, I spied a straight dirt road that connected two parts of the trail, eliminating a five-mile loop. Had I taken it, I would have deprived myself of the luminous meadow walk. Besides which, there was a compelling sign demanding we stay on trail as it was hunting season, and the PCT is adjunct to a regularly active gun club. I passed by the closed Hiker Town, normally a gathering point for thru-hikers to get to know one another better. For me it was joy enough to just be in the area due to the flat ground, wading through the expanse of wildflowers and side-stepping bum-wagging black beetles doing headstands. I presumed them to be the skunk of the insect world.

I was soon confronted by another sign, alongside a gate, warning me there was a danger of drowning. Oddly juxtaposed in the middle of the desert, a man-made and terribly straight canal is initially concealed by its banks. I knew the area to be a haven for vexed rattlesnakes, and so I declined to listen to any podcasts. What I hadn't expected was Insane Shopper to holler as I took a break at the point the watercourse, brimming with fresh water, was absorbed into an enormous rusty pipe. From this point on, gravity pushed the water hundreds of miles from its Owen River source to be quaffed and dispersed amongst Los Angeles' residents. I had arrived at the infamous Los Angeles Aqueduct, a very flat portion of the PCT.

Insane had pulled off trail ostensibly because her stove had seized, something that would be the undoing of me. By chance she'd met a couple of friendly natives who'd driven her around the hills where the blossoms were particularly thick and abundant. Back at her motel, she met up with Hotel Hopper, himself taking a break. It was his eighteenth motel stay since he had started his trek the day after me in March. Insane was keen to walk the Aqueduct herself, and so they contrived to return to the trail together. This was the place I had aspired to do one percent of the trail in a day: just over a full marathon. I'd figured it was perfectly possible given the long stretches of smooth dirt road walking ahead as we bypassed Death Valley.

Like us, it was Hotel Hopper's first attempt at a thru-hike. He'd opted to go 'ultra-light', a trend amongst long-distance hikers to carry a pack, which when devoid of food and water, combines to weigh between four and seven kilos, around nine to fifteen pounds for the imperialists. It means eschewing any and all luxury, like spare clothes and fears. Typically, the carrier renounces a cooking stove, preferring to cold-soak each meal in a plastic jar during the day. Given I was carrying a laptop, albeit a small one, I was topping out at the grossly overweight mark, about twelve kilos. The downside of being an ultra-light aspiree is that one is highly likely to get hypothermia. Hotel Hopper's longest day so far had been a thirty-miler, which had taken sixteen hours of slogging through snow and ice around San Jacinto. He'd been unable to stop due to insufficient gear to safely sleep at high elevations. It had taken several days to recover after that before he succumbed to carrying a few more layers, sensibly repudiating the ultralight way of life for a while.

The three of us climbed atop the riveted pipe and marched along but I swiftly declared it painful underfoot. The metal fastenings were an impediment to be dodged, forcing me to concentrate on my stride in ways I didn't want to focus. I opted for the alternative: traipsing along the sandy maintenance road where my footprints kicked up the dust, mixing it with foot sweat, bringing fresh blisters. The aqueduct section was shorter than I had envisaged. In my head, it went on for hours and hours, an assumption I'd formed from watching videos of people sleeping on the metal tube. In reality, the PCT veers off along a wide intersecting dirt road quite quickly.

With the combination of level ground, and the fact that the two of them had only just started their day following some rest, they set off at a speed I could only dream of. Astonishingly, Insane whizzed ahead, comfortably outpacing the taller and younger Hotel Hopper, even after the mid-morning temperatures soared. I learnt during a break that Hotel had started to struggle with *plantar fasciitis*, an inflammation of the sole common amongst long-distance runners. Still, he outwalked me.

All around us Joshua trees, the squat hunks of giant cacti, dotted the horizon and tumbleweed collected and tangled in dry stream beds. Lizards skittered and danced between shadows. Snakes were unlikely to be far away. Hives of bees bombinated in small holes in the shallow banks either side of the arenaceous road.

I lost a good hour scuttling back and forth trying to find my bearings, when the road split in several directions. I still had no way of determining my exact location. In my frustration, I opted to follow the tracks of two people similarly geographically challenged. The selection of shoes amongst thru-hikers rarely varied that the prints may have been from four different wearers. In the end, after too many debilitating hours in which I overcooked and over-cursed, I doddered towards the promised and much required water tank I refilled and said "hi" to the ever-cheerful legend that is 'Grateful'. He walks and vlogs his hikes to raise awareness that twenty-two US veterans *a day* take their own lives in America. He had opted, along with Insane and one other gentleman, to set up camp by the tank for the night and he was predictably grateful for it all.

Leaving the three of them behind, I crawled up the next mountain, ostensibly hoping to catch Hotel Hopper, who'd left about an hour prior. The hostile desert was now defined by its savage winds. Mound after mound of hillside was punctured with electric windmills. They whirred rhythmically, their gigantic blades swooshing through the air. The masts lit up the skies with their red eyes. As dusk began to threaten, I spotted what I thought was the tree similar to the picture on Guthook, denoting the two-tent campsite that I previously calculated was well over twenty-six and a half miles from my day's start.

I was spent, and yet, more than slightly impressed at roaming such a formidable distance under two very trying climatic conditions. The sun had baked me all morning, the winds dry-frying me all afternoon. The wind rallied on relentlessly throughout the evening as I greeted two women whose tents were only kept upright with the aid of the lonely tree's wafting branches. Their presence left just a small gap a few metres away for me to crush my tent between two quivering bushes. I roped the Castle to their ever-whacking stems in a bid to keep it tied down. It was the wrong tree, a mile too soon, I learned from one of the women as I heated up the night's dinner.

Overnight as I once again rebuilt my oft-collapsing tent, this time my attention was diverted by a mountain lion roaring its disapproval at our interloping. All I could think to do was to order it to piss off. I was incredibly surprised, and mightily cheered, when it listened and obeyed - something my own cat would never do. I then settled once again onto my ever-deflating sleeping mat. It was to become flabbier every night after that until finally it barely remained inflated for a half hour, offering no respite against the desert floor. Yet again, sleeping was something for another country.

Still, I trudged on, heading to Highway 58. There I could hitch a lift from a stranger willing to pick up a harmless tramp with an oversized rucksack. It would take over an hour to find such a kindness. The wait was made more discomforted by empty water bottles. To pass the time, and cope with the disappointment of repeated rejection, I perfected my Irish pronunciation. Quite why Irish I have no idea, but whilst standing forlornly roadside, to every car that whizzed by declining my implorations for a ride, I muttered, "Ye miserable fecking twats 'm jest a gentle fecking English woman."

****

Points of disinterest

I had never previously observed how well-intentioned advice often begins with the word 'Don't.' Much of my distraction as I was walking along listening to an AA podcast or three was noticing the words people chose. Sometimes the speakers fell into the trap of telling their audience what they should or shouldn't do rather than focusing on what worked best for them, describing their experience and how they came to learn from that. I found myself irked by some of their know-it-all, hectoring approaches with their proclamations of how we must all tread the exact same path.

I find the 'don'ts' the least helpful and the most dictatorial. Don't get hungry, angry, lonely or tired, the HALT acronym that informs a person why their next relapse is on the cards when new in. I spent a good portion of each day being at least one of those things, albeit less so hungry. I was not yet afflicted by the cavernous gnawing and ceaseless hiker hunger. Instead, I hurt. I fantasised about mummifying myself in KT tape, that magic sports aid that can take the stress off a vulnerable muscle or ligament. Getting up in the mornings, bearing weight on my feet for the first time in several hours, unfailingly induced a screeching agony rising from the soles up through my ankles to be dispersed by my calves. Some days I yearned to cry, and I hadn't yet got to heaving on my pack.

In Tehachapi I bought ten days' worth of food, hoping to claw back time lost heading to towns, tackling some of the deficit I'd built up the first month. I'd set myself a new target of a minimum of eighteen miles per day, every day, and just in case I couldn't maintain that I had two days' reserve of food. As I was packing up, Facebook messenger bleeped with a text from Insane who enquired whether I wanted her trail angels to take me back to the trail. Absolutely I did, especially when they offered to cook me pancakes at their home first!

Hunger is a physiological state, and for me, far easier to manage than psychological matters. I still carried a lot of repressed anger. I grew up in a home carpeted with eggshells and a volatile mother whose moods could switch in an instant. A smack was readily forthcoming for having an opinion, a thought, or an idea. It stopped when I was twelve because she went to whack me, and I pushed her away first. She looked aghast and erupted into floods of tears. I had spent the rest of the day anguished about what the consequences would be for my impertinence, and it turned out not being hit ever again. Today, if I think about the childhood violence, I can recall a healing moment in an AA meeting when the day's speaker had described how her mother would utter those familiar but utterly ludicrous words, "If you don't stop crying, I'll give you something to cry about." One by one my fellow attendees dissolved into laughter, starting as a low rumble, its contagion spread around the room. What had begun as a morose recollection, had morphed into a modicum of healing, and now had become a magical moment to supersede a bad memory. We had momentarily and collectively bonded over a shared experience, and it had provided me a liberation from a lifetime of silent resentment. It taught me that when something is no longer kept a family secret, one can come to talk about it as a matter of fact, and then it can be put in its proper place: the past.

But once my mother's strategy of control and mismanaged anger had ended, it was simply replaced with long lectures, but more often letters, on how I was ruining her life, her marriage or her day, practically anything unsatisfying she could attribute to me. Why couldn't I be more like...insert the name of sibling, neighbour's child, or fantasy perfect little girl. Her words were full of the *shoulds* and the *oughts* of life. For me, they are the most pernicious of verbs, often abused to compel or coerce others to change their behaviour to suit ourselves. Ultimately, I have adopted the same words to perpetuate the bullying of yonder year to judge and to condemn both myself and others, usually harshly and unforgivingly.

Getting honest in recovery meant I was now familiar with the lengths I'd go to in order to justify my own drinking, adopting the common refrain, "If you'd had my life, you'd drink too." No matter what, I could concoct an excuse, and then use it to validate my behaviour. I realised though, on reflection, I have been both blessed and cursed with a quick wit, and that was just one way I could cause enormous harm to everyone around me, as well as myself. This truth is tragic for all concerned but I was bloody lucky to have been given a respite from continuing on my destructive path. It meant, like it or not, I could accept that perhaps she was just as much a dysfunctional human being as I, the only difference is I didn't have children to carry on the family traditions with. It was only in recovery I discovered that 'accept' and 'like' are not words synonymous with each other. I can accept things I don't like more readily, although I'm still inclined to make an awful lot of noise about things I dislike before I accept them as they are.

Angry people frightened me, but it was my norm, and I too became a hostile, angry person myself. They say you grow up to become your parents or marry them, and I did both. Somehow, I'd blamed myself for everyone else's behaviour too over the years. The fourth step gave me the time and the focus to work through my issues and enabled me to separate out some ideas from the melee of noise and chaos I carry upstairs with me all the while. I can learn to take responsibility for my part, and my part alone, recognise that I wasn't a saint nor a victim, but I had developed my own defenses that were counterproductive, or self-sabotaging and at times just plain spiteful. They'd helped me survive a frenzied and confusing childhood, but they didn't permit me to thrive in adulthood.

I said goodbye to the lovely pancake-making ride-giving Tehachapi trail angels at the Barstow-Bakersfield Highway, the point where Cheryl Strayed took her first steps to a new life. It looked remarkably similar to what was depicted in the film - unsurprisingly. I'd left Instant lingering behind as we crawled our way up from four-thousand feet to six-thousand feet above sea level. As I hiked uphill and down dale, I was simultaneously despondent but grateful that I had to drink myself near to death in order to start to find me. The fourth step didn't tell me I was wrong for feeling what I felt, but it showed me I could change how I looked at stuff and try to reason it differently. I wasn't five years old anymore, I didn't need to keep re-feeling those feelings, but I did need a new way of looking at things. The problem, of course, was my head was an echo chamber and that alone made it a particularly fraught place to mull stuff over, worsened now as I ambled along on my own with no one to talk to nor distract myself with.

I camped up with the Belgians that night, a father and son team. The son had recently turned eleven I'd learnt as we'd dined together that evening. As was fast becoming a familiar ritual for me, I'd fallen over on my first day back on trail, this time smashing my nose, my glasses grazing up the bridge of it. The young lad and I compared battle scars, and shredded clothes, in a fading light. He beamed when his father told me they'd enjoyed a brief moment of television fame as their epic intentions had been broadcast by a local news magazine. Following that, the parents had been roundly criticised and called child abusers for taking their son out of school for a few months. Three weeks later, all schools in Belgium were closed down because of the virus. To my eyes, that boy was loving every second of his alternative childhood.

It reminded me of when my mother, having no teaching experience of her own, decided one day she was going to homeschool me. I wouldn't or couldn't behave properly so she told me and had me sent back to regular school. A few years later, off I went to boarding school - flinging me as far away from my sibling as she could. We suspected there'd be a new appreciation for teachers once the pandemic was over, but all this enforced homeschooling might have horrendous ramifications for teacher training schemes.

The next day, the Belgians romped away from me, the little lad's oversized pack bobbing up and down as he scampered up the hill ahead of his dad. A few hours later I briefly chatted with a couple who had also flipped up but were now heading south. They cautioned me that the next few days would be tough physically as the trail was in bad repair. After saying cheerio to them, I would become the loneliest I had ever been, not seeing or speaking to another soul for four consecutive days. Boredom set in for the first time. With the ongoing pandemic, there was not even the sight nor sound of aircraft above, making my mind wonder whether the world had been obliterated. Humanity was truly screwed if I was the last surviving member of it.

My isolation ended when I bumped into an elderly section hiker. He was loquacious, barely pausing for breath, with little or no interest in any contributions that I might make to the conversation.

Standing still exacerbated the toxins lurking in my overused joints, and I could only fidget from one foot to another. There was nothing to sit on, nor prop myself against as he droned on about his gear selection, nodding at his disparaging assessments of mine. I made my excuses and lumbered off.

At times, I was glad to be at higher elevations, leaving behind the low-lying desert, I followed a swathe through heavier woodland, blotting out the heat of the afternoon. Nonetheless each day remained a story of enervation, hour after hour of ascending and descending thousands of feet, hampered as the trail couldn't be maintained at all this year by the PCTA's volunteer army. One of their many roles is to organise teams to clear away the fallen trees that block hikers' passage through the forest. Each year, hundreds of trees are uprooted by winter storms, or perhaps from carrying an excess of snow. Some have just naturally succumbed to the passing of time and others to the voracious pine beetle. With few people on trail, rarely were new grooves worn in to indicate an alternative path. Each blowdown needed careful assessment as to the best way to overcome it. Sometimes it was easiest sliding down the steep mountain side, other times I'd claw my way up to circumvent the dying foliage or knots of roots. Most preferred was sitting astride them awhile, leaning back and resting against my rucksack as I clamoured over. Occasionally, I had no choice but to remove my pack and shove it forward as I scrambled underneath. I could only pray the trunk was stable in its repose. One of the days, I was dispirited to have made a little over six miles in seven hours.

It was a route with an abundance of points of disinterest: a broken radio mast; rusty and rotting gates, and the occasional signing of trail registers, last signed and dated by the Belgians. They were making huge distances. I saw my first bear prints: a mother and its cub, the most dangerous of bear encounters one could possibly have. A momma bear is thought to be fiercer when with its offspring. They can out-run, out-climb and out-fight most predators. I gave myself the redundant suggestion of 'Don't worry' on account it wasn't the real deal, that it was just a trace of, a hint at, the threat could be long gone. The tracks didn't even look that fresh, set in dried mud. The next day, I was jolted out of my mindful meanderings meeting my first snake, complete with a go-faster stripe along its side. A harmless gopher snake, nonetheless, it had scared the bejesus out of me as it bolted across inches from my feet. After that every stick presented as a potential venomous menace.

I arrived at Walker Pass, famed as an arid desert section with few water resources. Boulders and sand, rocks and dust, occasional scrub but no shade. There were no recent comments on Guthook to indicate whether the trail angels were active this year at all. One should never rely on water caches, and I was left with the choice of a mile-round road walk to an animal trough fed by a spring, or to remain on trail and hope someone had stashed a few gallons of water behind a monument as they would have in previous years. If I chanced it, and there weren't, it would make the trip to the guaranteed spring even longer. It was already the hottest part of the day. I opted to play it safe. I made the wrong choice. On the plus, I did pick up a carelessly discarded lighter on the side of the road, with enough gas in it that I no longer needed to worry about how I'd light my fuel can that night. My own lighter ailing. The next day, I couldn't be bothered trekking off a side trail to get water and figured I'd make do with what I had, not anticipating that I would be back in the stony desert for five hours, my dehydration making me slothful.

I took to night-hiking to extend my day. The wilderness is a different beast in the dark with who knows what monsters lurking. Inexplicably I stepped over two recently slayed foxes and a large dead rat. I also learnt my headlamp was a magnet for the night insects: I was twatted on the head by far too many moths to count.

My fortieth day had me climbing up from five and a half thousand feet to eight thousand feet without a jot of daytime shade. The unrelenting sunshine beat down on me as I staggered away part mile after part mile, from odd-shaped rock to odd-shaped rock, from kink to curve. Nourishment arrived in the late afternoon in the form of the Kern River slooshing through the desert, fed by ample snowmelt hurrying down from the Sierra mountains. Dotted along its banks a small number of weekend hiker tents. Couples, dogs and fishermen enjoyed a moment's recreation as I slogged on. The trail lurched away from the river towards a crop of desert oak where I found a rare flat spot riddled with mountain lion paw prints. My night's amenity only afforded by the thin yoga mat I was making do with until I could pick up my new sleeping pad. Predictably, I slept in fits and starts.

I packed up later than usual and walked on about eight miles, coming off the trail for three of them to check into Kennedy Meadows South. Awaiting me was Grumpy's Place, acclaimed because no matter what breakfast is ordered, they all come with a side-serving of the fattest, fluffiest frisbee-sized American pancake. If one finishes the first, and few do, one automatically receives a second. No one leaves Grumpy's hungry. What I hadn't expected was to be cheered in once again by the friendliest of smiles: Insane had quit the trail for good this time, but she'd wanted the Kennedy Meadow experience of camping at Triple Crown Outfitters. It's a gear and food supplier at the gates of the Sierra, owned and run by the renowned Yogi, a woman phenomenal for championing the rights and safety of PCT Hikers. She has completed eight long-distance hikes herself between Mexico and Canada, on the PCT and Continental Divide Trail, as well as the more famous, but shortest of the three, Appalachian Trail. They combine to form the 'triple crown' of American thru-hiking lore.

Her knowledge and wisdom are unsurpassable, dished out freely but only when asked for. Her shop offers free wi-fi, free camping, free liquid refreshments and free recycling to the veritable rabble of hikers who mingle there readying themselves to ascend the High Sierra. I arranged to leave Kennedy Meadows South, where I learnt there was a Kennedy Meadows North, and returned to Idyllwild to complete the previously skipped miles. She waved me off and as I picked up my pack, she bellowed out, "Just don't quit on a bad day." It's probably the best life advice going.

****

Fearful and careless

If it is pride that gives a swollen heart, and ego a swollen head, I am without doubt it was the log that gave me a swollen ankle, and the ice that caused my idiocy.

Back in Idyllwild, the temperatures had expanded the mercury considerably since I was last there. It had been a relief to pick up my latest gear: a fully inflating and unpunctured blow-up sleeping mat. This one was less bumpy than the previous, and substantially lighter too, albeit the green colour was putrid. I had also obtained a brand-new mobile phone, the unlock codes not having worked on my UK one. Finally, I could get an exact location of my whereabouts: Room ten, Silver Pines Lodge. This time, being alone, I took a small room rather than the cabin of before. With glee, I set about downloading Guthook, only to discover the maps wouldn't load, a result of the parent company doing a software upgrade or something, that did something, that meant nothing worked, or something like that. They expected it to be sorted in two to three weeks. I may have said something of an expletive nature.

A day's rest later, I set off once again to the one-hundred and fifty-first mile just as the mid-morning sun began to parch the earth in earnest, forcing an intake of a litre of water an hour, demanding more pitstops to keep supplies replenished. Shade was sparse and spying a flat rock, I plonked myself down, my chest heaving, to filter water for the umpteenth time that day. All the while hummingbirds zipped back and forth, buzzing like giant insurgent insects. No sooner had my backside connected with the rock, I leapt nearly a foot high when a male voice piped up. Resting nearby against a larger boulder, his face puffed red from the day's exertion, he introduced himself as a multiple thru-hiker and triple-crowner, Judge Dredd. Disheartened he felt this would be the one he couldn't complete on account he was now mid-sixties and getting past it. He was another of life's talkers, and before I knew it, I'd got his entire potted history. He was not one for sharing the conversation, he had no interest in mine, but he told a tale I was familiar with.

"I should have seen it coming, but I didn't. One day I was a happily married man, the next thing is she's gone, and eighteen years of marriage doesn't matter." He'd felt he'd done nothing to deserve that, nor the animosity that came with it after. The devastation, the stumbling around for years endlessly wondering why. The refusal to date, or try again with anyone, to just accept the unacceptable. "I had two children die on me," he'd added, "but it was being left so abruptly, so cruelly, without a single conversation, that destroyed me. I'm a religious man and I know I'll see my children in the future, but I'll never love another woman."

I too thought I'd never be able to look at that whole chapter of my life without resuming the bitter tears that had obliterated the following three years. Through AA I'd become accustomed to talking about it, slowly, carefully, euphemistically, without body-wracking sobs. I'd got to the point that I knew it was now safe for him to walk down the street again and I felt that was progress, albeit granted very far from perfection.

Bill Wilson, a founder of AA, once wrote that pride says you need not pass this way and fear says you dare not look, but a good sponsor taught me that in the land of the blind, the one-eyed man is king, and to just make a start, and not necessarily make a finish. The conversation with Judge Dredd brought my failed marriage to the fore of my daily thoughts. A part of me hoped that this trip would restore some of that self-esteem that divorce had extracted. Marriage can be a death by a thousand cuts and memories can be sharp and jagged. I'd counter the number of times he'd called me useless, the latter years his misogyny corrupting my own sense of person. "If women want to be equal to men, it's best they learn not to boast," he once told me when I said I was proud of some of my accomplishments. I could recall so many of his taunts, but I was less inclined to look at my own verbal abuses. When drunk I certainly provided an injection of malevolence into our marriage. As I walked along, I still felt the discomfort of some of my behaviour and was certain he still bore the scars. But words are to be played with, and in AA, pride is often a dirty word, but it is usually ego that is being referred to. Ego doesn't like being prodded. I learnt early on, primarily by taking on a sponsee who, like me, wasn't that enthusiastic about 'doing the work'. Through her, I saw how damaging perfectionism is, that personality trait that stopped me starting, and prevented me from finishing. It was a way of thinking, combined with frail self-confidence, that provided the toxicity that kept me drunk long after I put down the booze.

I was coming to accept that if the next water source was one mile off trail, down a steep gully, I'd be taking it although I might still grumble inwardly. Might? I would grumble outwardly often! Cedar Springs had been a mile and a half off the beaten track, and I'd cursed the entire way down, and all the way back up again, scrambling through bracken whilst watching out for wriggling ticks hanging off dangling branches, little legs scouring their surroundings desperate to latch on.

I proceeded to the ravine where Microsoft had slipped and fallen to his death. It was indeed steep, but no longer icy. My proximity to his last living moment of earth had me reflecting morbidly throughout the day. I wondered how his fellow hikers were coping - were they even carrying on? I'd learnt from a heart-breaking open letter written by his father, that the Australian I'd met my first day on trail had been there when it happened. I could only pray for his family, and that felt wholly inadequate.

My gloominess shattered when I approached a rockslide that had caused the PCT to be detoured for several years. The rubble of boulders was unmarked on Guthook but referred to along with the faux reassurance of 'it wasn't *that* bad'. Someone had affixed a rope which helped stability, but still my arse and rucksack hung far out into the expanse of the gully. I could feel my heart pounding in my mouth as I traversed it, especially alone with no one to watch me plunge into the abyss, should I have tumbled. My knees trembled for hours after I resumed my lumbering along the narrow path cut into the mountainside, the wind picking up by the hour.

I rested up that night behind a rock face standing fierce on the peak of the mountain, the wall of stone was my only protection from the horrendous bluster. I pitched the Castle not fifteen metres away from a fairly mute cowboy-camper. The kind of hiker that eschews tents, saving time and energy sleeping under the stars. He was not there for the scenery but rather to race against himself to complete the trail in the fastest possible time. My tent hammered around me, yet I slept like the stone. He was long gone by the time I awoke for a fresh day. I found myself ambling back the way I'd come the previous evening. Another couple of miles wasted.

I hit the remainder of the snowpack as the crests edged over eight thousand feet to familiarise myself with the horror that is postholing: a manner of walking that involves placing one foot on a patch or lump of snow, bearing weight on it, and then with great flourish, witnessing one's leg being devoured by the frozen snow underfoot. Several grunts later, in a vain attempt to dislodge it, I'd realise my spare leg was of little assistance, and soon enough I'd despair of ever getting my foreleg out from the vice-like ice. I'd finally dig my leg out with a combination of hands, trekking poles, a lot of frustrated cursing and even more grunting. A really bad posthole would see me foot out, bare of sock and shoe, necessitating more digging on already frostbitten fingers. And when I wasn't falling through the snow, I was introducing my arse to it. A lot of saking was fecked for!

91

I noted that not far further down the side of the hill lay a continual line of snow-free patches and, unfathomably, I decided life would be much easier over there. Of course, I hadn't planned on that also being the simplest way to get lost and lost I did get. Just after lunch, I finally saw another hiker, my first of the day, with a very red top, himself struggling to find the whited-out trail. We chatted about the Search-and-Rescue helicopter that had hovered for the best part of an hour overhead, both of us concerned we'd somehow accidentally pressed our SOS buttons. Soon after, he found his bearings and strode off, leaving me with his tracks to follow, his post holes to avoid and his splattered landing patterns to snort at.

The day was particularly notable for it taking me five hours to cover a distance of two miles, but it was even more remarkable for the log I fell beneath, shearing off the skin from my shin, and twisting my ankle into a position it did not want to be twisted into. Momentarily I feared I'd broken it, but then I am prone to high drama, and a scratch and a bruise doesn't make for a great tale. Either which way, the log had me beaten. I finally hacked my way into Saddle Junction, having completed a mere thirty miles in three days to find trails lunged off in every direction, leaving me flummoxed. With no Guthook, and no PCT signs that I could spot, I was distracted when a family of three on a day-hike turned up full of questions and curiosity. We chatted for a while, then acknowledging how sore and exhausted I was, I opted to join them for an exceptionally long walk down to the trailhead. There they had an RV and a willingness to drop me off back in Idyllwild, where I yet again checked into room ten, Silver Pines Lodge.

A friend of mine says that for him God exists in human skin. It's the people who pass fleetingly through one's life who can ignite the most profound change to one's outlook. I had enjoyed listening to the father of the family as I limped mile after mile down Devil's Slide as he relayed his story of becoming a born-again Christian. I didn't share many of his beliefs, some of them fundamentally fear-based, but I found his observation that many people believe in God, but few people believe God perceptive. That little word 'in' magnified for me the difference between having a faith and trusting that faith. I had no problem with the former, it was a lack of the latter which caused me so much mental distress. Today proved to me that every time I'd asked for help, it had arrived in human form and led me back to safety.

If I was going to make it to Canada, it would be more by luck than good judgement on my part. Moreover, I wouldn't be doing it perfectly, and I'd have to be okay with that. In the interim, I intended to rest up for a few days so my very-nearly-permanently-broken-leg and the impassable-for-me trail could clear, and me and my humbled arse could get some decent bed rest. As I checked in, I learnt that the helicopter had picked up a local man with a broken leg, having himself fallen beneath a snow-covered log.

****

Chapter five

Keeping it surreal

I rejoined the PCT at Fuller Ridge Junction facing an eight-mile slog uphill, reasoning with the two and a half mile walk down Devil's slide, I'd more than compensated for skipping the eleven miles of PCT hell in frozen form. It turned out to be a two-mile jaunt after I met a trio of hikers: Witchcraft on account he was using a broomstick in lieu of his lost hiking poles, Tom Cruise, for no other reason than he was a fan, and Kitchen Sink. Kitchen Sink had two sleeping bags, four sporks, a Nintendo, a second game console, two camping stoves, and even more bewilderingly no sleeping pad. He reckoned on off-loading the excess when he got to the Sierra so then he could marvel in his pack's lightness.

What astounded me most was the fact I'd caught them at all until I discovered they took long breaks to enjoy several cigarettes. I passively stood beside them, a street pervert inhaling the secondhand smoke. It was now four months since my last cigarette, a craving would still rudely interrupt my struggles uphill. Cresting a mountaintop could induce a post-coital urge like no other. All I could do was tell it to do one and sigh out my frustration.

The three men persuaded a reluctant boulder-dasher to give us a $10 ride in the back of his smart black pick-up to the top of the pitted dirt road. Each bash and bump reduced me in height, as my spine compressed further and further between the truck's bed, hammered down by my skull. My ischium ground through my gluteus not-quite-as-maximus-as-forty-eight-days-ago. Once we'd been dropped off at the top, they left me for dust, leaving just footprints, their detail quickly brushed away by the unrelenting gusts of southern California. I settled in that night, alone once again, unnerved by the sounds of a man coughing when dusk curtailed the day. None of my hellos echoed back at me, and I saw no evidence of another human being in the flat sandy spots around my tent as I went out for my evening pee.

The following day lay eight miles of continuous knee-destroying downhill over rugged terrain. I grabbed at my tent to stuff it into the bin liner, lifting it up revealed a large and very fluffy spider carrying an engorged sac of eggs, along with what I initially thought was a small scorpion the size of my pinky. It was missing its

94

stinger. They must have been having a thorough conflab, but they were quick to disperse as I folded the fabric away and stuffed it into my pack. My sluggishness overcome, I headed downwards towards Interstate 10, where it was rumoured trail magic could often be found. Also rumoured were swarms of savage bees just after the two-hundred-mile marker.

In the UK, bees are rescued and considered fluffy and precious. Some go so far as to buy expensive but dainty little burrows to put in gardens for them to hide away from summer drizzle, munching on their carefully collected pollen. We rescue them, feeding injured ones honey to rejuvenate them. Not so here. From tiny holes on the side of the hill, an advanced party of kamikaze bees savaged me, exploring under my hat flaps, looking for exposed flesh, getting locked into my braids, the buzzing obstreperous. Another found its way into my glove. I jabbed my hiking poles frantically, screeching as if being taken hostage and about to be dumped into the boot of a car. I nearly flung my trekking poles into the ravine trying to free my hand. More arrived and all I could do was try to flee, smashing the side of my head in a vain attempt to squash them through the side panels, my ears and cheeks aflame. Every buzz after that threatened, compelling me to bolt forward, working up more of a sweat as the blistering heat of the desert floor edged nearer and nearer, my perspiration seeping into the stings.

Arriving at the multi-laned interstate, the deafening noise of giant trucks and speeding cars combined with the obnoxious fumes of oil and diesel, rubber and tarmac. The overpass provided much needed shade despite the heat emanating from the motorway above. I rested up in what was otherwise a dumping ground for rubbish, amid a few old mattresses, and inspected my fellow hikers' signatures written on cardboard sheets affixed to the walls.

The elusive trail angel had left some cans of pop. Ordinarily I never drink coke or the like. I used to tell people I was allergic to it, and I am, it leaves me breathless. Perversely, if it had Bacardi or vodka in it somehow, I was miraculously cured of any reaction. These days I hated the artificial flavour, but my dehydration ensured I drank my Gatorade quickly enough to belch out my appreciation. I struggled to reason why I drank it in the first place: the drink itself was of no benefit given it was zero calorie. I really didn't wish to be ungrateful, but I was scraping the barrel trying to fathom why Diet Gatorade had been this trail angel's drink of choice.

There had once been fresh bottled water, but it had all been consumed. I also barely drink water in my usual life, but aside from a small decaf coffee first thing in the morning, and last thing at night, water was all there was. I'd discovered some powdered flavourings in Idyllwild's supermarket. I'd picked iced tea and berry juice, and both brought a joy to my daily drinking especially when added to filtered water from muddy rivulets or stagnant pools. I could readily detect the chemicals used to treat drinking water now, so I rarely enjoyed the bottled water, no matter how 'smart' or mineralled it claimed to be. A few dry pretzels scattered around the bottom of a plastic tub tempted me. Nothing else really kept me there. I headed onwards, and ultimately upwards, glad of the momentary diversion, as the day scorched away at well over one hundred degrees Fahrenheit.

At my twelfth hour of hiking, I spied a small piece of bare ground next to an old broken down fence. It was the first reasonable site I'd encountered for hours so the decision to pitch up was swift. Heaving my belongings into the tent, I left the inner fly open as I danced off behind a nearby bush. I clambered into my shelter, perplexed at the ominous clicking sound rebounding around me. Like a thousand computer mice going off all at once, I then noticed millions of small black flies tapping away both inside and outside the single-sheet fabric. Wearily, I re-packed my stuff, crushing my tent into my pack as forcefully as I could.

I headed uphill once again, tackling a series of very sandy and much eroded, switchbacks: quick tos and fros dug into the side of mountains to lessen the gradient of the ascents. As seven o'clock came and went, and I found no further camp spots, I was mugged by a second swarm of bees. Incandescent with rage, these ones were no less vicious than before. One shuffled inside my top. Yanking off my rucksack to free it, it left its calling card in the form of a large urtication on my back. Another zapped me on my naked hand. Wrecked by sobs as I faced the dying of the day, I could only hope the insect world might take pity on me and give me a wide berth.

Gone eight in the evening, I spied a faint trail leading behind some shrubbery which revealed a wide patch, free of scrub and grasses, not listed on Guthook. Surrounded by tarantula holes, and some larger ones of which I knew nothing, and suspected everything. I hurried to get me and my lumpy body into the tent before the pesky night squad arrived with God knows what grievances against humankind.

The next day was Mission Creek. It sounded wondrous, snaking through a valley carrying ice cold snow melt. The luxury of water on hand. At first, splashing through the river over and over again was bliss, cooling my feet as the rest of my body broiled. By the afternoon, damp socks housed the perfect blister cultivating farm within my shoes. The trail was frequently obscured by the rubble of previous year's floods and landslides, masking the path as it interweaved the river. I could only search for micro-cairns stacked up by uncredited visitors to indicate which side of the river I should be on. Guthook was now operating normally but the blue dot then unfathomably vanished once again. I spent many hundreds of metres disorientated trying to pick up traces of the trail, but usually I just marked someone's footprints, a stranger who was similarly discombobulated. Progress was lamentable, making less than a mile in an hour of hideous sweltering hour. Then the creek forked off, and I forked off with it, not realising it was taking me far from where I was supposed to be.

I camped up that night having managed a mere fourteen PCT miles. Three-quarters of the distance I needed to average daily, assuming no rest days, each and every day if I was to complete this journey north. Soon after, I was joined by a section-hiker doing a ten-day mope around the wilderness. She'd nearly stepped on a large rattlesnake and was as deathly pale as someone who had. I invited her to camp up with me - elated for her company. She changed into vivid pink snoopy-dog pyjamas, a civilised homely act so out of keeping with my norms. I remained in my sweat-infused top and bottoms as we dined out together. She asked me which section was my favourite. I could only think it was the bit just after I walked into Canada.

The following day, I ventured through the remaining two miles of Mission Creek, which I dubbed dramatically as "Mission: Creek!" The trail remained missing in action for the most part. Leaving it behind would have been wonderful, except it entailed climbing up four thousand feet, to a new height of eight and a half thousand feet. Worse, it was a stretch devoid of water for nineteen miles, forcing me to carry five litres with me, the maximum I could take.

I rudely introduced myself to my first rattlesnake. I spotted the fairly distinctive diamond shape lattice along its length as it bolted into the undergrowth of a squat tree. There it assumed its starkly upright strike pose but failed to rattle. I took this to mean it wasn't too bothered by my existence. Many weeks later, a biologist told me they were evolving to quietly wallop any threats, rather than ward them off with a shake of their tails. Glad I didn't know that from the get-go.

I had planned to stop at this appeasingly shady spot for lunch. Guthook's picture of a wide-rimmed tree was alluring, and I imagined myself settling beneath it and cooling off. Having taken a battering from the wildlife in recent times, I opted to not linger with the serpent so close by. Besides which, someone had left two pairs of socks and a pair of underpants on the fallen log, now used for seating, and I really didn't want to handle them. Around the next corner, I interrupted a brilliant orange King snake minding its own business. They look venomous but are merely skittish. They are, however, the only thing capable of defeating a rattlesnake, immune as they are to its venom. I visualised taking it as a pet - one I could put it down at my next confrontation with a rattler, but alas it was quickly gone. In reality I didn't care for the extra burden.

I headed that night for an abandoned cabin, imagining a shelter to be more hospitable. It appealed for having the ultimate in hiking luxury: a pit toilet. I staggered into the clearing, first inspecting the latrine - its doors were locked. The windowless cabin was chilly and foreboding: the perfect setting for a wilderness murder scene. Instead, I camped up in the dusty forecourt next to someone's forgotten tent pegs. From there, I headed into the alpine loveliness that surrounds Big Bear. I could only hope the Bear wasn't big, nor alive.

From there I migrated into the town itself for resupply. The mayor had made all public transport free for the duration of the pandemic. It struck me as an odd decision. I stayed a night at an illicit hostel also hosting yet another Kitchen Sink. There were quite a throng of people there, including a brother and sister duo from Virginia. He was called Snow White, and she Black Widow. I was rather glad of her company, not yet twenty-one, she wasn't willing to drink until it was legal. That made her practically an alien to my mind. She would also make a hopeless poker player, as she rolled her eyes, then her body around her mobile phone when a somewhat obnoxious fellow hiker deigned to patronise us with his presence, which happened with disappointing regularity. He called himself Trailblazer, but we called him Starburster. If you had a black cat, his was blacker. No, that's not right, his was a melanistic panther. He put the man into mansplainer, and worse, he much preferred the pleasure of female company. Unfortunately for me it was my second meeting with him. The previous time he'd prated on about my pack size and when I wearied of his opinion, he declared I shouldn't be on the trail. Now I had to spend the entire evening with him, stewed as he was. There are times I miss drinking, being comatose would have made his company bearable, or at the very least, I could have declared what I really thought. Mind you, with the demon drink in me, I might well have slept with him.

Breakfast the next day saw me introduced to biscuits and gravy. It was a combination I did not think would work well together, and they don't. I discovered biscuits and gravy aren't a cookie and beef sauce concoction, but more of a soggy scone smothered in sick combo. Allegedly, a southern delight. The rest of the stay, though, had been blooming marvellous.

****

Feelings are not meant to be felt

"I think I could live in an exoskeleton sometimes," said Jaywalker as SideSnack mused over who would have won the fight for her shoe after a scorpion had commandeered it as a home overnight. She'd remembered to shake it before putting it on, hence the formal introduction. We were talking about bugs. I'd met a lad the day prior, practically naked, slapping himself all over to rid his body of the thousands of centimetre-sized ants manducating him. He'd selected a rare tree to rest under halfway up the day's climb just as the mid-morning temperature surged, oblivious to the fact he'd squashed their nest. They were relentless in letting him know they were mighty aggrieved by their sudden eviction. I got the joy of seeing an extremely healthy young man in the prime of his life, jumping around, not having the best of days.

I had met Jaywalker and SideSnack straight out of Big Bear where we'd been collected from our various overnight homes by a trail angel. We'd been ferried back to the PCT together. They were the kind of couple that enjoyed other people's company, full of smiles and sincere interest, with great anecdotes to boot. They'd lived hundreds of miles apart but had found each other through a shared love of long-distance hiking and Twitter. This was their second attempt of the PCT, and I was now their gooseberry. Their company helped while away the miles, better still they were early risers, more so than me. I was no longer waking up at the crack of doom: their stentorian and cheery morning salutations got me up and gone by five, well before the sun emerged. It was gifting me the stunning delights of red and yellow smeared skies, which would turn purple then blue as the sun re-greeted the horizon, splashing its warmth all around.

We eased into a rhythm of walking together for an hour or so as we all twitched and shrugged trying to get sagging packs to rest on bruised shoulders. Once perky rucksacks had sat snug, but now our weight loss interfered with their fit. The paddings on our straps had compressed, no matter what they wouldn't hug as they previously had. My pack had gnawed several raw spots above my butt cheeks. Once the body had adjusted to the rucksack bedding into my back, then a shoe would need re-fitting, forcing a precarious totter forward to tighten or loosen the laces. After a while those nuisances would seep from my consciousness, the discomfort wouldn't so much as melt away but seemingly exist with less objectionable intrusion.

The three of us would relax into our own regimes before bundling up again for second-breakfast, or lunch. We'd then spread out again in the afternoons, before reassembling to camp together early evening. Each break was an ungainly collapse on the side of the trail for a ten- or twenty-minute reprieve. Being older meant every stop caused our bodies to stiffen up considerably, and for every rested minute, there was at least two minutes of internal rebellion as we coerced bound muscles and taut tendons to bend again. Jaywalker, lanky and long-legged, would pace off ahead then wait for us to catch up. SideSnack, as diminutive as Jaywalker was tall, would blast downhill and then crawl uphill, and I was the polar opposite. Like me, it was stamina, not speed, that was ensuring she was making the distances. Joining up with them, even though they were both my senior, was really stretching mileage out of me. I loved it and loathed it at the same time.

There is something about shared hardships such as expeditions that make a person bond with their fellows quicker than we might in ordinary life. People can work alongside each other for years, and yet know little beyond the person's surname, and a rough estimation of their family life or hobbies. In AA it's the reverse, everyone's surname in my address book is the name of the town that I meet them in. Sometimes I'll add another moniker that separates them out from all the other Claires and Chrisses in my phone. There are people who know some pretty dark stuff about me, and I haven't got a clue what their surname is, or where they actually live, let alone their job. AA's openness horrified me when I first started attending meetings. Grown men weeping confounded my narrow-minded belief systems and women confessing to drink-mothering revealed my own sexist expectations of parents. We all can confess to abuse both dished out and received. AA is a safe place to dispose of the shackles of shame, addiction dies in the sunlight. I love hanging out with some of my fellows in recovery as there's an implicit openness, an assumption that I won't be judged or advised. I like how we can just listen and more often than not share our own similar experience and what we learned from it. Subsequently, there's a lot of laughter, and a hell of a lot of gallows humour when AAs connect.

As I bumbled along, I sniggered at one of the podcasts when the speaker said, "If you like everyone in AA, clearly you're not going to enough meetings." I try to suppose it's an opportunity to expand my patience and tolerance, something I'm not particularly good at. At the same time, I can't live in AA all the time, as safe a haven as it may be. The twelve steps are an aspirational way of living - a mechanism for keeping me from running back down my escape route - the river of booze. Like all addicts, when I put down the drink, I picked up new distractions to compensate. Relationships and sex are common outlets, as are shopping, gaming, gambling or eating. I started with baking, which I was too terrified to share with others, so I ate a lot of muffins and soggy-bottomed cakes. I'd put the rest in the bin before cracking on with the next recipe. Then it morphed into jigsaw puzzles. I feared knitting would be next, so I

101

was rather glad now it turned out to be excessive walking. Like all addicts, I was learning I just replaced one extreme for another, substituting one compulsion for another. They may be less harmful and risky than the booze, but I realised it was easy to fall into the trap of believing, "I'm not drinking, what more do you want?" Then the head demons would go into full revolt, coming up with the contrary belief that seemingly the world wants the moon on a stick. They would churn away all day making one all or nothing argument after another.

The fifth step also teaches me not to overshare. Not everyone needs to know my problems, nor my despair of my secrets, especially not when I'm dealing with 'earthlings'. Earthlings is one of the better phrases I have heard for people who seemingly have it all together and can keep it that way. Being thrust into recovery is comparable to being a snail without its shell, and it is the fifth step that strips us of our exoskeletons. Living in the real-world means trying to find the balance between showing one's vulnerability yet keeping one's skin sufficiently thick.

Jaywalker, SideSnack and I connected over a shared love of culinary programmes and specifically the UK cookery shows that had made it to the States. A passion for the Great British Bake Off, renamed for the US as the Great British Baking Show, led to a discussion on how dislikeable Gordon Ramsey would be in real life. Then cruelly the conversation turned to our favourite recipes and meals, and what truly makes the best roast dinner. I argued persuasively that roast dinners are incomplete without cauliflower cheese. I asked for the secret to making a good American hash brown. They are nothing like the triangles of oily regret typically served in greasy spoons. In America, they are a half-plate size of crispy, crunchy, shredded spud, a deep bronze of fried calorific loveliness. They both admitted to buying pre-cut raw potato on the rare occasion they did make it. On the plus, I now know what a skillet is.

From there we tentatively discussed different political systems in our respective countries before explicitly querying how the hell both our nations had ended up with leaders with clownish attributes. Over dinner that night Jaywalker generated new conversation: "What do British people think of the Royal Family?" I was happy to answer that on behalf of the entire United Kingdom, man, woman and child, notwithstanding creed nor religious persuasion. I'm very good like that.

Within a day, we moved onto the essence of what had brought us to our knees in life. All three of us were the 'left behind' party in our divorces following lengthy marriages. We discovered we'd all hidden away in what was left of our homes until they too succumbed to the legal wrangling, and we were evicted into our after-lives. Shells. We'd all set about slowly killing ourselves with drink or drugs, barely making eye contact with the outside world, believing the sun had set on our lives for it never to rise again. How we all felt stripped of our identities and sense of self-worth. I was the only one who couldn't stop once I had made the decision to cut back on my boozing. There was a comfort in talking about that, and how awful I'd found the first few years post-marriage. Seeing them hooking up later in life was a tonic for the soul: still flush with the joy of finding one another. For the first time in years, I didn't envy their coupledom, but rather I loved observing it.

It was the fifth step where I had begun the process of unlearning the mantra of my life: don't ask, don't tell, and when under pressure, whether it's necessary or not, always opt to lie. I was the problem child of the family long before I could say the phrase, "If you'd been the firstborn, you'd have been an only." It was one I learned early. The fifth step helped me start to unpack that. As immature as I was, and am, emotionally at least, I could begin to make progress, and that way resemble someone who had at least a grasp on the rulebook on life. I no longer needed to bullshit and flap around pretending I knew what I was doing, instead I could ask for help and learn from others.

I had to learn that it was safe to open up; that I didn't need to swagger around on the defensive the whole time. Admitting my many flaws, my regrets, the house load of shame I carried around with me, without fluff or fluster, was probably the most human thing I have ever done. It kickstarted a process of learning how to trust another human being. Several, in fact. Getting honest and raw about my feelings, my thoughts and my memories has shown me the difference between self-pity, where I tell a story with me as a centrepiece of victimhood, and me as someone who is just grieving sometimes, sorrowful for everything that I've lost along the way. Not everything is always a result of my own carelessness, or someone else's. I didn't need to be angry all the time. Nor frightened. I was learning that taking responsibility for the mistakes I'd made didn't mean I couldn't feel a deep sadness about them. I no longer had to hate myself for them either.

It was step five that taught me how fascist I could be about other people's behaviours, but so ultra-liberal about my own. Who knew that hypocrisy could be a feeling? A darned uncomfortable one sneaking within me. Hardest still was learning to be at one with uncomfortable emotions, allowing them to dissipate naturally rather than getting stuffed down only to resurrect themselves another day in another way.

There is an amazing freedom about getting well, or getting better but it is a long, and at times, a laborious process. All I have to do is make a start each day, and from there I'd want it to take care of itself. Just as they say breakfast is the most important meal of the day, this journey also needed me to get up and get going early. In reality I could start my day at any time, and with these two, that any time was four o'clock in the jeffing morning. Yet, getting up and getting going in the dark allowed a sense of adventure to develop as day broke. Then came the distraction of watching colours unfurl and the sensations of temperature changes slowly creeping in, simultaneously annoying and pleasing me when I had to stop to de-layer. First removing the puffy jacket, then later the thin fleece, revealing just my stained merino-wool top. Each stop reignited the cycle of agony which eventually melted away so I could then again notice that recalcitrant crease under the straps of my backpack.

****

Whose wrongs are they anyway?

I'd been lonely going into Big Bear, but now as we headed away from it, time was pleasurable, even after SideSnack had to bear off for two days because her blisters had taken a turn for the worse. She'd said nothing of them, I'd only realised her suffering during a long break at the Hot Springs. It was a haven for weekend trippers and one that I felt uncomfortable in, unaccustomed as I was these days to gatherings of drunk, naked people. I've no need for skinny dipping now I'm sober, I was never that enamoured by the idea when intoxicated.

104

A fellow hiker had tended to SideSnack's feet, popping blisters one by one with her sewing needle, jamming it in deep. The next day they'd re-sealed and re-infected. The Ubers unwilling to come to the nearby highway, now desolate as lockdown was in full force. She limped unevenly down a dirt track where Jaywalker had flagged down a company car and persuaded the driver to wait and give her a lift. By mid-afternoon she was resting up at the roadside motel at Cajon Pass, a busy rest stop for motorists.

Jaywalker and I pushed out twenty-four miles that day where I collapsed in gratitude at a sub-par, very lumpy flat smudge of ground. There was just nowhere to place two tents until we were seven miles away from the tunnel that safely allowed hikers and the local wildlife to cross underneath the multi-laned Interstate 15, the bustling motorway which is a significantly more efficient and cheaper way of getting from Mexico to Canada.

The remaining seven miles took forever to grind out as I lumbered along the cute winding trails cutting across hillocks engorged with meadow flowers and swirling mists. In the latter miles, we plunged down into a canyon where the fumes of diesel, oil, brakes and other mechanical matters coagulated. Conversation ceased, incompatible with the roar of the heavy-duty traffic. We diverted to McDonalds; it even had its own trail sign. I had fully intended to boycott it, but when milkshake was mentioned any principles I may have, or snootiness to be more exact, rapidly vanished.

Jaywalker had forewarned me that the area was a centre for the homeless and destitute, living in cars and tents, or worse cardboard boxes, subsisting on whatever it was they could find. I'd expected drink and drug paraphernalia to be scattered here and there; and presumed it made this part of the PCT the most dangerous. In fact, it was apparent the coterie had been moved on to where I don't know. Perhaps the pandemic was benefiting them, but that would be a wild guess.

Jaywalker had made it his mission to arrive at Cajon Junction with as much McDonald's debris as he could gather. He victory-walked in with his dirt-ingrained trousers, grinning from ear to ear, his face unshaven and grimy, holding his trekking poles aloft pierced with several drink cups, like the slayed heads of his mortal enemies. Soon after I was stuffing myself with a McDonald's breakfast *sans* sausage and bacon, and nothing to compensate. McDonalds has a very inflexible menu, and clearly meat-eating is mandatory. I requested they forget to put the meat on, which was the only thing that was permissible. I had asked them to replace it with extra hash brown, but that was not agreeable. From the server's face, you'd think I'd demanded she spit on the scrambled egg. Seconds later I collected my aeroplane-type tray of egg, scoffing at the one soggy triangle of hash brown, familiar and greasy, lying limply next to the stale English muffin. It wasn't long before I stuffed my rubbish into the overfilled bin praying the wind didn't whip it out again.

We mooched about with French Guy who I'd already met a few times. Being a fellow European we'd greet each other like long-lost cousins, except without the cheek kissing or the more conservative British hand-shake. I slumped down on the curb of the road slurping my starchy milkshake, doubting it had ever been in contact with a strawberry. French Guy had spied an electrical socket on the outside of the building, behind the large drive-thru menu and took full advantage. He waited several hours for his battery pack to recharge. As McDonalds punters drove past to place their orders, he was frequently mistaken as a beggar, and given a wodge of cash by more than one generous benefactor.

Not wanting to lose Jaywalker and SideSnack's company I booked into the hotel at Cajon Pass, and I was given the room adjacent to theirs. Hotels are the single biggest expense of a thru-hike coming in at least one hundred American dollars per night, often more when taxes are added on. Californian prices are supplied without the VAT, but they have a double taxation system - a national and a more variable local tax, which adds around twenty percent to the tariffs, and then of course a fifteen percent tip is the norm. Service workers in America are not paid a living wage. It's a mistake to think living in a tent for six months is cheap, but it only is if one stays in the tent and eschews the luxuries of a hot meal and a cleansing shower along the way.

PCT hikers can be loved and loathed for this very reason. Typically, one or two people book a hotel room, whilst a posse hides away elsewhere. Competition for rooms can be fierce in normal years. Holidays and weekends push up prices further. Once a room is secured and the keys obtained, the group takes turns to shower. It saves on hiker's costs, but it exhausts goodwill. Hoteliers usually reserve their least appealing rooms for us hikers too. We are inured to our body odour and our general filth, as well as the sheer volume of rubbish we individually generate in re-packing of foodstuffs and not just from our take-aways. We carry the legacy of all previous thru-hikers. It reminds me that my decisions are mine, but the consequences may be borne by others. I am also blind to my own privileges. It is this reality that causes so much conflict, resulting in a long diatribe of 'shoulds' that my head demons use both to criminalise me and condemn others.

The managers of this hotel had just immigrated to America and they were unfamiliar with the workings of their booking-in system. Unusually, they were very accommodating about letting me check in well before the official opening time of four o'clock. Ten o'clock in fact. An unheard-of act of generosity; getting a room one hour before the official check-in time was a rarity no matter how much I amped up my charm or limped in forlornly. As they scanned my passport, we laughed about being foreigners in this place, wrangling over words as they too were appropriating Americanisms. Momentarily we shared the confusion of what constituted a first- or a second-floor room, as in the US there's no stairs to the first floor, being as they are on the ground.

A brief inspection of my room revealed three tiny bottles of body lotion but no shampoo. Above the microwave, standard in American hotel rooms, I smiled at the small sign propped up against the coffee maker. "Dear Guest, due to the popularity of guest room amenities, the housekeeping department now offers the following items for sale..." The cheapest purchase was a second-hand small towel for fifteen dollars. The comforter, whatever that was, was eighty dollars. I supposed tax would also be added after that. I made do with the small bar of hand soap to wash my hair in the disappointingly lukewarm shower, before drying myself with a solitary rough towel. It's a bugbear of mine: hotels that only supply one towel. I think it's a result of the patriarchal system of industry being run by men. Try drying your body, whilst your tresses continue to leak ever cooling water all down your back, before getting lost in a substantial creek.

The early check-in meant I could go to one of my usual UK AA meetings, courtesy of Zoom, and there I'd see several of my closest friends. We grabbed a few moments to chat before the meeting kicked off, and they all commented on how sleek and shiny my hair was. It might have looked good, but it felt like sellotape.

I gorged on hot oily Mexican style food of questionable quality from the service station, stuffing cheese-laden burritos and quesadilla down as we binged-watched culinary shows. Jaywalker and SideSnack taught me about yogi-ing, a strategy of brazenly asking day-hikers for food, begging just like Yogi Bear is apparently famed for. Oddly, I didn't feel I would have the courage for that. Besides, I'd most likely just get another cereal bar, a foodstuff I was already heartedly sick of. Plus, I would have to decline any pepperoni-type snacks. This beggar was somewhat fussy and had dietary requirements.

Another quirk of being a PCT hiker is the ability to replace or substitute possessions when we arrive in PCT-affiliated towns. Hotels and restaurants often have a designated 'hiker box', a sort of lost and found but more of an unwanted or unneeded assortment of other people's junk. Usually they contain odd socks, plastic bags filled with unfathomable green powders, nearly empty gas canisters, and the odd flavour of ramen noodles. It was always worth a rummage as occasionally something of great use could be found like cotton buds, shampoo, water sanitation syringes, electrolytes or Imodium.

As I whiled away the hours until we got going again, I read that the most common thing to lose on the PCT was one's spork, a hybrid cooking and eating utensil that saves weight but brings a game element to eating. Using a spork means food rarely makes it to the mouth without first visiting one's front. At Cajon Pass I became a PCT stereotype. I have no idea how it didn't end up leaving with me, especially now I was fastidious about packing up my belongings. I can only hope someone somewhere will discover it again and make use of it. It was a genuinely nice aluminium, or aluminum to use the local vernacular, spork. It's oft said that "the trail provides", throwing up serendipitous moments that cannot be reasoned but still provide a welcome solution to a problem. I'd hoped I'd magically find a spork growing out of a tree to replace it, but instead broke the taboo of self-sufficiency by asking Jaywalker and SideSnack to use theirs after they'd finished their dinner.

Our little threesome soon became a six-some when we were joined by Snow White, Black Widow and Penns State. The trail in the first month was mostly pairs and trios of hikers, but now groups were starting to form, gaggles of six to ten people. Collectively called the 'hive', this bubble starts as a result of people ignoring their formal permit start dates, choosing instead the optimal, and by far safest, start time of mid-April. The other reason, of course, is that the PCTA application system treats everyone as an individual, and thus 'fairly', so a married couple, for example, intent on hiking together, might have official start dates up to three months apart. It's something that fascinates us all on the PCT: whether or not the system truly works. We all agreed it doesn't whatsoever, but we haven't got a clue on how to make it work. Fairness, like beauty, is in the eye of the beholder.

The counter argument to this approach is it disperses the footfall more evenly, and prevents systemic overuse of amenities as well as, of course, reducing the impact on the trail. However, thru-hikers are not the only users of the trail, and not all of the trail actually requires a hiker to have a permit. The advantage of a PCTA-issued permit is that one applies only once, and it is valid for all national and local parks the entire way. If it's the hiker's misfortune to not be allocated one, they may apply individually to all the restricted national parks. It's complicated but doable - as many have worked out. The information is readily available amongst the thru-hiking community.

This year, the PCTA was nowhere to be seen, unable to enforce a plethora of rule changes that had been drafted in for the 2020 season. The most startling was the forbidding of flip-flopping around the Sierra. Previously one could avoid the worst of the snow and avalanche season by skipping further north and returning to it after much of the snowpack had melted, or at least, proper trails worn in. Conversations amongst passing groups would reveal our obsession with conditions 'up there' and we'd watch for news on Facebook with interest. This year, there was a four-person international team breaking trail, but one had just pulled off injured with a snapped little finger following a bad fall. He'd thrilled us by sharing his stark X-ray showing a clean break.

Despite the PCTA's withdrawal of support, they continued to send out missives condemning the thru-hikers who'd chosen to carry on. They removed any useful safeguarding information on their website and wouldn't comment at all on conditions. That struck me as particularly short-sighted. Moreover, they strongly advocated visitors use the trail for shorter distance hikes, even LASHes - Long Ass Section Hikes. With people now furloughed or being paid by a newly devised social benefit created to off-set the economic calamity of Covid, and the absence of jobs, plenty of people had slumped off to the mountains. The PCTA had taken their stand on it but in doing so had alienated a batch of their own supporters. I wondered if they realised that pissing in one's own drinking water is still contaminating one's own sources.

The PCTA took its opportunities to remind us that a thru-hike was not possible due to the closure of three national backcountry areas, the biggest and closest of which was Yosemite National Park. The fastest thru-hikers were just about to clear the snow-swamped high Sierra mountain range and presumably faced bypassing America's most famous area of outstanding national beauty. A few days before the leading trio faced that reality, the overlords at Yosemite National Park declared those with valid PCT thru-hiking permits would be allowed to hike through the region uninterrupted. Taking the directly opposing stance to the PCTA, Yosemite National Park would continue to decline any admission to day visitors or short-term visitors. I could only imagine that supporters of Yosemite were left with the same feelings of being under-appreciated in favour of another group. We were all walkers, but clearly some of us are more *flavoured* than others!

Had the threesome got to the invisible border of Yosemite four days earlier and carried on north, they would have broken the law, that ultimate barometer of right and wrong. The change coming in as timely as it did, meant they were welcomed in, and revered by those of us following in their footprints. Many felt that it was also one in the eye for the PCTA. Elsewhere in America, the pandemic had now become hugely politicised as the two dominant parties took quite different positions on how to manage the debacle, and the world at large was falling out about wearing, or not wearing, knickers on their faces. Reading the news was now enough to make anybody want to run for the hills.

****

110

Admit nothing

Traipsing along from Cajon Pass northwards, the PCT was becoming more sophisticated, albeit incredibly westbound. The Nevada mountain ranges weave between the vast cauldron that is the Mojave Desert on the east and swerve the megalopolis that is Los Angeles to the southwest. This area is rife with trails, giving us the luxury of a plethora of formal campsites complete with picnic tables and locked pit latrines, although randomly one or two of the toilets were open. Like hungry bears, we'd rattle at all the doors of the state-supplied amenities, which were supposed to be closed to prevent the transmission of Covid. We'd be able to jettison our rubbish too, reducing ounces of weight, which made a big difference psychologically, even if undetectably to the rational mind. Better still, this section was likely to have a profusion of worn, flat patches to pitch multiple tents.

I'd been unsure whether to divert to climb Mount Baden Powell. It's not officially on the PCT, but it's only a mile to its summit, offering the highest climb so far to just over nine-thousand, four hundred feet. It was rumoured to still be chock-a-block with snow and ice, and given my experience, I was undeniably terrified. The whole day was a horrific thirteen-mile uphiller, steep and unrelenting. My fear of deep snow threatened to rule me especially now the Sierra was looming large as I'd soon be flipping back to Kennedy Meadows South. SideSnack knew she would road-walk around it, having had a helicopter rescue the previous year when she'd tumbled and dislocated her shoulder in snowpack. Understandably, she risked no chances this year, and Jaywalker would be staying with her as they forged north in a lower elevation. They'd already covered this ground in their first attempt anyway.

The trio with whom we'd been camping were later risers, yet so agile and fit that they would catch me mid-morning, hurtling by not to be seen again until dusk. I could do nothing but envy them racing up the side of the mountain, all youth and bold strides, kicking at rubble on the loose trail, occasionally causing minor landslides. Spilling down from high up, rocks and debris scuttled around me, a small boulder nearly whacking my ankle as I followed them up the path zigzagging across the mountain wall. The last few miles offered nothing but a straight-up climb: the switch-backed trail buried deep

111

under the snow. The tall evergreen trees ensured the area remained a cool box long into Spring. There was no way to get one's bearings and I soon lost track of them.

I paused briefly to catch my location, phone in hand, as tobacco smoke twitched my nose. Metres away scrambled a pipe-smoking, four-toothed fellow whose name I didn't catch, and my accent he couldn't comprehend. He had old school gear on him: a formidable bulk and weight. He looked like he'd lived in these mountains all year round, all gnarly and wild. Someone who'd scare the bejesus out of me in any other context. He was my new best friend and together we tried to work out how to get to the top, mostly by grunting at each other, and pointing.

On the cusp of the ridge, I met Black Widow, Snow White and Penns State lunching in the weak midday sun just below the peak of Mount Baden Powell. They recommended I leave my rucksack and scamper along the knife-edge ridge with just my poles. There, at the end of a thin crease, I took the old man's photo by the memorial to the founder of the Boy Scouts and he mine. The old man indicated he was going to try a different way down off the mountain, so I crept back to collapse with the other three, chuffed as if I'd conquered Everest, and now starving with the additional exertion of the day. They were already preparing to make moves. Swallowing my pride, I asked if they'd mind going slowly downhill that way I might keep up until we met firmer ground. Admitting my need for help felt all kinds of wrong. I hate asking for help. It's like turning on a neon-light of inadequacy in me.

Alas, I lost them at the first swatch of dry land where they had sped off. It had been a false dawn. Soon I was back slipping and inching my way downhill when suddenly the four-toothed, pipe-smoking hiker was there again. Frequently stopping to refill his pipe, whenever I lost him, I could always follow his scent as he cut a new trail into the deep snow that I could follow. Eventually I re-caught the three of them, once again resting in a feeble sunny patch. We had more snow and ice to tackle. I never saw the old man after that, but I was pleased I had already thanked him profusely in my terribly British way, with far too much froth.

The end of the day saw me meet my nemesis: a mound of ground, buried under snow shielded by a frozen crust. It was no more than twenty yards from its base to the top, but it didn't yield to

112

footsteps, remaining obstinately icy. With little tread left on my shoes, it was like a game of *Snakes and Ladders*. I'd just get to the brow, and then slip back down and splatter into a bowl of sunken earth metres below. Three dismal attempts later, I finally sprawled atop of it, all the while observed by the much more capable trio. There are times I like being invisible, and this would have been one of those times.

By dusk, I discovered the backside of my trousers had ripped, loudly announcing the colour of my underwear - pink! It was the only available size in Walmart that fit. There was also a very odd stain that ran down from my crotch to my knees. I hadn't pissed myself, but I'd be hard-pressed to convince anyone of that. As savage as I looked outwardly, inside a little ember of success glowed within me.

****

The false prophet

Because of my flip-flopping, I celebrated two months of hiking, a third of my visa allowance, by completing my personal six hundred and fiftieth mile. It left me with approximately two thousand to go, and just four months to do them. It seemed a tall order: averaging nearly seventeen miles a day, without a single day off, five hundred miles a month. The climb up Mount Baden Powell and descent of it had covered a mere fourteen PCT miles, indicative of what I could achieve if I ventured into the High Sierra. Having already visited Kennedy Meadows South, the entrance to that region, I had already learnt from Yogi's considerable experience that eight to fourteen PCT miles per day was typical through that section at the time of year I was due to arrive there.

I struggled to right myself, sore and over-exercised on my sixty-first day, having woken up only a couple of times in the night to turn over and reposition, taking next to no time to re-settle. Having other people around allowed me to relax sufficient enough to induce a much deeper slumber. I figured that my tendency to sleep light when alone must be something primordial - that somehow my psyche expected the worst, yet hoped for the best, much like my woken mind does.

My sleep rhythms and patterns had gone to whack in my drinking years, I didn't sleep so much as pass out. It had surprised me that it had taken several years to level out again. I'd either be zonking out all the time or barely mustering four hours a night. But the last year or so, I'd been consistent and normal, and able to remember dreams, which were less likely to be uncontrollable ventures into a past I'd rather forget. They could once again be random and sometimes whimsical, like dreams are supposed to be. On the PCT, the night-time delusions returned which I took as a sign that all was getting well. More often than not I'd wake up feeling refreshed, although a morning stretch remained an act of torture as I'd checked to see if any of my limbs were capable of movement.

"This too shall pass," is one of AAs most oft-said sayings. I loathe it as I'm programmed to believe that this too shall stay, unless it's good times, then I expect it to evaporate imminently. Alcohol always promised me that 'this time will be different' and it was. After all, I could never be sure what was going to happen, that's why I preferred in the end, my own company. Less opportunity to make a prat of myself or say a patently regrettable thing. Alcohol told me I'd have a great time, and I believed that long after it ceased to be. My anticipation of drinking booze turned me into an eternal optimist, whereas a hangover had me suicidally pessimistic.

The day's PCT hike included a detour to avoid contaminating the habitat of an endangered species: the garlic-smelling Yellow Legged Mountain Frog. It is now mostly captive-bred with periodic releases into the wild. Strenuous efforts are afforded to its recovery. Yet despite this, it retains an imperiled status, and it is especially vulnerable to contact with humans. To use another AA term, "I strongly identify with it." It's a phrase I'd never used in my life until I got into the swing of AA meetings, and suddenly I identified with everyone when it came to my time to speak. Now I was out and about with 'earthlings', I'd stop short of saying, "I identify with you," whenever they said something I could relate to, lest I outed myself as a recovering alcoholic.

The road-based detour added another third of a mile to the trail - an excruciating amount to my mind. The absolute purist, Black Widow argued, needed to take the twenty-and-a-half-mile South Fork Trail. Someone had posted on Guthook they'd rather accidentally step on the last endangered frog than walk the fast-flowing Angeles Crest Highway alternative. But we'd all agreed to take the road option and then ambitiously set out to do a twenty-mile day. The highway intertwined with the PCT so frequently it was possible to pick up the trail four miles further south than strictly necessary. It was a compromise sparing my knees the winding and hilly path but off-set against risking life and limb encountering fast-flying motor vehicles and further hammering my worn shoes, and therefore feet, on the hardened asphalt.

Jaywalker and SideSnack managed to blag a lift the entire way. I kicked myself for not doing the same. They spent much of the day lolling about the car park beside the highway where the six of us had agreed to reconvene once we'd all taken our respective routes less travelled. I arrived long after them but plenty before Snow White, Black Widow and Penns State who'd opted to do the four-mile trail detour.

I rapidly settled myself at the one empty picnic table just as rapidly unsettled myself as a rattlesnake slithered in to share the shade. One of Jaywalker's friends lived not far away and brought a car full of hot pizza and beer so instead I plonked myself down in the adjacent car parking space. The pizza, deep-panned, smothered with gooey cheese, housed a thorough scattering of pineapple and olives. I'm in the camp that thinks putting an exotic fruit on pizza is perfectly reasonable, but it's the work of the devil putting an olive on one. It baffles me that the world thinks that's acceptable. Worst of all, it's standard on a vegetarian pizza no matter where one is on the globe. I have lost hours of my life picking them off.

Black Widow joined me in the vacant parking space, "I hate olives on pizza normally, I can't believe I'm eating them," she spluttered. "I so identify with that," I retorted as I put my contempt to one side and devoured the sodding lot with a hefty swig of gratitude, washed down by some hideously chemical-tasting mineral water.

By six o'clock I was shattered. I made my excuses and readied myself for bed: my first time sleeping in a car park. It wasn't something I'd ever aspired to do. We'd located enough flattish spots on the perimeter amongst the rubbish and rubble to tightly ram in our tents. I woke a few times to snoring, but nothing really disturbed my night's slumber. A gunshot going off just outside my tent at three-thirty in the morning did though. My American counterparts deemed it appropriate to roll over and drift back to sleep.

An effective alarm, it guaranteed I got up early. Jaywalker and SideSnack caught up as I ate my brunch eight miles into my day. There was a rare spring surrounded by thick desert brush in which one could easily hide an elephant. I needed to obtain enough water for the next seven and half miles on yet another blisteringly hot Californian day. "Don't forget snakes come in to drink the water too," Jaywalker helpfully cautioned as I began to bushwhack in to find the stream. Not long after, I realised it wasn't the snakes that were the day's nemesis, but rather poodle dog bush. This most friendly-sounding plant reeks of marijuana. A mass of stems each houses clusters of thin finger-length leaves. Later in the year, the plant would bloom beautifully topped with large purple heads, but for now it was the dank smell that set it apart from other similarly-looking harmless vegetation. It is not because people try to smoke it that makes it so pernicious, but the millions of delicate hairs bonded to its leaves. Even the gentlest brushes against it with clothes or a hiking pole can be enough to ensure just one hair is transferred from plant to skin later in the day. The reaction might not begin for a few days, but sometimes weeks or years later red welts can emerge. The plant is so irritating that blisters can sit for months. It truly was a terrifying triffid and common to areas formerly ravished by wildfires.

We'd planned a sixteen mile walk to the fire station, where we'd get yet more pizza that night for dinner, this time via online delivery, and hopefully *sans* olives. I'd made sure I'd let everyone know if they got there ahead of me, which was entirely expected, exactly what I craved. Except they didn't. Mystifyingly, I got there first. I hung around at one of the picnic tables. It was still early afternoon. An hour later, I heard SideSnack yelling my name. They'd annexed a different picnic table higher up. To fill the eternity of waiting for hot nourishing food, we debated whether or not the shrub next to it was a baby poodle dog bush. A p*oodle dog puppy* perhaps. Snow White was keen to touch it but didn't. Clearly, I am not alone in having an inner-lemming gene.

We'd pushed on a few miles after but walking on a bloated stomach is a brutal pastime. I struggled to keep up with the other five, all of us aiming for a spot two and a half miles ahead. We knew it was unlikely to accommodate four two-person tents. It was a relief when Jaywalker stopped at a decent enough place about a mile and a half later. I say decent, it was terrible. I slept on a slope, a guaranteed way of ensuring insomnia as every time I nodded off, the floor seemingly moved, and I'd jolt awake.

The sleep deprivation did not really matter. There were only twenty-five miles between us and Acton KOA which we'd split over the next two days. After that I'd have a few days rest before I flipped back up to the Sierra. Jaywalker figured we should do eleven miles to a closed campsite, meet for lunch, and then head on another seven miles to a ranger's station where we'd camp that night. That was the plan, except it derailed for Jaywalker before he'd taken one step on the trail. He face-planted himself onto it instead. It started the day off with mirth, despite the drizzle. As he rubbed off the damp sand that had affixed itself all up his front, he gestured towards the non-existent view. "It's only a mist cloud," he'd said optimistically as he and SideSnack embarked on the day's hiking, leaving me to gather up the rest of my stuff.

It wasn't a mist cloud. It was the obvious sign of the deluge to come. By first light, rain, not mist, was pelting me almost horizontally. The foliage sodden. Shortly after, so was I. The trail was dreadfully overgrown, each time I squeezed through the shrubbery, I was splattered by freezing blobs of what should have been sparse water. Before long, every inch of me was soaked, right through to my pink underwear. Nothing, and I mean nothing, lightweight is waterproof despite what the adverts claim. Water repellent and waterproof are synonyms for absorbent I learnt.

It wasn't so much a desert hike; this was more like paddling in the deep sea. Or, as they say in the Pennines: a normal day's walk. By the time I'd got to the Mill Creek Campsite, with its locked toilets and 'crime scene investigation tape' surrounding its solitary picnic table, placed to ward off people wishing to sit for a moment and defy the 'closed campground' government order, I was blast-chilled. There was no sign of any of the others. I huddled under the roof of the toilet block, opting to make myself a rare daytime hot coffee. My hands riddled with the shakes; I was barely able to ignite the damned stove. I made a second because as every alcoholic knows, one is never enough, but nor is a thousand. It failed to warm me up. As I emptied my rucksack to retrieve my puffy jacket, the only dry attire I had, I noticed the Ziploc containing my electronics was filled with water. As expected, the rucksack was more sponge than water-resistant.

For much of the afternoon there was also this all-pervading smell of cats' piss emanating from one of the plants. The only good thing about the rain was that it washed out the embarrassing stain between my legs that made it look like I'd wet myself days before. I propelled down in elevation to around two thousand feet. We'd dropped seven thousand feet since the summit of Mount Baden Powell three days prior, and suddenly I felt fitter and healthier than usual, upping my average mileage to well over two miles per hour. I could see my destination from six miles out creating a new form of torment. Twelve hours later I arrived once again at Acton KOA to find the other five had made the very same decision, pushing out a full twenty-five miles.

Beaten but euphoric, the six of us booked into a six-berth cabin. Black Widow jumped in the shower, then it was my turn. I delighted in the scalding hot water, embellished with oodles of shampoo and liquid soap, even hair conditioner. SideSnack jumped in third as Jaywalker waited, fluffy towel in hand. "That's the best feeling ever," she announced as she exited the shower, swapping places with Jaywalker. "I can't wait to warm up," he shivered as he entered the bathroom.

It was no wonder his Appalachian Trail name was False Prophet. He really shouldn't have been surprised when just after he turned the taps on, the boiler packed up.

****

Chapter six

Pick up and play God

Hiking with a 'tramily' had been a very pleasing experience, pushing me further than I would have compelled myself, left to my own devices. But in the last two days, that old mindset of not quite fitting in had snuck back in. I'd always put it down to being an expat kid. I'm not from 'here', and not from 'there' either. Now I was a Brit in a group of Americans. I struggled sometimes to relate to others' life experiences, those cultural in-jokes and references that fly past my head. I grew up without TV or much music anyway, cringing all through my school years when people asked what bands I liked. My first all-girls boarding school had deemed popular culture unladylike and banned the sodding lot of it. Nonetheless, I'm great at embroidery. I live in the vain hope that one day making pretty handkerchiefs will be considered an essential life skill.

My painful shyness at times is read as aloofness and I can inadvertently alienate people. I've learnt to override it, but sometimes I've overshot and come across as too keen to be a new best friend. I knew nothing of codependency before getting into recovery, that all too often I've needed someone, or something, to make me feel okay, rooted in a belief that I'm not okay at all.

Regardless, my tramily was now about to fracture: I was to fling myself back to the entrance of the Sierra, picking up where I'd left off previously at Kennedy Meadows South. SideSnack admitted she wasn't finding it all that much fun. She went on to explore bits of the Appalachian Trail and the Continental Divide Trail, the two other long-distance north-south paths that comprise the Triple Crown of American Hiking. Jaywalker, and the trio, with their youth and physical fitness, I presumed would overtake me probably on the third pass of the Sierra so it was more 'au revoir' than goodbye as far as I could foresee.

I checked in for two nights in Ridgecrest, a nondescript town by most accounts, and extended my stay for a third night. I was back in my element: slobbing around half naked, stuffing myself silly. I only ventured out, dressed - I hasten to add, to get an omelette for breakfast, then later in the day I'd hobble back down the main drag for take-out pizza or similar, and tank myself up with coffee, chocolate cake and milkshakes. I spent the rest of the time picnicking

119

in bed, dozing on and off, mindlessly watching junk on TV or listening to an AA Zoom meeting. I was adept at lockdown long before it became de rigueur, but unsurprised that my favourite pastime had finally become en vogue just as I had decided to go all 'action woman'.

The pandemic had truly become an introverts' paradise. Masks were exemplifying those with pretty eyes. Glasses for my shortsightedness shrink my small eyes further, my mask steaming them up obscured my upper face altogether. I'd leave the supermarket, tearing off my blue face mask as if I'd just completed heart surgery on a particularly vulnerable patient. "He'll live!" I'd want to exclaim to the imagined worry-stricken family. The world at large was also discovering whether one's collars matched the cuffs, as finally we knew everyone's true hair colour. TV presenters suddenly looked like pre-teens experimenting with their mother's make-up, and presidents and prime ministers already adorned with floppy hair became positively hippified.

In recent years, I have come to love my auburn hair. I consider it natural justice as I've not an ounce of grey, but I'd dyed it for years, shamed by its colour. These days, I keep it defiantly long, and so it doesn't need cutting that often anyway. Long hair is supposed to be a sign of vitality, once upon a time a transgression for middle-aged women. I struggled to remember when I last had a period. I learnt that younger women on long distance hikes often get a sabbatical from the menses too. My menstruation cycle had been slowing down for years, only boldly announcing its existence approximately every eleven months. Each time I was about to make a doctor's appointment to confirm my graduation to my senior womanhood, I had to cancel the visit. Leaving me feeling like the class dunce sent back to re-sit the year.

It had been a wrench leaving the hotel, my legs no less stiffened despite the rest. Going into the Sierra alone was unquestionably advised against so, whether I liked it or not, I'd have to find a new tramily that would adopt me. It meant facing the fear of feeling utterly unadoptable. In truth, it was only going to happen when I got my procrastinating, albeit slightly slimmer, arse out of my motel room and back into my tent at the haven that is Kennedy Meadows South. It's one of those places where groups of hikers tend to concertina before embarking on the second stage of the PCT.

Step Six is about getting ready to let go of the stuff that causes our lives to be out of balance: the excessive guilt, the perfectionism, the manipulative people-pleasing, the desire for control, the smouldering self-hatred and the non-stop blaming of other people, places or things. It's about preparing to make changes so that one's insides and outsides start to align a bit better. It's also about learning new ways of being and doing, and it is supposed to be exciting but daunting.

Ernest Shackleton believed successful explorers have four qualities - optimism, patience, idealism and courage. None of those things are innate to me. I'm more over-reactive, petulant, idiosyncratic and full of claptrap. Or perhaps it's just my perception that is skewed. A lifetime of hearing the 'you're so...' remarks: *you're so brave; you're so lucky; you're so strong*. I feel none of those things underneath. I'm riddled with the inner voices of ghosts of the past who'd bellow, "you're so lazy; you're so useless; you're not clever enough." Born of a lifetime of rejection and insecurity perhaps - who cares. "An alcoholic is just an egomaniac with a chronic inferiority complex," someone had said recently, and I could accept that as a very perceptive view of me.

If Step Six was about losing the emotional baggage, then Kennedy Meadows South was the place to go for physical baggage. From Triple Crown Outfitters, I rented the mandatory bear canister, a one-kilogram bear-resistant barrel of monstrously thick blue plastic. It is cumbersome to pack although rumoured to be good for sitting on. I disagree. I could only manage one arse cheek, and even then, it was a short fall to the ground. The bear can is supposed to contain all of one's food but only if one has the appetite of a three-year-old. In reality, it only carried about half of my anticipated calorific intake, let alone be roomy enough to stuff in anything else scented like used toilet paper, Deet, toothpaste or baby wipes. The clever peeps, or the realists I supposed, bought half-sized canisters merely to comply with the regulations should we be inspected. They, like me, had the rest stuffed in carrier bags deep within their packs. Quite frankly, the bear canister merely adds to the impression one is about to be mauled to death.

I also acquired an ice-axe and a pair of micro-spikes: ultralight crampons which slipped over my shoes, contributing further to my sense of impending doom. After seven hundred miles of hiking, I'd only just got to grips with this walking malarky. With legs already so sore, I barely felt competent enough to climb stairs with any degree of confidence. Yet here I was getting specialist mountaineering equipment. I also purchased some bulky waterproof socks for the inevitable river crossings - who knew such things existed? The snow was now melting fast and listening to the general hubbub about snow melt had me believing I'd be meeting Noah soon enough out there. The shop didn't stock life-rings, however.

All of these items, along with nine days' worth of food needed stuffing into my fifty-eight-litre rucksack, already packed to the gills. I'd experimented with the bear canister tied up to the outside of my rucksack, but it would drop off before I'd walked fifty feet. Whilst I still had an ample supply of calories in my rear end to get me to Kennedy Meadows North, over three hundred miles ahead, I preferred to eat multiple times a day: anything to break up the monotony of continuously putting one foot in front of the other. In the end, I shoved it inside my pack, and attached my tent to the outside, hoping it wouldn't snare and tear.

As people were leaving the camp, they'd take the opportunity to weigh their packs, most coming in around twenty-five kilograms or so. I'd intended to send on my laptop, a beast of burden, although very small and compact, I had worried about smashing it, or drowning it in a river crossing. I'd armed myself with paper and pen instead but when my phone battery pack failed to recharge, I opted to rely on the supply from my laptop to charge my phone. I double-wrapped the slim laptop in plastic bags to waterproof it best I could. I didn't dare weigh my pack. A heatwave was due to arrive any day, nonetheless we all had to carry several layers on top of our thick weighty sleeping bags for when we entered snow country, with its highest pass at a formidable thirteen thousand feet.

A mish-mash of couples and loners came together and that would be my new tramily. The two 'Jays' who were a not-a-couple couple; Darkness - a second timer on the PCT; a US marine in the prime of physical fitness called HeadHat. He'd arrived with Drill Sergeant, who wasn't actually in the army but she'd all the organisational abilities of someone who was. Then there was me and a very drunk German, who smoked large spliffs, and swallowed edibles of varying colours. I passively got stoned whenever he stood next to me.

122

We'd mingle for hours, then pad back and forth between Grumpy's restaurant and the picnic area outside the shop, occasionally breaking out into conversation. Poo seemed to feature a lot as we traded misadventures with the bushes. Of course, these incidents only happened to 'someone I know'. We'd compare pains and scars, and appraise our general physical robustness, or lack thereof in my case. But for the most part, we'd stare mindlessly at our phones lost in our own little thoughts, studiously ignoring each other, whilst connecting with the wider world.

Somehow we'd agreed, I don't know how as I wasn't there, that we'd be leaving the following day at eleven in the morning to do a sixteen-and-a-half-mile jaunt. On my way to my bed, I received the message that two of the group needed to do some 'adulting', whatever that was, and so I'd be spending a third night at Kennedy Meadows resting up. The delay enabled me to greet WildCat who staggered in the following day. For the sixth day running, I enjoyed the shakes from overdosing on way too much caffeinated coffee. Then I was dismayed to discover it would be another year before I could call myself post-menopausal.

By now the advanced party of Swedes had vacated the High Sierra. It was no surprise they'd done so well, being young, robust and coming as they did from a giant ice lolly. A second group had followed them in, but injuries or demoralisation had forced them out again. Since then, dribs and drabs had traipsed in, even though it was still a few weeks ahead of the ideal hiking window. I'd spent the last three weeks waiting on news of hikers popping out again for resupply and fervently hoped they'd remember to update our Facebook group, or Guthook, of the latest conditions on each pass. There was no phone reception to be found up there at all. Reports varied from hell to not too bad. I had to assess their perception based only on a reductionist stereotype. If they were young and athletic, I ruled them out for talking shite.

Cramming as much breakfast as we could that morning, we waited for Grumpy to do whatever it is Grumpy does in the mornings before he ferried us back to the trail at noon to commence a simple enough climb from six thousand feet to eight thousand feet. "It's like day one again," Jay One panted a few hours in, struggling to find any rhythm. The afternoon temperature burnt well over a hundred degrees. My Achilles screamed at me, a new pain that I'd not previously had, my heels felt like slabs of stone. Every footstep became a drudgery in itself.

In the morning I'd convinced the Drill Sergeant that sixteen and a half miles in a heatwave, going up in altitude in just a half day might be a bit ambitious. At least it was for me. Collectively, we'd all re-settled on a campsite around twelve miles ahead. By mid-afternoon, I happened upon the two Jays larking around in one of the rivers. Shortly after HeadHat found his stride and marched off, while the rest of us filtered water, snacked or got high. As the afternoon wore on, I was bemused that no one had passed me at all. I set my tent up in a lovely shaded wooded area just after the twelfth mile. It offered a delightful recess from the glowering sun, I wondered where HeadHat had got to.

The drunk German arrived next, taking an age to assemble his small one-person tent. He was an ultralight hiker, eschewing most weighty things like stoves, and extra warm clothes. He grinned and showed me he still had four litres of beer left in three of his water bottles. I left him to recharge his Zen in his own inimitable way and clambered into my own tent to start dinner, my stuff strewn all around me in organised piles. Darkness passed by and said he wasn't ready for stopping yet, preferring a campsite with a stream. Drill Sergeant arrived next, but said that there'd be a change of plan, that they'd be camping about a mile and a half ahead on account that Jay One had diarrhoea that day and understandably wanted to be near water. Finally, the two Jays passed by too. I couldn't be bothered to dismantle everything and figured I'd most likely be up first anyway. I'd easily pass them in the morning, and we'd regroup after that.

It transpired that the tramily had got engaged and divorced that night, having completely omitted the wedding part. By the end of the first day everyone dispersed all over the place. I never saw the two Jays again, nor the drunk German. I passed HeadHat at around ten the next morning at Kern River where he'd decided to spend the night. He was waiting for Drill Sergeant to turn up, but I hadn't seen hide nor hair of her when I'd walked the first four miles between us. Later in the afternoon, HeadHat and I chatted briefly as I'd paused to catch my breath going up a long lung-busting incline. Whilst he stood still, I was able to keep up with him. He turned to resume his hike, leaving his parting words to hang in the air, "Whatever you do," he said, "don't do Forrester on your own."

124

****

Swerving the top of the rock

The trail snaked up and over gentle rolling hills, but the increasing altitude was a thief of stamina. I was sluggish, lugging one foot after the other, to rise and fall between nine and ten thousand feet above sea level. The dust and sand of the desert was now a pest of the past. Gnarly bushes and horny lizards were replaced by pines congregating in ever increasing numbers. The trail wound around the peaks of craggy rocks, and across flat meadows banked with tall grasses, still dry and beige from the long winter. Boulders, some the size of houses, imposed upon the landscape. Trout-filled rivers demarked the end of one hill and the beginning of the next. A hare whipped past me so sizeable, I could have saddled it and ridden the damned thing to Canada. An hour later, I spooked three deer, who spooked me back, before bouncing away. I spotted my first marmot, an oversized gerbil, the size of a domestic cat. It squealed a high-pitched yell as if being abducted. Shortly after, another marmot return-squealed their own sense of despair. A black squirrel had me agog, whilst the black and white stripes on a small squirrel revealed my first chipmunk. It barely paused long enough to give me a glimpse as it ran full tilt for cover under a rotting log. The day was a cacophony of meeps and beeps, and screeches and screams.

The rustle of trees could sound like the rush of water, which I had assumed would be plentiful. That assumption had left me without any for a good portion of the morning, before I'd spied a few long strips of snow a few hundred feet off trail. A decaying tree laying prostrate provided the excuse to rest up a while and boil some of it down. The abundance of thawing water brought with it even greater abundance of mosquitoes and flies, lusting after flesh or food. They hammered at my tent in the evenings and by the third night I was in a mood most foul as I set up camp next to a raging river. Fording it had left me with soggy feet and even soggier trousers. I'd thought about lighting a campfire, but the marauding bloodsuckers compelled me to seek refuge in my tent. The night's entertainment was hunting down every one that had followed me in and putting it out of my misery.

The site I'd targeted was supposed to have bear boxes where one could lock one's canisters away from hungry bears, but they had clearly been removed if they were ever there in the first place. I'd spent a good half hour looking and I resented every tender wasted step. I'd lost any sense of impetus. Each day I would set myself a goal of around seventeen miles and I was failing to reach it, quitting on average two miles short.

My axe-ice, parked in a pocket on the right-hand side of my rucksack, had taken to tapping me continuously on the shoulder. I resorted to putting one of my pairs of socks over its head. My new trousers had chaffed the lower part of my backside, and I'd had diarrhoea draining me further. The mosquitoes were frequently treated to a humongous smorgasbord of alabaster flesh. I could feel every single network of nerves from my feet up, all crying out for some reprieve. Each day had become a matter of grinding out one long mile after another, and I'd taken to crying for most of them.

Homesickness washed over me, more of a flood than a light shower. I learnt in Ridgecrest that someone I supported in AA, a sponsee as we would say, had taken to drinking again, which made me mad and sad at the same time. I felt somewhat responsible and selfish for leaving her, even though I know that I can't prevent anyone from drinking, just as no one could have stopped me. I've learnt it's best not to be someone's cushion as they hurtle towards rock bottom. It's all one can really do: stand to one side and hope they survive to tell the tale. It feels vicious but it's better than the crazy-making of trying to help someone in the throes of addiction.

The podcast speaker had told a story of the man stuck in the well. How a well-meaning businessman had thrown the man some dollars, telling him to buy a ladder. Then a doctor came by and prescribed him some pills that would alleviate his anxiety. Despite both encounters, he was still stuck in the hole. Soon a psychiatrist heard the man's feeble screams for help and asked him how he'd got there, whether he'd been treated kindly by his parents, and encouraged him to talk about his feelings. That still didn't get him out of his pickle though. A priest came and prayed for him, but to no practical avail. Until finally a recovering alcoholic discovered him and promptly jumped into the well without a moment's hesitation. "Now we're both stuck here," said the drunk. "Yes," answered the recovering alcoholic, "but follow me because I've been here before and I know the way out." I adored the story and so I wept over it too. I missed having someone to cogitate with now back to seeing no one from one day to the next. I wondered what happened to the others. Did Jay One get so sick she had to turn back? How come they hadn't overtaken me? Was I really back to being the last surviving member of humanity once again?

I'd expected snow after about forty-five miles into this section, but there was none on the trail for the first sixty miles. An expectation is said to be a resentment waiting to happen, but this was a great delight. The alpine wilderness, with its cooler daytime temperatures, was rapidly becoming a home to a vast array of lakes big and small. Its beauty failed profoundly to raise my gloom.

Many PCT hikers divert off to climb Mount Whitney at this juncture but I was steadfastly against it. Mount Whitney is the highest mountain in the contiguous United States. As a Brit, this does not give me bragging rights, because by and large the vast majority of people I know won't know what the tallest mountain is in the first place. Worse, merely describing the detour would render me pretentious simply for using the word 'contiguous.' But the real reason was because I simply could not be arsed, so I plodded on beyond the trail marker pointing the way to the summit, just eight miles away.

A few hours later, my prayers for the company of fellow man were answered as a mildly Scottish-sounding woman from Japan introduced herself as Skyscraper. Flush with success having conquered Mount Whitney, she proudly told me how it had been full of snow, and she'd had to christen her axe and microspikes. Even better, there were others ahead of her and to keep pushing on until I found them. That way we could all tackle the foreboding Forrester Pass the next day together. She sped off to catch them up, and I limped onwards my body in revolt but insides reeling with optimism.

As was becoming typical, the end of the day meant another fording, this time of Tyndall Creek. It was a raging torrent of ferocious water that rushed well above my hips. In the distance I could hear the yelps of a man frantically waving, gesturing for me to go further upstream. People in pairs are able to form structural support for one another, clasping each other's shoulders, stepping one foot at a time, repositioning each foot to guarantee a solid stance

127

between the hidden underwater rocks. Only when they are stock still can the second person move their foot slightly across too, searching for unsighted purchase, and so on until they've crabbed across the dangerous flow. I had two lightweight trekking poles for balance, each with a snow basket on the end to prevent them from piercing through mounds of snow, and no water-fording partner. It took me three attempts to find my way across, the river splashing up over my breasts, and into my face. My feet fumbling to find stability amongst the large uneven rocks deeply submerged, the water's current racing to trip me up. To my amazement I discovered I had core abdominal muscles that kept me from tottering over twice but inside my heart hammered with abject fear. I was over halfway through when suddenly it got much deeper, but less fast-flowing and I was able then to scramble to the other side, hauling myself out with extraordinarily little dignity. A dripping mess, but not a drowned one. It was then I noticed my trekking pole was missing a snow basket. It would be half-way to the Pacific Ocean by the time I introduced myself to my guide, a cheery Finn and his Finnish girlfriend, basking in a sunspot.

I pushed on and on and on to spend the night with fifteen other people, squeezing in as best we could in a spot designed for five tents. It was the last snow-free camp site, a mere five miles from Forrester Pass, the highest point of the PCT at just over thirteen thousand feet. That night my tent was delightfully free of mosquitoes. It was a relief to crash out before it had even got dark.

****

Sorting the Woodsmen from the Forresters

Being one of the last to the campsite had me pitched on a tilt once again. That wasn't the bad news, that was delivered in the form of a storm beginning its full rage overhead.

Fear is a difficult master, and Forrester commanded fear. My neighbour, Eyes, from the adjacent tent asked me how I'd slept. "Fine," I lied out of habit. He gently chided me for sleeping with my bear canister and not leaving a few hundred metres away as we are supposed to. "They can still smell food, they just can't get at it," he explained. I noticed as I was brushing my teeth that everyone else had slept far apart from their bear canisters. I'd fancied a second hot drink before bed and once I had fallen into my pit, there was no way I was coming out of it. The pain of getting back on one's feet was excruciating, and the wind whipping up didn't make the day any more welcoming.

I shlepped off soon after, long before anyone else had collapsed their tents, and immediately commenced the five-mile climb. Breaking rivulets frozen over, I shuffled on, my breathing laboured, despite the gradient being barely detectable. Icy water crept into my shoes - my new 'waterproof socks' were not remotely waterproof: already the rubber insides were causing friction burns. It seemed like no time had passed before the train of the night's campers whizzed by. I had to push hard just to remain within sight. Surrounding us, the barren rocky ground left little to distract me from mulling over how awful Forrester Pass was likely to be.

I caught the others as they coaxed wet shoes into microspikes and crampons. Eyes issued a reminder on how to wield our ice-axes, cautioning us to never let go. Shortly after, the path was lost to the hardened snow and I could only complain about how steep it was becoming to the hiker behind me. As we ascended the last mile, we had to haul ourselves up more vertically. In an ordinary year there'd be footsteps of several hundred people flooding through each week, providing a clear route and some traction, but the gale had blown away any traces of anyone having ever visited at all this year.

I started to wither. I felt so inept that I couldn't do more than a plod, counting to six or ten or twelve, then taking regular breathing breaks. Goblin, from the Czech Republic, had lived in Birmingham for several years. It puzzled me how he'd not acquired the correct *Burming'um* pronunciation, a riddle solved as he talked non-stop of working for sixty-five hours a week, seven days a week, every week, even holidays. It was paying for this trip of a lifetime, so it had been worth it for him. He'd worked in a processing plant that supplied every damned high street store and supermarket he could recall, he carefully listed them all one by one. He'd learnt their names from the labels, causing me to ponder exactly which stores he meant. He went into intricate detail on how the production line worked. He'd just completed, in minute fashion, his first year's work record, from there he'd been promoted to label printing. He was interrupted just as he commenced his monologue of his second year when Eyes yelled,

"Don't follow the footsteps," pointing at a clear patch of snow, suggesting I take it as an alternative.

There was just sheer ice ahead of me, and Goblin behind. "But there's no footsteps," I pointed out utterly baffled. I found myself gripping onto my ice-axe having slipped and nearly fallen, digging my spikes into the wall of ice. After an age, Eyes chiselled his way over to me using the back of his ice axe, and I followed him out and back to the rock where he'd previously waited. Up we crawled some more. I wondered if this horror would ever end.

Everyone hollered and clapped as I made it across another ridge of ice but as soon as I reached them, they all muttered about the cold, and off they took again. The problem of being the tortoise is one never gets a damned break. I couldn't complain: they had to do things their way, that's what expeditions are about. Behind me, Goblin, having paused to take a photograph, dropped his phone providing simultaneous levity and panic, as we watched it fall nearly a hundred feet down, stopping only when it clattered into a gap between a boulder and the ice. I was simply glad of a moment's rest. Amazingly, he retrieved it undamaged. I'd had mishaps with both my phones on the trail, both now cracked to hell. His wasn't at all tarnished for its escapades.

There were more sheer ice packs to navigate, and then the famous one, the final icy chute below a cornice, straddled between two walls of bare rock. The wind blasted upwards and swirled unpredictably, with intermittent heavy gusts threatening to throw us off our feet. One slip and it was a long, accelerating descent to death. We crossed one at a time, me second to last with just Goblin behind me. He scurried across it without an ice-axe, revealing for the first time that he didn't think one was necessary.

Soon after, I staggered over the top of the pass. Someone had thoughtfully taken the time to dig out the snow-covered sign announcing: 'Forrester Pass, Ele: 13,200.' We took it in turns to snap a quick round of photographs, set to a backdrop of waves of snow-matted mountains. It was not long before our stasis invoked violent shivering. My legs still trembled with the toxicity of adrenaline. It was then I looked down the other side to the descent we now had to face, and my knees recommenced their knocking in fear. The storm of last night had obliterated all the routes down too, presenting us with a protracted, steep slide. Eyes opted to glissade down, plunging in his axe as a brake, he announced after thirty metres or so that it was "very hard on the ass!". His wife chose to hike down conventionally in wobbly, physically-demanding steps. Taking time to observe them both, it made glissading perceivably less exerting. The Finns went third and fourth, on their backsides, then Skyscraper sat on a small pillow, which promptly took off ahead of her. I followed second to last, I was just gathering momentum when below me Skyscraper's scream pierced the air, and in the distance, I watched her barrel-roll over and over, stopping at the feet of Eyes.

I plunged my ice-axe into the hardened snow and held myself about one-third of the way down. Goblin, having no ice-axe, smashed into the back of me. I watched as our two water bottles, and other stuff of his, careered down the mountainside, and was oddly proud when my water bottle won the race. Now I was holding the two of us, patiently waiting to see if Skyscraper was going to get up. I didn't dare release my ice-axe until she'd cleared the path. For a long while I was apprehensive for her welfare, but it turned out she was, thankfully, unhurt and merely resting to compose herself. I began a tightly controlled glissade down. Hard on the ass it was indeed. Later, I discovered I'd scorched a large hole in my new trousers.

The impact of Goblin had also blown the insides of my rucksack out. The pockets were no longer usable, and the collision had burst rips into the main body of the rucksack. Because of all the river crossings, I'd taken the precaution of packing everything in bin-liners, which for now just about kept everything contained. I silently fretted for the laptop. The rucksack, however, was undeniably toast.

We were soon in waist-deep snow, frozen on top with a melting crust. On the opposite mountain, an avalanche roared downhill ominously, as we all battled through newly-formed snowdrifts on the slope of the mountain. I had to self-arrest quite often. The rock-climbs, the ice, the postholing all consumed energy I didn't wish to expend. At one point, Eyes again pointed to an alternative route and told me to take it, only then had to come over and give me a lesson on how to post-hole and fall forward without twisting. He tried to give me a positive pep talk. More frustrated than scared deep down, something buzzed within that I was going to be okay. I noticed, however, the top of my fingers on my right hand had frozen solid and were ice-white. The beginnings of frostbite.

131

I was a now-not-so-novice hiker, not a mountaineer. This was way beyond my skill set. I was miserable. Miserable about always playing catch-up. Miserable to be told to go a different way from the others when I didn't have the confidence to break trail. Miserable about how goddamned hard this was. Just plain miserable. We managed to make it to a crop of exposed rocks, jutting out from under the ice, it was a recent rockslide and horrifically unstable. "The rocks are moving," Goblin said. I didn't know if he meant they were in motion at this moment in time, or just a bit loose. I did my best to scramble across them, but scampering wasn't exactly how it was. I lacked the agility of the others and took considerable time to be sure-footed. If one believes in reincarnation this was irrefutable proof I have never been a mountain goat.

Once the going got slightly better, the pack took off again. I was left to tip-toe my way across the remainder of the downhill. At the bottom, once it had smoothed out, I was to cross a large ice field. Now completely alone, I postholed regularly once up to my hip. Trying to get my leg out from the icy vice, I left my shoe behind, forcing me to dig for it with already frozen hands, obliterating nearly twenty minutes. It happened again not five minutes later. By the time I'd done the traverse of the snow field, many of my group's tracks were dissolving but occasionally I could shunt one leg into a hole that they'd previously dropped through, grinding out one giant footstep after another.

The views had been outstanding, yet I felt overwhelmingly traumatised. My split bag meant that somewhere along the way I lost my water bottle which housed my filtered drink. Now all I had for a container was an old two litre bottle that I had previously used to gather water directly from the source. I didn't dare take off my rucksack to retrieve my water filter. Risking giardia, E-coli and God only knows what else, I had no option but to drink from springs directly using the contaminated bottle, storing only enough to keep me going.

Eventually I picked out some traces of trail between snowfields where they vanished once more. More rocky outcrops were scuttled, my hands now red-raw, the rest of me shook like blancmange. Physically, I was beat and yet knew that I'd have hours of hiking ahead of me. I have never, ever in my life been 'sporty'. I'd go so far as to assert I have no natural sporting talents whatsoever.

Even in primary school, I was the undisputed winner of the game of 'last to be picked' in the school yard selections. Yet, I've always had tenacity and a notion to try novel stuff; that's why I've travelled the world and I'm drawn to bonkers things like this. But when it comes to more normal pastimes, they are scuppered by an acute fear of failure coupled with a phobia of judgement, which proves to be a powerful deterrent. I've found myself signing up for all sorts of community-based sports and events, gone once, felt exposed and never returned. I understand why women tend to do things in pairs, rather than alone, a sort of gender co-dependence that's been instilled in us for no other reason than 'people might think we're Billy No-Mates if we go alone'.

Back in reality, the altitude had zapped whatever pace I had managed to build up previously. Everything smouldered: my hands, my feet, my rear. I was getting waves of nausea each time I ate or drank. I presumed it was altitude sickness rather than the start of something more sinister. My rucksack sat heavy on my back. I figured the rules of gravity, which are supposed to ease the higher one goes, didn't apply here. Yet when I got to lower elevations, I was suddenly aware of just how much heavier everything was on my shoulders. That there is a very plausible explanation as to why I didn't get a very high grade in physics GCSE.

Hours later, the ground had flattened out and the trail was visible once again. I stumbled on the two Finns, sunbathing in the warming afternoon, looking rather replete. They reminded me the next best stop was at the exit for Kearsarge Pass, another five miles away. It was mid-afternoon and five miles seemed very doable. I hadn't, however, factored in that two and a half miles of it was a tremendously hefty climb.

For much of the day, I was conscious that I was sandbagging the group. Worse, I was unwittingly putting them in danger with my inexperience. I realised, sadly, that I was out of my depth. Eyes and his wife had taken the time to point out that Glen and Mathers Passes were still ahead, and would likely be more arduous, despite their slightly lower elevations. A substantial part of me decided it was time to quit.

The PCT explicitly forbids one from flip-flopping around this section, so if anyone leaves for any reason beyond a re-supply or brief sojourn, they cannot return without a new local permit. Perhaps, one way forward was to road walk, or find other lower elevation trails that might get one to Sonora Pass. What was not a palatable idea was being another group's liability, nor indeed going forward on my own.

Somewhat sexist, the sixth-step is known as the one that sorts the men from the boys. It is the step which asks us to start growing up and take responsibility for our own behaviour. We learn how to focus on our part in matters, rather than always permitting ourselves excuses or planting irrational justifications. If instincts are what help us to stay alive, the ego is what motivates a person to act rashly or willfully. Most of the time, I find it hard to distinguish between the two. My ego was clearly writing cheques my body couldn't cash, but quitting seemed so utterly repulsive. All I could do, then, was hand it over, ask for a sign or something to tell me what to do next.

The last two and a half miles of the day were a non-stop exercise in demoralisation as I rose up another thousand feet. I got to the first of three exits, escape trails that would take me off the PCT, and eventually to a trailhead where I could get a hitch to a nearby town. Someone had scratched out 'Kearsarge' on the sign, utterly confounding me. Exhaustion impelled me to take my chances with this route rather than press on another Herculean half mile to the next exit. Shortly after, I approached another sign forbidding camping at Bullfrog lakes compelling me to keep moving on, despite my head tormenting me with the mantra I had nothing left in me. Having done another mile, the uphill mildly less agonising than before, I promised myself that I was going to stop as soon as I could find dry ground. I trudged by a stunning but very swollen pond, which I assumed to be the second of the two lakes. With any luck, I half-pleaded, I'd find someplace acceptable soon after. It was then I heard the howl of a single wolf. Seconds later, came a considerably longer howl. I had not factored in being devoured by rabid wolves in my list of things to fear on the PCT, but at this moment, they topped it.

Never before have I regretted my innate laziness so much. That extra half mile I'd previously shunned suddenly appeared incredibly alluring, but only now I had an added couple of miles to romp back. After the trauma of the day, I really needed to be around people to sleep. The idea of being alone was awful, but with a pack of wolves circling, it was insufferable. I had no way of googling how many people are exterminated by wolves per annum but the head monkeys created an entire collage of images.

Leaving the area with more speed than I mustered coming into it, I found my way back to the PCT, only to be confronted by yet more strenuous acclivity. Stopping every thirty paces or so, I eked my way back to nearly eleven thousand feet. I discovered quite by glance, Skyscraper and the Finns collecting stones to better staple their tents to the ground. Despite sheer debility, we chatted until long after dark. Nausea had interfered with my ability to eat my dinner, but I couldn't have cared less.

****

Fear is a friendly foe

Short of rest, I made to pack up my belongings only to discover my running shoes frozen solid, leaving me unable to manipulate them onto my feet until they melted. I smacked one then the other around, trying to make them pliable. One of the Finns came across and casually mentioned it was nearly eight miles to Onion Valley, the trailhead where we'd hopefully get a ride out to one of the towns. I'd presumed it was between three and five miles. My morale plummeted.

There are trail miles and town miles: those that we have to do to get re-supply. In my head I discounted town miles as being useful for getting to Canada. I was still adjusting to the fact that in the Sierra the trails to car parks are substantially longer than the side trails in the desert. Walking off the PCT makes every step seem twice as hard to do, take twice as long, and appear on the surface to be at least twice as gnarly. Time seemed to expand considerably; my head crammed full of the 'what ifs'. What if the car park is empty? What if they've closed the road? What if I don't get a lift? What will I do if I'm stuck in a vacant trail head forever? And what happens if all the hotels are full? What will I do if all the cafes and restaurants are closed? What if they've banned takeaways?

This particular side-trail was, for the most part, horrifically uphill for quite some time, then just as horrifically downhill, with fat rocks impeding any rhythm. My poor battered body wasn't countering any of it. Skyscraper and the Finns zoomed past me about an hour after I left camp. A few miles later, the side-trail merged with the lower trail that I'd u-turned away from the previous night. I caught the three of them resting, snacking and rehydrating as they introduced me to a fourth man called Wolf, so called because he does a realistic 'coyote' howl. He'd been baying for Goblin who he'd agreed to camp with the previous night. Only Goblin hadn't turned up. Had he not howled, I would have had the pleasure of his company. Fear is a terribly cruel master, and my faith is seemingly incredibly flimsy. One of the many hideous clichés some AAs have adopted from the alma mater of many a rehab is that fear forces a choice between, 'Forget Everything And Run, or Face Everything And Recover.' It was only my dilapidated rucksack that had prevented me from running in the first place. That, and my lack of physical prowess.

I staggered towards Onion Valley, Goblin, now reunited with Wolf, along with the Finns and Skyscraper had overtaken me on the descent into the trailhead and were now long gone. I'd rung several trail angels on the way down, but none were available for giving rides that day, leaving me to take my chances with a hitch-hike. I could see a smattering of parked cars in the distance. As I neared the end of the side-trail, a woman was heading up for a day-hike with her dog. "You don't want to come out," she said, "you really don't. It's carnage out there." I presumed the pandemic.

Soon after, I saw Eyes and his wife come down perching themselves in front of a locked pit latrine waiting for a car sent by their hotel. They weren't going to Bishop, which was my preferred destination, but to the smaller town of Independence. We nattered a while expressing our astonishment that the car park was so steaming hot in contrast to the freezing temperatures we'd experienced just five hours earlier. With no phone reception at the trailhead, I'd have to rely on the goodwill of a day-hiker and approach them directly. I had to trust things would work out exactly as they should, rather than how I think it might. I practiced patience, a virtue I'm not renowned for. A group of three arrived and I tentatively asked them for a hitch to Bishop, overcoming my self-consciousness. They asserted their car was full to the brim and I gracefully backed away and wished them a nice day. Of course, I felt the need to inspect their car as they left, revealing a sense of entitlement I was not proud of.

I found my next encounter substantially easier: two couples, with two cars, and accompanied by two dogs. It always amuses me that if one compliments someone on the beauty of their dog, they will readily take unmerited credit for it, but tell the human they are gorgeous, they rapidly back away avoiding all eye contact! Alas, my tactic of ingratiating myself with them by fawning over the canines, had little impact. They shook their heads stating they were not heading to Bishop that day before adding that it was a fifty-mile trip. I hadn't realised at that point what I was asking of potential lift-givers. I'd got it in my head that Independence and Bishop were more or less equi-distance from the trailhead. Most day hikers here would likely have come from Independence. I apologised and went to walk away, and just then one of the couples changed their mind. Not only that, but they were also emphatic: they would not consider taking payment.

As the women helped me haul my broken pack into the boot, shunting dog and human paraphernalia all around to accommodate it, they passed me a phone charger, thrust a bottle of water into my hand, as well as some snacks. They insisted I take the passenger seat and make myself at home. I was stunned but delighted when they then announced they were going to take me to their favourite coffee shop and treat me to whatever cake I liked. In truth, at this point there wasn't a cake I wouldn't have liked, even coffee and walnut. They were my new best friends.

They'd both been furloughed in the pandemic, and one had recently been made redundant. Avid outdoor enthusiasts, and equally avid cake-eaters, they were glad that life on the streets appeared to be opening up again, but now there'd been this killing of a man in Minnesota. They described how half of America was gearing up for riots and protests, and there was talk of civil disobedience being put down by the National Guard. There was now blanket coverage on the national news, momentarily pushing the Covid-related obsession to second place. Nearby street protestors were flooding highways across California, and curfews were being introduced to contain the reaction of an angry and cabin-fevered population. Bishop, for now, was unaffected, they assured me.

When we arrived in the attractive town, the coffee shop had taken to closing early, leaving me with nothing to do but say goodbye to check into a motel nearby. Relieved yet still despondent about the circumstances that I was facing, and clueless as to what to do about it, I was not entirely ready to admit defeat. It is at these times that I am reminded that praying is a possible remedy, and better still, being willing to accept whatever will be, is the way it must be. I find acceptance difficult, and my sponsor noted early on that I bargain over outcomes continuously. I fight tooth and nail to resist letting go until things get unbearably bad. He always said that if I can face things as they are, and not as I'd like them to be, I'll be a substantially happier person. He may be right, but still I argue.

I mooched along the pavement, head down, sore, hobbling and hungry searching for something appetising. In doing so I stepped over some chalky scrawls on the cement: *Don't give up, look up*. The following day, I went to the coffee shop, the women's favourite, and there on the wall in the biggest lettering, 'Courage is fear that has said its prayers.' It's a phrase I hear a lot in AA and a timely reminder. On a recent podcast I'd heard a new phrase, "God is never late, but I'm usually early," and I adopted it. It summed up my impatience and I committed it to memory as a mantra so I could remind myself frequently that all is exactly as it needs to be. That I am the problem, the solution will be forthcoming, and I may even prefer it. It was a salutary and timely, but humbling lesson.

After breakfast, I'd scrolled through Guthook and realised that if I skipped forward forty miles and rejoined via Bishop pass, a thirteen-mile side trail, I could circumvent Mathers Pass, Glen and Pinchot. Mathers is the mean one, although the snow fields around Muir are horrific, there could be no avoiding those without a substantial leap forward. It was an option, not a perfect outcome, but an option. The perfectionist in me rallied, but the realist in me persevered.

My insistence on coming to Bishop meant I could get a replacement backpack at one of the outdoor specialist stores. Non-essential shops had just been given permission to open up again from June 1st, and I just happened to have arrived on the 31st of May. Had I gone to Independence, forty-odd miles south, I'd have had to come to Bishop anyway. One of the outdoor shops had my exact rucksack in stock, although pricey. I'd wanted to try a new style rucksack, but I wasn't willing to compromise on weight that much. I paid the full whack.

The following day, I sought out a hearty American breakfast, which I'd fallen deeply in love with. I recognise that I may well be exiled if I dare to admit that American breakfasts are far superior to most English fry-ups. It was lovely to sit down inside and dine at a proper table again, rather than on a park bench or a hotel bed, any desk space would always be swamped by my belongings. For the first time in two months, I got the benefit of bottomless cups of coffee, as is typical in the US, because like me, they agree one is never enough. It gave me several hours to catch up on the news. I learned the protests had spread to major cities within the UK. A few hours later, I stepped out of the restaurant to see the main drag had filled up with bannered students chanting *Black Lives Matter*. On the road car horns honked out support, the small town now in full clangour. The thought of walking through protesting crowds was intimidating but if I wanted to return to my hotel, I'd need to combat that notion. I soon discovered it was nothing more than a warm-hearted coming together of people disgusted by the terrifying suffocation of George Floyd at the knee of the arresting officer. They had mostly melted away about four hours later when I'd headed out again to the Post Office to retrieve a new battery pack and to send my laptop further north. I'd always planned to come to Bishop to do that, but the pandemic meant there were now considerable postal delays, and my kit wasn't there. Assured by the battery company it would be there within two days, I opted to stay a further two nights.

Just after I'd renewed my stay with the manager, who offered a discount, I got a private message from a woman called Delightful who I'd crossed paths with a couple of times back in the desert, wondering where I was. Her hiking partner, also bound by a visa, didn't want to waste time and energy doing the full horror of the Sierra. Yet, Delightful wanted to give it as much of a go as she could. She'd worried about finding a new partner to continue with, everyone else she was in contact with had been abominably fit and capable. She was nervous she'd be left alone to face Forrester Pass. Currently, she said she was managing around fifteen to seventeen miles a day, which wasn't wildly different from my own average. So just like that, the four days I had taken in Bishop, saw me leaving with a brand-new battery pack, a brand-new rucksack, brand new tear-free trousers and a brand-new hiking partner, slightly worn out, as she was two years older than I.

Thrilled, I took off for the launderette. As I waited for the spin cycle to finish, Darkness turned up. I learnt that they'd just dilly-dallied for several days, went fishing in the lakes and generally didn't push out much mileage. Jay One hadn't been ill at all. Just as he vanished, Drill Sergeant turned up, angry about the constant rearranging of plans. She was frustrated that every time something had been agreed each day, the metaphorical agreements had just as rapidly been torn up when the two Jays got distracted. She was hurting, and pissed off her hiking partner, HeadHat, had abandoned her as well. Realising the experience had revealed her considerable control-issues I readily empathised with her mixed feelings. She told me how she'd come across a podcast quite randomly, and when she began listening to it, it had been all about perfectionism and the fear of letting go. I told her I didn't believe in coincidences and that perhaps she should take that as a sign. My hypocrisy naturally burned a hole within me.

****

Not remotely willing

The climb back on to the PCT took the best part of a day and a half. A kindly trail angel had picked us up some four hours later than scheduled, her car already packed to the rafters with her partner, son and boot full of stuff. Delightful, diminutive with an oversized pack shunted herself to the centre of the back seat, and I rammed myself in next to her. Within minutes my weighty rucksack had cut off the blood supply to my legs.

It was quite the adventure returning to the trail as our driver shrieked and hyperventilated throughout the hour-long journey. All because, as I saw it, cars drove on the correct side of the road, and traffic remained appropriately stationary at red lights. I could only imagine that having an entire support network around her, including us two unbecoming strangers, was in some way helping her overcome her fear of all things automobile, just like her loud and frantic self-talk requiring her to 'focus' and 'breathe deep' might. It was a relief to cascade out of the car at Bishops Pass, not least because it had been a good half hour since blood had found its way to my ankles. Alas, the joy evaporated when my knees discovered the large steps and boulders they had to yank me and the contents of my current life up and over.

Behind me, Delightful seemed slightly underdressed for the conditions she was to encounter, exactly as I had been. Acclimatising

140

to an entirely new section, radically different from the desert conditions she'd just left was going to take time. She was already wowed by the additional weight of the bear can, ice-axe and microspikes. It had yet to occur to her to jettison the extra water.

Within a few hours of setting off, lightning struck overhead, and the ominous rumbling of a storm took hold of the entire area. Seeking refuge under one of the few remaining fir trees, hail lashed down stinging whenever it made contact with bare skin. I was celebrating my sobriety birthday, and I was astonished to find myself tearfully homesick, as we huddled together wishing the weather system to move on. I counted the seconds between the roar of thunder and the sudden flashes, but soon enough the worst of it rolled away. Within a half hour or so we'd be above the tree line and exposed, ever-thickening patches of snow becoming the norm. The unrelenting path took us higher and higher, peering over deep-frozen lakes, our lower limbs doused by tiny waterfalls landing on the side of the trail. We struggled to locate a suitable place to camp, but eventually came across a tiny harbour next to a small seasonal pond, less than a mile short of the top of the pass. Above eleven thousand feet where no mosquitoes could plague us, Delightful was less than delighted to find her gas canister not working but oddly enough it did with my gas nozzle.

Lugging ourselves and our wares over the saddle early morning was a feast of post-holing and swearing, particularly as the summit levelled out. Leading the way, I didn't dare let her know that my sense of direction was diabolical. Legs weary from the exertion, we rested at the first exposed rock, gasping at the wintry scene encompassing us. "Where do you plan to resupply?" Delightful asked nonchalantly. "Well, it'll have to be Mammoth next, then Sonora Pass. What with pretty much everything else still closed," I replied. The trail to Mammoth was about seventy miles ahead, and then about one hundred miles further north, Sonora Pass signified the end of the High Sierra, and with it the much-maligned requirement for carrying a bear canister. "I'm not doing a ten-day food carry to Sonora," she snapped. It puzzled me how she'd calculated that, but she insisted it would take that long. I'd figured once we'd overcome Jim Muir, we weren't likely to be traversing that many intense snow fields. Information was scarce, but summer was inching its way in. I figured we needed to get to Mammoth first and then see where conditions were at. Things could change quickly in the Sierra.

It was downhill for much of the remaining time on the side trail until we finally rejoined the PCT. To my envy, Delightful practically glided down whilst I staggered and floundered foot by foot. I overtook halfway up the next four-mile ascent, where a virtually snow-free campsite awaited us. Exhausted, my knees and back on fire, I pitched my tent and set about filtering water from the adjacent river, itself fed by a thundering waterfall a hundred feet away. I heated up some lentil dahl. The pre-made wet meal, designed for people who don't hike, was thus delicious. It had weighed a ton, but the warmth of the spices was simply fabulous, though considerably spicier than I was used to. I justified it as a good restorer of energy, readying me to tackle the horror that was the formidable and much-feared Muir Pass the next day. According to the notes, deep snow fields stretched for miles, beginning pretty much right from where we were. The trick, most supposed, was to get up in the middle of the night to make sure that one was up and over well before mid-morning. After that, the surface of the snow would start to thaw, and one could easily find oneself falling through, devouring energy reserves and squandering time digging legs and shoes out. I'd seen a picture of a fellow hiker up to his armpits in one snap, the caption claimed he was six foot four. If that was true, Delightful at five-foot-one wouldn't get out before August. Some had called it a slog, others hell frozen over. It really didn't matter; I was dreading it.

As I was about to go for my pre-bed pee, I heard a sobbing Delightful lurch in. "I'm not doing Muir tomorrow, I'm going to take a zero," she yelled at me. "Today was just too much," which obliterated the plan of getting up by two in the morning. I helped her erect her tent, an identical one to mine, that used our trekking poles instead of rods. Novelly, she turned hers upside-down the tips skyward, for what benefit I had no idea. Her tent, her rules.

I brought across some sizable stones to better hold the stakes in place and then she promptly threw herself into her tent, whipping the vestibule cover shut. A "for fuck's sake," muttered here and there emanated from beneath the fabric. Later, she told me she'd burnt the fabric doors of the vestibule lighting her stove. I'd always left one of mine as a precaution because I didn't know how flammable these tents could be. It was a relief to learn from Delightful they are not inclined to combust like shrink-wrap.

As we were going to bed, I asked her if she was certain she wasn't walking in the morning, and she expressed some doubt. "How about I wake up at two, and then you can see how you feel then?" She was non-committal. I've learnt in AA to break things down into baby steps, and to postpone a decision until the emotion of the situation has dissipated. "You can start your day at any time," is a frequent refrain - but clearly not when stuck on the edge of a gigantic snow field. As I was readying myself for bed, I broke the day down a bit. "If you do change your mind, perhaps we could just get the hut on the top of Muir, and then if you want, we could rest up then, we don't necessarily have to do the whole thing tomorrow." Strictly speaking, sleeping overnight in the hut is not allowed, but then who the hell was going to check?

AA's twelve steps are read out at almost every meeting, with its immortal lines of, "Many of us exclaim: 'What an order, I can't through with it!'" I frequently remind everyone that is not what I exclaimed. I silently thought, "You can jeff off if you think I'm doing any of that," But slowly one by one, I started to incorporate the steps into my daily life, urged not to worry about the fourth or nineth steps, the truly yucky ones, until I got there, and I didn't need to rush to get there in the first place. Better to make a bad start, than not to make a start at all. Besides which, I could always come back. I don't need to live an 'all or nothing life' these days, which meant that barely anything got done out of fear. The steps are, after all, merely suggestions, albeit ones given with all the earnestness at one's command!

At two in the morning, my alarm sang out its unwelcome news. Not that I'd needed it to wake me, another storm had crashed in even before darkness had descended, bringing tent splattering hail. I doubted it was the weight of the icy stones that caused my tent to collapse, rather the shoddy way I'd pushed the tent pegs in on one side, leaving it vulnerable to the fierce blasts of wind. It repeatedly ripped out the central stake tethering the trekking pole to the ground. The whole structure toppled onto me several more times.

Delightful agreed to give the day a go. Lying around thinking about doing Muir was surely infinitely worse than doing it, and I felt a day idling in our tents would just heighten that fear. I didn't know if the sub-zero temperatures, and the storm with its driving rain and wind, would make conditions better or worse. I did know that if I didn't get a move on, no miles would be done at all.

Packing up a tent in the dark, and trying to pick out one's way, with only the weak beams of two head torches made the going slow. Shoving our feet into a wide icy river crossing in the first ten minutes, revealed an absence of trail on the other side, forcing us to cross and re-cross. For the first mile, the uphill was sharp. Delightful asked to lead the way, better to control the pace, and that seemed sensible to both of us. Her hyperventilating inexplicably had a relieving effect on me, but her panic made her deaf to suggestions. For once, I was not the weakest link in the chain, now I was the voice of reassurance. Although, actually, it is just another admission that I'm well practised with bullshit.

As dawn broke several hours later, the ice fields stretched out ahead of us. We slipped on our microspikes once the rocky outcrops had reduced to small interludes. As usual any previous traces of people had been extirpated by the storm. We rounded a lake the wrong way, wasting a precious hour having to creep back. Delightful was terribly vocal about her suffering. Anger for some can be incredibly motivating, but it easily renders me intimidated, and I'm inclined to take responsibility for other people's feelings. I had to remind myself mentally that some people just make a lot of noise to dissipate their fear. I could have cried with relief when we were suddenly overtaken by Eyes and his wife, shortly followed by a New York couple. Their enviably long legs bounced them through the snow, leaving us giant footprints to straddle between, exercising hips and upper thighs in ways hips and upper thighs do not enjoy being exploited. Muir isn't overly vertical, unlike Forrester, rather it just is one elongated knoll after another. Motivation saps away and turns to despair as one quietly creeps up to the apex of each mound, only to discover another gently revealing itself. The monotony of it all gives the impression one is not making much by way of progress. Our microspikes bit into the snow, but they were cumbersome to walk in. Having an ice-axe in one hand, a trekking pole in the other, left me off-set and unbalanced. I played a mental game of estimating how many footsteps were between each mound, then set off to count, pausing after each fifty or twenty footsteps to alleviate the buildup of lactic acid.

Delightful shouted up at me to wait at the top of the next hill as she wanted her fleece hood pulled over her head to cover the woollen hat she was already wearing. When she caught up, her teeth battering away. I suspected she had made the same mistake I had on Forrester: wrongly assuming that the day would warm up once we'd got moving. It doesn't, if anything it gets colder. She'd likely have more layers in her rucksack, but when I was in the same position the idea of stopping to pull everything out was an ordeal too difficult to bear. Strangely her hood was already over her beanie, and even more confusingly she declined the option of putting her puffy hood on as well. She was clearly utterly cheerless.

I pressed on not wishing to stop for a moment longer than was necessary to regulate my breathing and give my legs some respite. A few more ice-trapped hills later, I neared the top of yet another morale-sucking, lung-busting, ice-bound ascent wondering when on earth this beasting would end only to spot the unmistakable circular stone roof of the Jim Muir Hut. A hundred metres or so behind me stood Delightful mentally gearing herself up to follow in my footsteps. I frantically waved my arms around and gestured back to her what I could see, my voice likely lost in the wind. She motioned back to me. I couldn't catch her words, but I rather suspected they weren't, "What an order, I can't go through with it."

****

Chapter seven

Quietly demanding

I lurched up the steps into the solitude of the hut, escaping the unrelenting southerly squalls, the unheated stone structure was a balm. I crumpled onto the wooden bench affixed to the wall, leaning back to remove my rucksack. In time, I'd read the copper-plated plinth about John Muir, a Scottish-American conservational philosopher and father of the national parks, who sought to illuminate the spirituality of the wilderness to materially-absorbed city-dwelling folk.

I set about warming water for a much-deserved cup of coffee, an absolute treat: I'd never otherwise indulge during my daytime hikes. On the other side of the hut, Delightful rehydrated a vegetable soup, which tantalised my nose. I'd bought a block of cheese, and a small tub of mayonnaise, reasoning our environment would be a sufficient refrigerator. The burger buns were crushed, but perfectly fine to shove roughly sliced cheese on top with a squirt of fatty mayonnaise. I wolfed the 'sandwiches' down, disappointed by a horrendously eggy after-taste loitering from the cheese.

Within the hour, restituted, I longed for a good sweat back to warm me, the hut's reprieve now dwindling. I looked to Delightful to see if she was ready to make a move. She snipped that she hadn't decided whether she wanted to carry on yet, reminding me that I'd given her the option of staying the night. The roof leaked but nonetheless enough dry spots could be found on the stone floor. She continued to shiver and shake, which I took as an indication she was chilled but not hypothermic.

She'd lost her svelte figure on the PCT, and had muscled up, much to her chagrin. None of her hiking clothes fit her particularly well now. Her husband was following her by road in their RV, their permanent home, but her changing shape put paid to the idea that she could readily swap things around rather than buying new. She was hiking in leggings, perhaps not the best choice of attire in the snow-ridden Sierra, where drying clothes was near impossible. She had spare layers but preferred to keep them for bedtime. I'd got rid of anything extra, probably foolishly, opting not to carry spare clothing beyond socks and knickers, and my puffy trousers and jacket. Bizarrely my waterproof socks had become impermeable - perhaps a result of having their first proper wash. I'd picked up new trousers at Bishop not realising they had water-repelling properties - an absolute Godsend. They were dark, so no more dodgy-looking groin stains. Alas, somehow, I'd already managed to put a fist-sized hole in the rear - once again revealing to the world the colour of my underwear.

She flung the remainder of her soup out of the hut and reluctantly indicated she was ready to return to the assault course that was the John Muir trail. Outside the footprints of Eyes and his wife, and the New York couple, were rapidly diminishing. I feared having to break trail all over again. We could presume the snow fields would be several miles long, but thankfully the descent was slow and gradual so much so we were quickly overtaken by a film-maker in his seventies wearing old-fashioned crampons, carrying a bright red canvas rucksack. He nattered away, but the winds confiscated so many of his words. Later he filmed me crossing stepping stones, all wobbly and without any agility whatsoever. He snickered as I quipped, "and that's probably an instruction on how not to do it."

It had taken us five tortuous hours to get up Muir, but just three and a half hours to come down to the stunningly pristine Evolution lake. I slumped on the wet bank alongside Delightful, replenishing my water bottle from a trickle of snowmelt racing down the hill. I watched her filter one litre of water after another, filling up four bottles to the brink. She plonked three of them back in the panels of her pack, leaving the last litre beside her to affix to her front. I intimated she might want to tip three of them away, but she shook her head. As she picked up the fourth bottle, the one filled with pink electrolytes, it slipped from her grip, barrelling down towards the frozen lake, shattering through the ice and submerging with a satisfying plop. "Well, that's one way of reducing your pack weight," I managed to spit out, battling to stifle the inevitable fit of giggles that brewed within me. Delightful was most definitely not amused.

We carried on until six that evening covering a mere ten and a half miles, cheered most of all that the worst of the High Sierra was confined to the past, to find a campsite sufficiently snow free. I felt terrible that I'd pushed on so hard and decided that it might be best if Delightful were in charge the following day. She could better balance things and I could fulfil my promise to her of "having an easy day the day after."

The night, though, was long. Placing my face against my tent bag, stuffed with the currently empty bin liners in lieu of a pillow, it tore at my skin, scorched, no doubt as a result of the unremitting snow glare on Muir. Perhaps too I had given myself frostbite on my lips, a simple lick of them stung. I woke the next day only able to lisp my morning salutations to Delightful. Although I had lathered myself in sunscreen factor fifty, I had failed to top up at all. My head ballooned with sunburn.

Taking our time getting up. I shared my hot coffee, apologising for it being instant and, worse, decaf. To an American, it would look like I was trying to poison her. Our bodies ached more than usual from the demands of Muir, making the first incursion into nearby woods an excruciating hobble. I selected fresh dry socks, not daring to put back on the waterproof ones worn the day previously. They were so stiff with ice I could stand them upright. It was a decision I hastily reversed after the first river crossing of the morning, fearing the iciness would amputate my feet. I howled in pain, then sobbed in despair. We'd barely been going a half hour, a smooth boulder splayed in sunlight beckoned for me to warm my toes in the weak rays. The skin from my calloused feet peeling away in thick shards.

Each night-time was spent contemplating the anticipated horror of the next day, with a fervent wish that all would pass well. After Muir, Evolution Creek seemed unutterably misnamed. It is not a creek but a rather wide, and sometimes fast-flowing motorway of snow-melt. We'd been told to try to do engorged river crossings in the morning when the volume flowing through is lessened, a fantastic theory that fails pragmatically. I dashed in first, being five inches taller, it would inform the shorter Delightful whether or not she would drown traversing it. As it was, my crotch was given a thorough wash and the quicksand was not remotely hungry, spectacularly failing to suck me in. It was just a bit squelchy, nothing like the saga of childhood nightmares.

After that, we came to breach Selden Pass, sitting a little under eleven thousand feet. In the notes, someone had wryly dubbed it Seldom Pass given the sheer number of false summits it boasts. It was Muir-like albeit with considerably less snow, although not completely devoid of the loathsome stuff. For those so inclined, it made for a stunning hike and it struck me as nowhere near as brutal as previous passes. I'd rested frequently waiting for Delightful to catch up. She observed that whenever she neared, I'd take off again: a reverse of my experience of Forrester. I was finding myself more and more weary of the constant grumbling of how heavy her pack was, how short her legs were, how tough this mountain was and on and on. It was becoming the norm to announce her imminent presence with a kind of 'urgent moan'. Hijacking my ears, she'd download her frustrations forthwith.

At the top of Seldon, I fell in love with a fat marmot who was having a squeaky bunfight with his neighbour. Delightful spilled her packet of M&Ms and in true hiker style thought nothing of picking up and devouring them straight from the ground, leaving a few morsels for the marmot. I imagined from the friendliness of this creature, it was benefitting from a lot of titbits carelessly dropped from adrenaline-rushed hands. I absorbed myself looking at peak after peak of mountain, rippling across the horizon.

As each day unfurled, I had become accustomed to, although no less galvanised by, removing myself from my snug sleeping bag, shoving sore feet into frozen shoes, battling to tighten solid laces. My morning ritual only completed with the brushing of ice off my tent. I'd then stuff it into a bin-liner, avoiding the futility of trying to coerce it into the small bag it had initially arrived in, minimising the intensity with which the frost would burn my hands. Delightful would also begin her day cursing at immovable items refusing to tuck themselves in an orderly way. I'd given her a spare bin-liner to put her tent in and showed her that it makes life easier when it's on the outside of her rucksack, but she didn't favour the idea. I left her to her wrangling, confident she'd catch me soon enough.

As I bimbled along, readying my podcast for the morning, I innocently disturbed a bear, oblivious as I was to its slumbering on the side of the trail. I didn't know much about bears, aside from they are big, brown and hairy; and the ones in this region are called Black Bears. The one whose morning I'd interrupted was on the lighter shade of brown. I assumed if we'd have anything in common, it would be a shared grumpiness at having one's sleep interfered with. I backed away steadily then stood stock still as it stretched before ambling off down the trail. Out of sight, I 'phewed' and then immediately shat myself a second time as yet another bear, stretched and then too sauntered off. Just as it vanished, I sang my national anthem loudly to ward off any other idling ursine as I tentatively continued to traipse along the path. Under pressure, "God save the Queen," was the only song I could bring to mind that I knew all the words for. And at that moment, I was demanding the crown.

Delightful and I fell into a rhythm together: she was truly a whizz going downhill, yet invariably at least once a day she'd take quite a spectacular tumble with trekking poles clattering all over the place. I'd then overtake her on the uphills. When she thrashed me up Silver Pass, I took it as proof she had gotten to grips with it all. I heaved myself up the final few metres of the pass, panting like a lustful dog, enthusiastically yelling my delight for her, with my newly acquired Americanisms of 'awesome' and 'great job' and 'woo-hoo for you!' I spied her rucksack and those of two others propped against a small flat-topped boulder, the vista around me yawning out for miles, grabbing my breath and holding it in the still air. Moments like these are the enviable rewards of the hardships. The rock was perfect for resting my derriere on and drinking in the view; as well as an opportune place for throwing some sustenance into me. Alas, as Delightful saw me staggering towards it, she broke conversation with the New Yorkers, and intercepted my beeline, announcing we'd be stopping at three o'clock in the afternoon because she was not doing the mile hill, which I'd dubbed a hump, no matter what. All I could do between heavy gasps was say, "I just need to sit and get my pack off my back." She marched back to the two New Yorkers to tell them more about her hypothermia on Muir. The man could only frequently apologise for not realising it and staying with her on the ascent. I was merely glad he was getting the tough time and not me for a change.

Each evening we'd embark on a merry charade of, "What are we doing tomorrow?" Typically, we'd be camping part way downhill, so she'd set up long before I crashed in. I'd barely have erected the tent, let alone started cooking and unpacking, before the inevitable conversation would start. I'd scan Guthook suggesting a few ideas, and each one would be battered back with, "I'm not doing *that!*" So far, the 'I'm nots,' were: week-long food carries; not sleeping at elevation; not doing more than one uphill a day; not doing more than fourteen miles in a day; not pushing on to a further campsite further along the downhill. My own views starkly differed. The time it takes to come off trail makes longer carries more

150

efficient. Sleeping at elevation meant avoiding the rampant mosquitoes. Doing two uphills in a day is just how it is. Even if one simply does a mile or two, a start is made on the next day's mountain, and one is in the best conditions in the morning to do inevitable ice-capped summits. She'd argued that doing a river crossing, which would always come as we moved from one mountain to the next, would leave us with wet feet before bed. My feet seemed permanently wet.

I much preferred to walk without any excess of water, and I'd always opt for a campsite with a steady stream or raging torrents for all it mattered. Once we'd dropped below the snow-line, which was usually around ten and a half thousand feet, finding spots to camp was a doddle. There were far more sites than listed on Guthook. In my head, I silently screamed back my objections. Yet, I tried to remain mindful about not reacting, but rather responding, just like suggested. "Does this need saying? Does this need saying by you? And does this need saying by you right now?" It's a common refrain in AA to silently chant when one's heckles are flaring up. I'm often criticised for believing myself to be right, and I find it hard to know how to be wrong. Bosses have previously called me out for being a lone wolf, and more than one friend has noted that I'm very matter of fact about things. The criticism, if that's what it is, stings. I'm left with the quandary of feeling like I'm always in the wrong for thinking or seeing things differently, like I'm supposed to just agree for the sake of pacifism. Worse, I've often done exactly that often enough and it's left me in a puddle of resentment. I try diplomacy, but somehow, I feel a suffocating expectation to just 'fall into line'. I can only put it down to having so many angry, volatile significant others in my life since childhood. I have spent a lifetime walking around on eggshells, and then when I explode, I shock the shit out of people. I suppose this makes me the archetypal passive-aggressive. Perhaps though I'm just too sensitive. I live in a perennial state of bewilderment: why having my own views and feelings seems so outrageous to others, and yet I'm utterly frustrated when I keep stumm listening to theirs.

****

151

Baffling situations

"Delightful?" How did you end up with that as a trail name?" I'd asked that morning by way of distracting her from the endless hardship she was enduring. She was too breathless to answer. Later, when we'd stopped to filter water, she recalled how a boss had taken a shine to her years ago. "He found me really upbeat and cheerful, so he'd always say, 'Good Morning, Delightful!' That's why I chose that as my trail name." She was great at conversation when she was going downhill, funny and more chipper, but she freely admitted that she wasn't remotely upbeat in the heights of the Sierra.

Over lunch, to my horror, she announced she was going to buy freshly roasted turkey for sandwiches next week, having watched me inhale my cheese buns with great envy. "With a side serving of salmonella?" I'd asked incredulously, wondering how she would keep it sufficiently cold. "You have cheese," she countered. "Might be best if you go for the processed stuff," I urged. "I don't like processed meat," she replied then added "You make me laugh, PI."

I revelled in the day's hike. In my diary, I'd noted it was *"Sunny. Decent temperature, if one overlooked the 5am freezing ones again. Lots and lots of alpine walking, enough switchbacks to keep my mind occupied. I count steps, set targets and just push. Beautiful views."* At lunch, 'I'm Not', as I silently started calling in my head, was convinced we would be facing three more miles of snow later in the afternoon. "I'm not doing more snow today!" she declared. She'd read that someone called Snacks had reckoned on three miles of snow at least a week prior. The very same Snacks had reckoned Evolution Creek was very doable, barely knee deep, but Delightful had reasoned it would be twice as bad just one week later because of all the snow melt.

I love how the human mind can twist anything, and especially how immutable pessimism flings reason out of the window. I'm prone to that myself but the Sierra was showing me that situations could change rapidly and unexpectedly. The only reliable source of conditions, I was discovering, was my own eyes and first-hand experiences. Somehow, I was becoming inherently more optimistic. On the trail, I'd tell myself that when I'd round the next corner it would ease. I'd remind myself that as one nears the top of the mountain the going would slacken, more so than at the bottom or the centre. I'd persuade myself that the painful rocky path, crippling my feet, and jarring my knees, would rarely stretch on for more than ten minutes, then promise myself it would smooth out again.

Conversely, when I thought of my future, returning to the UK; my finances and my lack of a home, love and life, I presumed it was going to get tougher. I'd found the first few years in recovery indescribably brutal, wrapped as I was in a sea of clinical depression. Undeniably it had lightened as the months clocked up into years. I was aghast when I first heard someone say they "had another drink in them, but not another recovery," but it made sense after a while. The old-timers promise life goes in mostly an upward trajectory, but there's plenty of dips and valleys too. I'd put down the drink believing that everything would magically improve. It didn't. It left me with me and no anaesthetic to escape me. I am certain I am not the only one to have gone around grinning like a Cheshire cat, masking an overwhelming desire to be dead, in the early years. Sometimes listening to the podcasts, one can be left with a false expectation of glittery unicorn farts, but that is not life. Recent speakers I listened to had been very much more phlegmatic, reminding me that, "Life is not fair. If it was fair, it'd be called fair." The next one was more upbeat with, "The fair only comes to town once a year!" Clearly this one was from a pre-pandemic era, and things had taken a downward turn since then.

I was starting to quickly turn off any podcast that took a didactic, and often condescending approach. Some took to preaching, rather than speaking. They'd argue that if one is not leaping around full of the joys of spring, one must be doing something wrong. The podcasts I listened to were overwhelmingly produced by the Pacific Group in the 1980s and 1990s. They practice a more radical form of AA than I am comfortable with. When they came to Britain, they took over a few established meetings, changing the formats, and bringing with them rules on dress and strict behavioural modification practices. The debate of the 'recovered versus recovering' alcoholic rumbles on to this day. I find the recovered lot incredibly angry-sounding when they've popped into my regular meetings, so I mostly avoid those kinds of meetings. I didn't like every pub I ever went to, so I don't expect to like every AA meeting I go to. I find the ones that resonate for me. I'm lucky because I can drive so that helps.

I realise that some people thrive in rule-based systems, but I am not one of them. I go to AA out of choice, I stay in AA out of choice. That's the freedom of sobriety. AA has given me the choice to drink or not to drink today, but it extends much further than that. I have a sponsor who I rely on for insight and wisdom, encouragement and gentle chiding when I'm veering off the rails. I don't ring at a prescribed time, which if missed by a minute, I can expect him to slam the phone down. I'm never yelled at to be more grateful or told off for not getting on to my knees twice daily. I don't photograph my tenth step and send it via WhatsApp. I did sit down and discuss my fears of becoming a dry drunk, a self-obsessed maniac in the wilderness, when I took myself away from our regular meetings. At times this week, I felt very much that fear had materialised.

"Eventually you learn that the twelve steps are the easier, softer way," Today's Podcast speaker had gone seventeen years without adopting the programme. He was hilarious. I hadn't shirked the steps for anything like that long, but I certainly am not a poster child for doing them brilliantly either, perhaps if I did, climbing these mountains would be significantly easier. Still, Delightful and I were now through all the eleven-thousand-foot passes, which was something to be cheerful about. Delightful was less than thrilled by my announcement though.

We were now a full day away from the side trail leading us off the PCT to the town of Mammoth, where we'd planned to resupply. "You'll have to sleep in your tent, because I want two nights with my husband," Delightful informed me. "I'm very tired and I didn't have enough rest before I came to the Sierra." That was inarguable, she hadn't. She deserved a good zero, but I didn't see the point of lounging around in my tent. Again, I felt the pressure of a visa deadline rise up in me, and all I was doing each day was adding to my deficit, and not coming close to maintaining or reducing it.

I was rather hoping to find the hotels had re-opened up but if not reasoned there would be a place in Lee Vining that could accommodate me. "Would you or your husband be able to give me a lift there?" I'd enquired. She came back with a long explanation on how she'd put up her previous hiking partner in her RV, but it interfered with her sex life. Now she needed a darn good shag. She also felt she'd had to run her around the post office, and the shops, the launderette and such like. It gave her little time to relax and unwind. As 'noes' go, this was quite substantial.

"A ride to Mammoth would be just great," I told her, "I'm not expecting anything like that level of support." At least, then I could find my way to a nearby town. It left me with the distinct impression I was pushing my luck even asking for a ride to Mammoth, a view confirmed when she suggested I ring the trail angel who'd previously brought us from Bishop to get me from the trailhead.

The remainder of the day's trek struck me as fun. There'd been smatterings of snow, but certainly no postholing. I did those three miles in two hours, and from what I could glean, it was the last of the snow in this section, delivering an absolutely stunning walk. As I arrived, once again late, at the night's campsite I was surprised to be greeted by the smiley couple I'd previously met during the day of horrendous blowdowns back in Southern California. They too pondered how to tackle the mammoth Mammoth problem. There were no cars coming to the trail head, nor buses, as would be typical for this usually heavily populated ski resort area. It would be eleven miles of road-walking to get to the town. Uber and Lyft had been banned from operating. Many thru-hikers had opted to resupply at VVR and then do a ten-day hike, avoiding Mammoth altogether. It was a town that was clear it didn't want tourists arriving, and the local mayor had shut down all hotels with hefty fines to deter any rebellion. I'd made a huge error of judgement opting to resupply there.

The trail was thorough in its teaching of me to take things as they came. I was getting used to practising the belief that things would work out in their own way. I'd have been delighted if Delightful would have made this easier for me, of course I would, but on balance, I was left with a sinking feeling that might be best to march on a further thirty-seven miles. I reasoned I might be better placed to hitch into Lee Vining from the Highway there. I had enough food, having over-supplied, although I'd have to limit myself with snacks. I ran this idea past the couple, but they thought that particular road may also be closed. It was a conundrum to sleep on.

I was around six miles into my day's trek when I spotted Delightful waiting up ahead for me. She said she wanted a 'pow

155

wow', which sounded like violent assault to my ears. She'd passed a day-hiker, who was taking in emergency rations to a pair who'd badly miscalculated their needs. He'd come up via Duck's Pass, which wasn't on Guthook, he explained to Delightful. It led to the very same trailhead as Mammoth Pass. The only difference was we'd arrive there this very evening, rather than the next day. She'd already contacted her husband who was available to pick us up. She'd happily put me up in the RV for the night, and then they'd drop me off at Lee Vining the next day. I thought the idea was brilliant. The only downside was we didn't have a map of Duck's pass, but the day-hiker assured her it was fairly straightforward. Amazingly, we had phone reception, permitting us access to Google Maps, which seemed to give a trace of a trail. I was all for taking it. We'd both get to re-set. Delightful was now full of ideas of how she could get me everything I needed the next day, then drop me off for two further nights in a hotel. That was absolutely fine by me.

It took us five and a half hours to stagger off the mountain, proving a much better alternative than Mammoth Pass, which would have taken us seven to ten hours, unknown conditions depending. The last four miles were tarmac road walking, shattering my joints. Oddly, Delightful had no end of speed and stamina. "Town Legs" her previous partner had called them. She could go like a train on 'nero days', uphill or downhill. It just proved to me that so much of one's ability is limited by the 'can'ts, won'ts and don'ts' we tell ourselves.

I need to see those traits in others to recognise them in me. "When you're pointing the finger at others, always remember there's three fingers pointing back at you." It's another of those cringe-inducing clichés lobbed at you by a sponsor or old hand when one is criticising the behaviour of others. I'd swore I'd never repeat them to anyone. Then I got my own sponsees, and of course, I too started trotting them out all willy-nilly.

****

Shortcomings and goings

Overnight, yet another storm raged its way across the Sierra, pebbling the trail with thousands of hailstones. We crunched our way back to the PCT, through legions of pines which had previously shed

156

millions of needles, making the trail oddly bouncy underfoot. I revelled in it with my well-rested legs and a stomach full of town food and good coffee.

"I'm within five beats of calling my husband and going home," Delightful wailed. I'd left my ice-axe in her RV to flog if she wanted, confident I'd no longer need it now but not so confident that I wouldn't need my microspikes. I'd bought a ton of food just in case the next stint took the eight days Delightful argued it would, rather than the seven I hoped for. Delightful had also got rid of the same, but had added a large 'brain', as she called it, an extra bag attached to the top of her rucksack. She'd rammed it full of food on top of the three of litres of water she still carried. Her pack was huge, and she was clearly paying the consequences. All I could think to say by reply was, "oh."

We paused for lunch and within a minute she'd whipped out her phone and proceeded with the usual, "Where are we stopping tonight?" The few days spent resting had got me and my sponsor exploring the notion of 'instant obligation.' Why I feel so compelled to assist people all the time, when I should be focusing on myself. I flit around a triangle of persecutor, victim and rescuer - the classic co-dependent. I'd realised that Delightful wasn't doing this to me. She was whinging and it was aggravating, but her issues weren't anything to do with me. Unless she asked for my help, and she wasn't, I didn't need to involve myself in her stuff. She'd already had a fit that it was too cold, and now she was too hot, stripping off layers as the mercury rose faster than we were climbing back up to the snow-bound mountains. It was a matter for her how she wanted to express herself. It was nothing I could or should be taking personally.

My heart had thundered within me, but I was adamant, "I'm not doing all these 'I'm nots' this week. I'm going to get up, walk, keep walking for about twelve hours, and then settle down for the night." To my astonishment she accepted the idea. Learning to say 'no' takes courage. I'd calculated that I needed to be doing nineteen miles per day for the remainder of my time here, and that didn't include any rest days. I could no longer afford to do anything less than that without abandoning my hopes to get to Canada. Her previous hiking partner, she told me, had estimated she needed to do twenty-two miles a day, that's why she'd skipped the Sierra. They'd both started early in March, two weeks before me, and Delightful had already skipped a good ninety miles more than I had. "I'll have to bust ass to keep up," she acknowledged.

In case she did make the last mile uphill I'd collected some stones for her tent. She never arrived. It was okay with me, I figured she would either catch me in the morning, or not at all. It was strange having a night alone again. I'd woken up to pee three times, a strange legacy of having a town day. I guessed I just over-hydrated before I set off again or the burning off of all those extra calories I'd imbibed. Perhaps all the caffeine from the hotel's percolated coffee machines irritated my bladder. Stupidly, I left my toilet paper in my vestibule and I was disturbed by a party of mice shredding it, bounding around back and forth, clattering across my cooking pot. I spent the rest of the night fretting that they would chew through the bathtub of the tent to nab my food.

The spot I'd chosen to camp at had internet reception providing a rare night of electronic entertainment. The headlines were immutable: Corona had simply morphed into Covid. I hate to admit it, but I was utterly underwhelmed by the numbers, they didn't quite seem to fit the overwrought headlines. Coupled with the on-going fear-mongering on social media, I could easily understand why factions were starting to emerge. I always believed that societies needed a common enemy to unite against, but this was patently not true. It simply provided the catalyst to spark the classic 'us' versus 'them'; you're either with me or you're against me.

Not being able to access the Internet removed a source of worry from my life. Years earlier I'd made a rule that I'd not put on the television or radio, nor read any news websites until it had gone six in the evening. A tactic I'd employed to reduce anxiety and help motivate me to get on with my day, rather than getting sucked into the latest drama real or induced by ratings-chasing producers. I missed having access to the web on tap, but at the same time, I was glad to be checked out for the most part. The other benefit, I'd discovered, was having little else to do but to go to sleep as soon as it got dark. I've a tendency to lose myself down rabbit holes reading late at night.

I'd read with interest on our own dedicated Facebook page from a fellow who claimed he'd only got his feet wet three times in the section I was about to embark on. He must have been Jesus because by mid-morning I had sploshed through my thirtieth stream, much of the trail submerged, channelling water from higher up towards rivers I was yet to cross.

The day's goal was to manage two passes in a day: Island and Donohue. The latter served as the entrance to Yosemite National Park. Excited to have got Island behind me pre-lunch, I strode off all cock-sure and full of ambition, before retreating an hour later having ambled off down a side trail. Much to Delightful's astonishment, I arrived back on the PCT just as she was passing. "I've just fallen over," she told me, wincing. She wasn't hurt but it had clearly rattled her cage. "I went the wrong way," I laughed "for nearly an hour!" I told her I was going to crack on, it was plenty early enough to do the second of the two saddles, even if I had to do some night-hiking, the terrain after looked pretty reasonable on the flat screen of my phone. "Donohue frightens me," Delightful chipped in, "I'm not going over it today." Two men had just passed by and I was intending to take advantage of their fresh footprints. "I'd rather have fear behind me than ahead of me," I replied, with no idea where that philosophy had magicked itself up from. It was barely two o'clock when she set up her tent next to a tinkling stream. In part I envied her. I would definitely miss Delightful's superior navigational skills, especially when I got lost three times coming down from Donohue when the snow had turned patchy.

****

It's all out to get me

I was dispirited to spend my ninetieth day, half my visa allowance, not having ticked off a thousand miles of hiking. People say to not panic, but I quite like to do the panicking thing. It makes me feel busy and somehow in control. The seventh step is all about taking the right action whilst letting go of results. I can't force me or anyone else to change, and no matter how I'd like it to be different, the power to change is out of my hands. I can only do what I can, and what happens next is what happens next. It's often called the forgotten step, and it's frequently mistaken as the one that sets up the expectation that somehow all our wishes will suddenly materialise.

"Take the action, and the feelings will follow," is a common refrain, urging me not to wait for miraculous, earth-shattering revelations or personality transplants. I still felt uncomfortable about leaving Delightful behind, but I knew deep down it was the right thing for me. I kept reminding myself that it's not for me to apologise continually for being me, and for having my own purpose and ambitions. Being British and a woman means I'm a double winner when it comes to saying sorry. I can even apologise when I walk into a lamppost. I'm not even Catholic yet I'd been mired in guilt and shame. I read once that alcoholics hang on to these emotions for far longer than non-addicts. I don't suppose it matters whether it's true or not, I just know I can retain resentments long after they should be forgotten. I can, and do, while away hours arguing stuff in my head with people who are not there. If I could only give that up, I would but then I would have no idea how I'd keep myself entertained as I plodded out each mile.

I do like the seventh step though, it teaches me to try stuff I wouldn't ordinarily try, and to avoid dismissing ideas out of hand for not being 'me'. I can only ask for what I want in a day, and if I get it, I get it, but if I don't, then I remind myself that's okay too. I like that, it's learning to practice acceptance. It's the stuff of the Serenity Prayer: *'God, Grant me the serenity to accept the things I cannot change, the courage to change the things I can and the wisdom to know the difference.'* I just fall short when it comes to wisdom. I don't always know what I'm praying to, just a notion of something grander than I. "The only thing one needs to know about God, is that you're not it," I smiled when I heard that on the podcast. It was a reminder that I should 'live and let live.'

The equivalent trail jargon is to, 'Hike your own hike,' I supposed. To walk in a good northerly direction, unfettered by anyone else's needs or wants. I was both staggered and elated to have completed twenty-two miles all the way into Yosemite National Park. It is the only national reserve in America I'd previously heard of. I assumed it was because of Yogi Bear, but then I learnt he resided in Yellowstone National Park in Wyoming, wherever that is. Yosemite, though, is every bit as beautiful as promised. Long meadows cracked open by gently-flowing streams, thronging with wildlife near and far. Deer gallivant all over the place. The ground is also amazingly level up at nine thousand feet, the ultimate tonic after the high saddles of the Sierra. Best of all it had bridges: real ones that spared one's feet from yet more icy drenches.

The park had now opened up to day hikers, one of whom greeted me loudly, "I can tell you are a thru-hiker by the state of your lips!" Although they were no longer swollen, they were still black from bruising and with at least eight scabs and various cracks which split each time I ate. Blowing up my mattress each evening had been a feat of endurance in itself, just trying to form a seal with my mouth. Vaseline came to my rescue more than once.

I met the first of many beige-coloured rangers; their first day back off furlough. They were all smiles and genuine bonhomie. I was honoured to be their first inspection of the season, laughing as I stood six feet away, holding up my paper permit, which I'd retrieved with great difficulty from the liner of my rucksack. He squinted to check its validity. He had no chance of doing so from that distance: one truly needed binoculars. Ordinarily they'd sign and date it, ensuring that I vacated the Sierra in a timely fashion, and didn't revisit it later. Covid meant they couldn't even touch the document. They remarked they could see my bear canister through the flimsy pack material. We chatted about how I was finding the trail, they were particularly interested in the conditions on Donohue. "It wasn't bad at all," I said. Two weeks ago, I'd have cried over it but now I was somewhat phlegmatic when it came to ice and snow. It was great to be around such enthusiastic officials, not remotely dogmatic or austere. They were clearly relieved to be back doing a job they loved, but I didn't want to linger. Time is miles.

If I expected Yosemite to be heaven, it so nearly was except for that one guarantee that can suck the joy out of anything: Mosquitoes. I have never in my life, and I have travelled far and exotically, ever experienced anything similar to the horror of those in Yosemite. Every limb was matted with their attention, despite my long-sleeved tops and full-legged trousers. Deet, the proper stuff, not the herbal ecological potion I'd previously tried, failed miserably to repel their bloodthirst. I wore a head net over my cap, but still they penetrated my ears and jawline, bumps raised upon bumps. My fingers, poking out of fingerless gloves, itched relentlessly. Sparingly I used toothpaste to rid myself of the most incessant aggravations. As a child I'd discovered the cool mint is an itching cure.

Scraggy had passed by in the morning wearing shorts, practically slapping out 'This Old Man' on his bare legs as we'd briefly chewed the cud. He'd also given up hiking with his partner,

161

who'd been so obsessed with mileage and distances that he didn't have time to stop and smell the roses as it were. Now on his own, Scraggy got into a routine of starting extremely late morning and night-hiking through to around midnight. Without anyone to wake me up in the morning, I was rousing around seven o'clock and pushing on until around seven at night, giving me a good hour and a half before darkness fell to cook and write my diary. I'd have preferred to rouse myself earlier, but I couldn't be bothered setting an alarm, the electronic noises increasingly incongruent with the sounds of the deep forest.

I spent my final night in Yosemite with Amsterdam, another long-legged beast timebound by a visa. An American in Holland for over a decade, it occurred to him one day how much he missed mountains and giant trees. I was getting to the point of hoping never to encounter another hill in my life, but I was still ambivalent about trees. I'd caught him filtering water at a stream and we chatted for a while, despite him being quite a reticent man. It meant I chatted quite a bit. We had both been bogged-down by the day: quite literally, we'd waded through miles and miles of thick, often knee-deep mud.

A fog of mozzies stalked me as I constructed my tent a good ten metres away from Amsterdam's. I opted to cook inside my tent that night, something I swore I'd never do. Spending another moment outside covered in skeeters, as the American called them, had me finally admitting defeat, so I took my chances. Amsterdam told me he'd had several unfortunate experiences with bears and ambled off to cook elsewhere, ruining yet another night's slumber.

The next night I hunkered down with a family of four under a wide patch of trees, along with Amsterdam, somewhat astonished at this newfound pace I was gathering. Finding a group to camp with overnight had been an unexpected bonus. I figured the teen-aged sons would be more appetising to any hungry bears roaming through the wilderness. The family also opted to cowboy camp - sleeping *sans* tents, making them delightfully easy prey. I would sleep like the proverbial log.

At dinner time we had mellowed out around the campfire, I inspected the likely conditions of the following day. How big the climbs might be; whether I'd need to carry much water; were there any red triangles forewarning us of some hazard or other. "Prepare yourself for a massive change in scenery," the notes had said. They weren't kidding, someone had truly turned the views off the second I'd left Yosemite. The ground was sparse, nothing but a few knobbly, decaying trees knocking around and the odd patch of white snow. Otherwise, it was utterly beige and barren. Water was long gone, forcing me to stock up again before I commenced up a ginormous zig-zag toward a stony pass. Above me, Amsterdam, zigged to my zag and then disappeared over the horizon onto yet another empty mountain. From the bottom of the ascent, with the huge trail above me snaking back and forth, I could only conclude this section would zap morale. And it did.

I crested the pass where the terrain became more and more desert-like, with only sparse rocky cairns occasionally keeping a sign or two upright, most had withered away in the harsh conditions. There was little by way of vegetation. The few plants that were clinging on in the arid land were a dull green or grey. Periodically, and oddly, I would be plunged into woodland, where impossibly tall, thin trees stretched up, their thick canopy blotted out the vast blue sky. The ground around me was simply bare brown nothingness. No chirping of chipmunks nor squirrels, no screeches from up high either. It was almost too pristine: no rotting logs, no ferns, no evidence of any eco-systems in existence, merely exposed dirt. Even the mosquitoes had abandoned the area. The only pleasing event was ambling past an arrangement of pebbles, outlining one thousand miles.

That night, I again camped with the family of four, plus another young couple who also abjured tent life, I was thrilled to greet Goblin, the Czech-Republican-cum-Brummie backpack-smashing-life-saviour from Forrester. He had no choice but to cowboy camp on account a bear in Red Meadows had demolished his tent. "You'd need a kilometre of duct-tape to repair it," he mourned. He'd left no food in his tent, nor toiletries, when he'd gone off to use the showers. Seemingly, the bear, in a fit of bad temperedness, had slashed it to bits for no other reason than it could. A week later someone posted footage of a strikingly similar occurrence. The ferociousness with which the bear had swiped at the fabric left little to the imagination. Thank God no one had been home.

As dusk descended the glow of a lit campfire kept everyone warm and snug, with the group convening around it. The smoke persecuted me: whatever place I opted to sit in, it was determined to asphyxiate me. Intent on an early start, I left everyone to it, drifting off to sleep with the young lads swapping serial killer stories, naturally all set in the backcountry and involving hitch-hiking.

****

Fortune favours the deeply flawed

Goblin overtook me, predictably, on the long descent down to Sonora Pass. We trudged the last few miles together, enjoying each other's company, trading tales about our hikes. He had eaten his only remaining snack bar for breakfast and was eager to get food at Kennedy Meadows North Resort, running, as he was, on empty. We hitched together, using the deceptive technique of hiding the man in the bushes, projecting myself as a lone woman. I thumbed away at every passing car. They shot around the corner at such high speed, they would inevitably blast me with choking dust. One man reversed back, then took a photograph of me, and raced off again, leaving me bemused and bewildered. I noticed he'd sniggered when he re-engaged first gear. It prompted the notion I could fill the waiting time by playing word games. How many synonyms can I think of for 'Knob-end'? The game was abruptly curtailed when I got lucky with a couple who'd pulled over to check some maps, and once they'd agreed I introduced my 'friend' who needed a ride as well.

Within seconds of arriving at Kennedy Meadows North we both jettisoned the much-maligned bear canisters, no longer legally required, and got our refunds within the hour. After much mental debate, I also left my microspikes in the hiker box, anything to lighten my load. Unusually, the hiker box offered nothing by way of food replenishments, it was mostly just junk.

The resort was thronging with tourists, now fully released from stay-at-home orders. The area heaved with over-sized, multi-roomed tents and RVs of various shapes and sizes, dwarfing the caravans and motorhomes typically found in the UK. Every space was over-run with madly grinning dogs frantically wagging and sniffing wildly in all directions. The receptionist checking us into the multiple-occupancy dedicated thru-hiker dormitory, simultaneously fielded an endless stream of the phone calls and in-person enquiries from people hoping to reserve a cabin, or one of the first-come, first-

164

serve camping sites. It was bedlam, or at least it seemed that way, after days in the impoverished wilderness.

We were warned the restaurant was closing imminently so we ordered burgers and fries before we'd finished checking in. I regretted not ordering two portions. My hiker-hunger had at long-last emerged, giving me an insatiable and unwelcome desire to eat and not ever stop. I contented myself with ice-cream, crisps, chocolate and coffee from the adjacent store, grazing absentmindedly until the restaurant reopened for dinner. The menu had slim pickings for a vegetarian. There was a noticeable shortage of staff: unsurprisingly most had been let go in the lockdown. My meal was lukewarm, but I didn't really care to complain. Breakfast was similarly cool. Not a jot could rub the shine from the joy of the place, the staff friendly and enthusiastic, and its visitors rejoicing in being sort of normal again. The collective cabin fever had broken far and wide, and for us northbound thru-hikers, we could relax knowing that the most gruelling part of the PCT was now firmly behind us. It seemed as if the pandemic was melting away too.

It was to be a short pit stop. Time enough to obtain four days' supply of food and some much-needed rejuvenation. The resort is truly geared up for the thru-hiker, despite being a business for the more conventional recreationalists. We could use the laundry for a small fee after dinner that evening, and the hot showers were a fabulous luxury too. I took one of the five beds in the dormitory, Goblin another, we were sharing the room with Amsterdam, and SatNav, who I'd previously seen in Julian. No one else arrived. Amsterdam and SatNav were intent on spending two nights there. Goblin, like me, was worried about the amount of time he had before his visa expired. I figured with his fitness levels and youth being far superior to mine, he'd surely make it. He then showed me how we'd actually have three extra days, because although one is only allowed one hundred and eighty days in the US, they calculate it as six calendar months. I felt as if I'd won the lottery.

The following morning, the caretaker, a devout republican, gave us a cheap ride back to the trail, all the while educating us on how democrats were plotting to destroy America. The day was blisteringly hot. Within moments Goblin romped off over the hill. My morning was particularly active: I fell over three times, twice on ice, and once on rocks, skidding down on to my backside in slow-motion, unable to prevent the inevitable. It didn't initially occur to me that my stumbling was because my pack had changed weight. Carrying only four days of food, no bear can and no microspikes, and the subsequent rearranging of my belongings had an impact on my gait. I slept alone once again, having managed yet another twenty-miler. This was to become my new normal.

The following day I admonished myself for leaving my spikes behind as the trail weaved up high on an acute slope of mountain. The path was buried beneath a half-mile long curve of ice stuck fast to the mountain walls. The foothills below swamped in a barely thawed lake. The tread had nearly worn off my shoes. I tentatively put one foot in front of me, before jabbing in a trekking pole, then I'd move the next foot dragging it back and forth trying to get a firm purchase. Then I would ram the second trekking pole into the ice. Four dainty manoeuvres shuffled me across. Occasionally I'd have confidence to stride in the depressions left by previous hikers, but more often I was following a faint line of verglas. Painstaking and time-consuming, one slip and my heart would be pounding around my ears, my stomach having flipped up to where my heart should reside. It would settle down a few steps, then I'd lurch again. The only plus of it all was the intense concentration provided a distraction on four otherwise monotonous days. Other diversions included bumping into day-hikers, a guide-led group of twenty stood courteously to one side to avoid impeding my progress. I was astonished that my pace outstripped theirs. They emitted a stench of chemicals from deodorant and perfume. Having been cigarette free for nearly six months, my sense of smell had returned and then the wilderness had honed it still further.

Another group of five asked the increasingly familiar, "Are you a thru-hiker?" and even though I couldn't claim to have thru-hiked my local bridleway, I answered yes. People seemed bowled over, and my ego gorged itself silly on the acclaim. Others would comment on how beautiful the scenery was and I would try to mask how deranged I thought they were. It was, to my eyes, sterile. The shrubs were tiny, the hillsides mostly hoary or boring beige. There was nothing that could register on the wow factor as far as I could adduce. A lone man on his own chatted with me for a while. I stood salivating as he crunched away on an apple. As I turned to resume my trek, he offered me his second one. I practically bit his hand off. I could have kicked myself for missing the opportunity to 'yogi': asking a day-hiker for some goodies and scoring that off my 'You're not a proper thru-hiker until you've...list'. It was divine. Fresh fruit is a rarity when thru-hiking, and its absence truly makes the heart grow fonder. This apple was twice the size of any I'd eaten in England, the sweet acidity made my hair stand on end. It was vanquished all too quickly.

The long winding trail, slowly making its way down to six thousand feet, had me increasingly irritated at my belly button. It was inflamed. I don't have an 'outy', it's always been a deep 'inny', buried beneath a crevasse of stomach fat. I couldn't fathom why it had become so red-raw until I realised that the crevasse was becoming more of a crease. I would smear the raging redness with a wet-wipe each evening, then squirt in a dollop of anti-bacterial cream but the infection raged on regardless. My little toe was now jutting out of the side of my trainers, sometimes snagging on rocks. I still wore my dark blue water-resistant trousers with the hole on the right butt cheek advertising my pink knickers to anyone who dared look. My top quickly became sweat-stained, salt circles highlighting my armpits, and splodges of pasta sauces ran down my front. I was still not immune to the fetor of my own body odour.

From ten miles out, after days of brown and grey hues, the colossal Lake Tahoe twinkled a marvellous turquoise. It is said to hold the best-tasting water in the world. With amazingly unpolluted purity, it is as close to refined mineral water as one can get. Allegedly. I never sampled any of it. The surroundings were now luxuriant once I descended once more. As a teen, I'd first heard of Lake Tahoe in a Danielle Steel novel. It sounded terribly high-end, a place for the sophisticated and well-heeled. It is famous for being the second deepest lake in America: a third of it bulges into Nevada, providing miles of sandy beaches, secluded though they are in the forest which engulfs it. The lake is rumoured to have its own Loch Ness Monster, imaginatively called Nessie, but I say bollocks to that - if the lake is that bloody clear you can see to the bottom, noticing a fat, frolicking lake-dwelling dinosaur would be a cinch.

I booked into a budget motel far from the shores, but close to the more important amenities in the surprisingly deserted town. I was disgruntled, waiting two hours after the hotel was supposed to open at four o'clock. They had misplaced the keys during the shutdown and were only re-opening for my booking. I was to be their only occupant. I was led down a small path to the room. There the receptionist requested I remain outside while she inspected the room, unsure whether the room was even habitable. Pretty it was not.

I'd been thrilled to plunge myself into a forceful shower: such things truly helped me tackle my long, matted hair. Detangling my locks with a light-weight brush would ordinarily produce a furball the size of a small pet. The shower had been gloriously hot at the first visit, but it never fully reheated again, though it reminded me of its presence with a constant rhythmic drip. I drew the curtains despite the daylight, and lay on the strangely cosy bed, swathed in the small, crispy towel provided. I casually explored my exposed midriff with gentle fingers as I lay post-shower contemplating the ceiling. I stroked away whatever it was that had been tickling me, thinking it was a strand from the towel or perhaps a snag of shed hair. With that, I unleashed the full aggression of a wasp the size of my little finger. It slashed a large wheal across the flesh of my abdomen, a third nipple, which I added to my ever-growing list of injuries. Most torturously, the room was not equipped with a coffee percolator, forcing me to get on my feet and limp to a nearby Taco Bell every time the urge took me. None of this truly mattered as all I needed was a day free from the trail, and some respite from the sheer tedium of walking twenty miles a day, every single damn day.

****

Chapter eight

See no harm, hear no harm, speak no harm

The local trail angel rang to see if I'd be amenable to going back to the PCT a few hours earlier than we'd previously arranged. She'd been booked by two hikers who had failed to show up, and she wondered if I could spare her one journey. She hauls strangers and their packs back and forth, day after day, year after year, and yet refuses any form of donation. I was piqued on her behalf but she herself was equanimous about it. As she pulled up to the trail head, she informed us that by way of compensation, we'd be litter-picking around the public toilets, and with that she thrust white bin liners into our hands. The toilet cubicles were a mess of discarded food and its wrappings, soiled toilet paper and nappies, cigarette ends - the detritus of humankind. It took little time to fill the entire bag, and satisfied with my efforts, I was free to return to the pristine wilderness, albeit with the stench of wheelie bin to accompany me.

Lake Tahoe gave way to Desolation Wilderness, which despite sounding bleak and abandoned, was everything but. The one hundred and seventy-mile Tahoe Rim Trail and the PCT convene for around fifty miles, making it a spot which pulsed with all kinds of visitors. We jostled around one another, trying, and largely failing to keep six feet apart. Some wore masks, but most didn't. I passed some large families, enough to start a small school, and wondered if they had the rule of six in California. If so, which ones would be put up for adoption? Large families would line the route, occasionally in height order, as I gingerly placed my feet on the rocky trail. As with the road, deference is given to those going up, but often as an overloaded thru-hiker, I found deference was just given regardless of the gradient. I'd frequently fling myself to one side as faster, younger limbs strode up behind me long before they'd even announced their need to get by. I'd tell myself I was being courteous, but the truth was I was just glad of a chance to catch my breath. The heatwave spreading across Northern California was becoming insufferable. That, plus I hate the idea of people staring at my arse.

In populous areas such as this one, I was starting to meet walkers with unleashed and over-enthusiastic dogs, some of whom would bark just as ferociously as they wagged their tails. Some call them nuisances, but as this was my one hundredth day, I was simply glad of the many sounds of mankind. The isolation of long-distance hiking was perhaps too uncomfortable even for my level of introversion. Dog owners were particularly vulnerable to my need for attention. I took to complimenting every canine I met as I determined I should become an expert on breeds.

"Is that a blue heeler?" I'd ask.

"Yes," they'd affirm.

"Very intelligent dogs," I'd say knowingly.

"Oh, yes," they would agree.

"But very stupid," I'd add wickedly.

"Oh, yes," they'd laugh.

At the next interception, I'd be off again.

"Is that a golden doodle?"

"Yes." was the usual answer, occasionally it was a labradoodle but who cared.

"Very intelligent dogs," I'd say earnestly.

"Oh, yes," without hesitation they'd agree.

"But very stupid," I'd add again.

"Oh, yes," they'd laugh, clearly oblivious to the fact that I was insulting every dog I successfully identified along the way. My behaviour as a passive-aggressive cat owner kept me thoroughly entertained.

As I left the massive body of water behind me, I was again accosted by a ranger. He let through all the other walkers, be they day-hiking or doing the shorter Tahoe Rim Trail. Much relieved he declined my offer to retrieve my permit from innards of my rucksack. Instead, he sought to remind me of the *Leave No Trace* principles. These are the well-established code of seven ethical behaviours designed to compel all backcountry visitors to be considerate of others be they human, plant or animal.

The ranger had wanted me to understand that I should pack out, not bury, my toilet paper. They'd been having problems with animals digging it up, leaving shreds of tissue to mar the popular camping sites, worsened further by human waste not being buried effectively. I wafted my hands in the direction of the small lightweight trowel I'd acquired for that very purpose. He reminded me to go at least two hundred feet off trail, but not to deviate from the trail otherwise. He also mentioned I should only put my tent down on durable surfaces, sites that are well worn by previous campers, lest I suffocate any fledgling plants, and especially not on pretty meadows. I confirmed I had a copy of the California Fire Permit with me. He declined to see it, but carrying it acted as proof that I've understood the myriad of rules governing stoves, campfires and smoking. I actually never had a clue when I could or couldn't start a fire, I simply didn't bother at all the entire trip. I just assumed everyone else knew what they were doing.

He was, exactly as the previous Rangers were, cordial and affable, thrilled to have met a PCT hiker in this year of confusion. No one knew how many of us were out there, and I was the first he'd intercepted that year. He too had just resumed work, released for now from furlough. I myself wondered how he'd concluded the violation of principles was a PCT thru-hiker issue, and not one generated by our more shorter-bound fellows. Litter seemingly increased the closer one came to civilisation, but most PCT hikers I'd met made a point of picking up trash when walking deep in the wilderness. I'd adopted the policy myself, but I always assumed that anything I collected had been accidentally lost, rather than carelessly discarded. I declined to gather up old trousers, socks and underwear that I saw occasionally hung forlornly from trees. I was still carrying my cold weather clothing despite no longer using it, and I'd been reunited with my trusty laptop, so I had little spare space for others' forgotten attire. I would, however, routinely bend down, groaning as I fought against the weight of my pack threatening to topple me over to snatch up drinking bottle lids, empty wrappers, and the occasional water bags snared on branches. I'd stuff them into a pocket until I could add them more permanently to my dedicated Ziplock. In reality, I'd only pick one or two pieces of rubbish up a day, it was hardly a fulltime job, but it was my little contribution to caring for the wilderness.

I was soon released and on my way. I fell in love with Desolation Wilderness, so called because there's very little beyond bulging bright-blue tarns and granite rock formations. The mountain ranges were set alight by strips of stark white snow. The region struck me as a magical but secluded oasis after the wan landscape of the previous week. Above my head thunder raged, but no storm was forthcoming. The mercury soared into the nineties, whatever that meant. I have no real familiarity with Fahrenheit. Weather forecasts sounded to me more like time-travel, as people would comment that we were in the nineties, the eighties or the seventies. Each day, I started rising at four, and found by mid-afternoon the temperature had dropped by ten degrees on the previous day. Partly, I supposed, because I'd regained elevation, but more so after forceful winds rushed in blowing away the heatwave.

It was a tad unfortunate that the ferocious gales arrived just as I had to traverse miles of ridges, with both sides of the mountain falling away abruptly. I'd walk as if inebriated, tottering along, the might of the gusts forcing me to lean in. They would cease their fierce exhales momentarily to regenerate, and then blast me again, as I staggered right and left trying to keep myself centred along the thin line that was the rugged footpath. Hair-raising stuff, quite literally:

my hat, despite the tie being tightly knotted under my chin, whipped off, snagging along the edge of the cliff. Not wanting to add sunburn to my already fragile skin, I tentatively crept towards it on my hands and knees, grabbing it and stuffing it down the neck of my fleece. There it couldn't drop out because the belt of the rucksack was already trapping off the blood supply to my hips. The tassels from my hood lashed against my face, and the straps of my rucksack whipped incessantly on my thighs, like a cruel jockey beating its horse. None of it made me find another gear. I was definitely more Model T Ford than Ferrari as I scooted along.

On the second day of ridge-walking, the elastic on my trousers failed and I sported a 'MC Hammer' look as my outerwear drooped down, threatening to moon any misfortunates who might be bearing down on me. I'd try to hoik the top of my trousers into the belt of the rucksack, but no matter how tight the belt was, they'd be dragged down again in the next squall. Thankfully, by now the Tahoe Rim Trail and the PCT had separated, and once again it was a rare occurrence to see a fellow hiker, but of course rare does not mean never. I shouldn't have been too disappointed to see a couple bearing down on me. It was all I could do to keep my clothing to myself as I took refuge behind a large boulder.

****

The legacies that haunt

The couple rapidly chasing me down were a man-woman pair. On average, sixty-five percent of thru-hikers commence their hike alone, although they rarely remain that way in a typical year. These two were outdoor, as well as romantic, enthusiasts: well-acquainted with spending intense amounts of time with one another. Overwhelmingly hikers who start in pairs are heterosexual couples, whether they end as such is anyone's guess. It's fair to say, though, the stereotypical thru-hiker was traditionally a white male in his twenties. The last decade has changed all that. Forty percent of thru-hikers are women, and the ratio is levelling out. Surprisingly though, in a typical year, around thirty percent of us are from other countries, most likely Europe, Australia or Canada. Hiking is still largely a white person's pastime, but not exclusively so.

"Are you hiking alone?" is an innocent enough question when it comes from a fellow female and I was happy enough to affirm I was. It can be slightly intimidating when asked by a male stranger, one of those unfortunate double standards that hog-tie us in different ways. My answer revealed we shared British origins. "Are you going to Donner Ski Resort?" was her next question. I wasn't planning on stopping at all, obsessed as I was with mileage. "You get a free pint if you're a thru-hiker," the guy with her mentioned. Torn because I couldn't bear not doing my self-imposed mandatory minimum of twenty miles per day, the thought of proper coffee had me hankering.

I have always felt guilty about having fun. It's remarkable because in my regular life I spend a lot of time procrastinating and avoiding things I ought to be doing. At my first boarding school, if we were caught playing even during times when nothing had been prescribed, it would inevitably follow with some kind of punishment on top of the confiscation of any contraband, which was usually walkmans, electronic games or similar sources of childhood pleasure. I have always been an avid card player, yet they were prohibited altogether for the travesty of being unladylike. Air hostesses, as they usually were called back in the 1980s, used to give packs of cards out for free to bored travellers, back when seats didn't have built-in 'entertainment systems.' Being an inveterate rule breaker, I'd convince them to give me several packs on each flight I took as I flew unaccompanied across the world. I'd smuggle them back to school, distributing them in the nooks and crannies in the cellar of the stately home. Like a squirrel I'd often forget where I'd hidden them from prying eyes. I could usually get through a term without losing the entirety.

I wonder now how much of that created a sense of gamesmanship with which I fight authority, that sneakiness that is typical of the alcoholic who gaslights the poor suffering spouse. My ex-husband had been the same, leaving me baffled or outraged when I'd discover his poorly-constructed mistruths. These days I can depersonalise so much of his behaviour and see it in the same light as I see my own - a legacy of a disjointed upbringing that never quite prepared either of us to become responsible, considerate grown-ups. Alcohol, I learned through a podcast, strips a person of their ability to empathise. It is such a popular chemical but if used in sufficient quantities changes one from being overly sensitive to a fully-fledged psychopath. The process begins to reverse when one gets into recovery. For the most part, at least. Learning stuff like that really helped me move towards forgiveness, both of myself and him, both victims of the torrent force of alcoholism and family dysfunction.

The adventurous, like alcoholics, are commonly depicted as young, white men, or old white men with grizzled beards. The history of this section of the Sierra Nevada is rich with the derring-do of the pioneers. Donner Pass, and its nearby lake, is named in recognition of the Donner tragedy: the demise of several family members and their employees trapped in the Sierra by the torrid winter conditions of 1846 to 1847. The fathers heading up two of the largest families were George Donner and James F. Reed. On Wikipedia their names are hyperlinked so more of them can be discovered. Their spouses, and numerous children, are listed in age order, sounding like appendages unworthy of their own individual histories, even though it is from the diaries written by the wives that so much of the experience is known. Are we less brave because we are women, or more? Subtly conveyed to the unwitting, women's roles in history are subjugated through the order of words chosen by the authors. I find it both fascinating and infuriating. Even now, if I ask someone to name people on television who are role models for undertaking far-flung escapades, they'll list the *Top Gear presenters, Michael Palin, Bear Grylls, Ben Fogle, ad white male infinitum.* If

174

you ask them about women travellers, you might get lucky with *Anneka Rice* from the 1980s or *Amelia Earhart,* who is still MIA, presumed dead. Women TV presenters who travel have tended to show off the hotel amenities. There are so many things I don't notice until I start looking.

The PCT is also a history of men hiking alone. The first woman credited for completing it was chaperoned by a man. Perhaps that's why *Wild* was so inspiring for me: financed and acted by Reese Witherspoon, Cheryl Strayed did this unsupported at a time when technology was weaker and gender prejudices far stronger. The fear-mongering around the safety of women was significantly more intense and coercive. The chief criticism I hear of Cheryl Strayed amongst thru-hikers is that she didn't walk enough of the trail, but I salute her endeavours. Too many women still comment they wouldn't feel safe doing this alone, and too often we're casually asked about serial killers and innocuously reminded to fear sexual assault. The joy of divorce and remaining single is learning how little you need another person, but all too often the absence of a significant, or interested, other can be a psychological barrier for women to partake in life's thrills.

In the end, I relented and gave myself permission to have lunch at Donner Ski Resort. The fast-food junk was proper nourishment: deep-fried jalapeño poppers, a grilled burger with fat chips, and creamy coffee. Over lunch, taking advantage of the free internet, I discovered the world had moved onto discussing the impact of Black Lives Matter. Some had taken to tearing at one another over a notion that 'all lives matter'.

I determined to make it to Peter Grubb Hut, a rare shelter on the PCT, promising me a comparative night of luxury. Named after an intrepid eighteen-year-old who'd died of exposure touring Europe in 1937, the hut is, in fact, an entire house. It is constructed so access can be gained either through the back door at ground level, or the first floor when the winter snow has engulfed the lower floor entirely. Behind the house, stood a separate two storey latrine for the same reason. The downstairs has a wood burner, a series of gas-fired hot plates for cooking, and solar-powered electricity on a timer to feed the bare lightbulbs. Two parallel runs of benches and wooden tables occupy the bulk of the room: making dinner a more sophisticated affair than usual. Upstairs is accessed internally by a vertical step ladder. The sleeping quarters offered nothing other than a flat dusty floor and a single stool for sitting on. I blew up my mattress and laid out my sleeping bag, leaving the rest of my belongings below.

At dusk I heard a gathering of male voices creeping around. The provision of a solid structure perversely made me feel more vulnerable than if I had heard them at a campsite from within my tent, where I would have welcomed their company. In the end, they moved off without inspecting inside. Darkness fell, and I reset the timer so I could continue to write my diary in dim lighting. I went to bed not long after, listening to an audiobook to distract me from the ghosts I fretted the house might hold.

****

Let me list the ways

In the small hours I reluctantly concluded it had been a mistake leaving my pack unattended downstairs. The rustle wasn't a draught nor a ghost, but a tiny mouse delighting in its luck finding my bags of groceries atop one of the benches.

Intent on making up the miles I'd sacrificed the previous day, I set off early, sleep-deprived and cranky. The terrain was flatter than usual, tempting me to push out twenty-four continuous miles of laborious plodding. By mid-morning SatNav had caught me. I'd bumped into him several times, usually at various towns and stops along the way, but I'd barely conversed with him before.

"So, I'm thinking of getting to Sierra City by twelve, I can be out of there by two, then I'm going to Quincy, but then there's Bucks Lake too." He was insistent on telling all about his potential resupply strategies in meticulous detail every single time we took a break. "But what happens if I can't get a ride? Then I'll probably stay," he asked and answered himself. I soon realised it was his only topic of conversation. "Well, that's all I have to think about all day," he said by way of explanation. I envied the simplicity of the inner workings of his mind.

In the day's AA podcast, I'd laughed out loud along with the audience when the speaker said, "once I've stopped arguing with all people in my head, I find I have a lot of free time." I spend an extraordinary amount of time conversing with invisible foes.

Everyone and anyone can get it with both barrels. It was astonishing how often I was right, and they would concede. I loved it especially when they became stumped for words at the sheer genius of my point. Half the people were long gone from my life, but I keep them alive within the parameters of my mind. My tendency to ruminate could squander any absorption of my surroundings. When I did remember to soak it all in, it was only because I was noting the never-ending woodlands were easier on the feet and knees.

"I get my resupply sorted within two hours," SatNav boasted at lunch, "but Quincy is ten miles away and I might not get a ride." We greeted a local hiker who SatNav accosted to inform him of his resupply strategy. By the afternoon Quincy was off the menu, instead he was going to make do with Sierra City and then Belden. Then along came another walker, and Quincy was back on the agenda because apparently Sierra City had nothing for the thru-hiker. That evening we camped together, and I was updated to the latest goings on. "I met a guy and he said Belden was right on trail, is it right on trail?" I checked on Guthook and confirmed it was. The next day, along came another hiker, and Belden was consigned to the bin again. Amusingly, it occurred to me that what SatNav was doing is called Forum Shopping, but he'd twisted it to Forum Resupply Shopping. That habit of asking a multitude of people about a dilemma, only to do what the hell one likes after all. It's a form of attention-seeking, and bloody annoying when you're not the shopper, but the shop. I've certainly been guilty many a time of soliciting a raft of well-meaning opinions only to ultimately ignore the advice unless, of course, I find the person who would tell me to do exactly what I'd intended to do all along.

I'd planned on doing one hundred and fifty miles between Sierra City and Chester to maximise my mileage. He seemed to prefer going in and out of every town. If that were my strategy, I'd never make it to Oregon, let alone Canada. I always wanted a full day to get chores done, and time was now my worst enemy. I had substantially over-supplied in South Lake Tahoe when my hiker hunger had kicked in. Now I was miffed to find my appetite had vanished once again. I'd be arriving in Sierra City with enough food for four more days. I'd only need three days' supply to propel me to my next overnight stop. As it was the night before a 'nero' town day, I did my quick ten-minute pre-town chore: inspecting the squashed remains of the carrier bags for a stocktake. I'd type into my phone, "3 Lun 3 Din 6 BFast 9 Snacks," or similar. I had become less and less willing to try new foods and utterly indifferent to what I was eating.

Traipsing nearly two miles into Sierra City with a retired reverend, we'd assumed a hitch was unlikely. My head was full of all the food I was hoping to eat: eggs preferably, but pizza if not, and burger as a great third choice. Dismayed does not adequately plumb the depths of my feelings discovering everything, including the grocery store, closed. SatNav, who had arrived an hour before, was hovering about the porch of the local shop looking utterly pole-axed. It was a Tuesday for Jeff's sake. There was simply nothing by way of people moving anywhere, not even a car cruising along the main drag in this out of the way backwater town. The post office, ostensibly shut at first glance, was, in fact, the only amenity open. SatNav went in to grill the man behind the counter on what to do about his resupply. If he'd come back to apprise me the entire town had been abducted by aliens, I would have believed him.

I'd previously ordered a new water filter and replacement trousers, hoping they'd be waiting for me in the store. A night in a hotel it would have to be. Alas, my booking app revealed all the hotels in the area to be full despite the place presenting as a ghost town. Whilst I mulled over my options, I figured I could pack up my puffy jacket and trousers and send them on to the Cascade Locks Post Office on the border between Oregon and Washington. It was mind-blowing that I still had five hundred miles of California to navigate, and then a second state before I'd see them again, if indeed I got that far. The Pastor flagged down the first and only passing car, and quickly hitched to a nearby town. On a whim I rang two of the local hotels directly. The first didn't answer, but the second had just that moment put the phone down on a cancellation, bagging me the last remaining hotel room.

SatNav returned and it became clear he wasn't au fait with using the Internet for information, or if he was, he hid it well. The post office worker had tried to book him a hotel, but with no success. Perhaps he just thought it would be easier to play helpless, I don't know. SatNav let me know that the shop would reopen at five in the evening for an hour if we hung around, but with no cafe or restaurants open, it would be a long wait given it wasn't yet noon.

Briefly I thought about letting SatNav sleep on the floor, but whenever I had seen him in towns, he'd been enthusiastic about drinking, very enthusiastic, in fact. Step eight is about asking ourselves: who is owed the truth, and determining which relationships deserve attention and need repairing. It's about making peace with oneself and others by looking at how and where we'd been neglectful or abusive. I often use the Woman's Way through the Twelve Steps being significantly less patriarchal and intimidating than the horrifically misogynistic but much lauded *Big Book*. I tire of men telling me the Big Book of Alcoholics Anonymous is the only book I need. I prefer the Woman's Way because it cautions us to not take responsibility for shit that isn't ours. It talks more about boundaries and space to grow. I am not to blame for everything in the world nor do I owe everyone an apology for being me, as I suspected I did when I first started this step.

When I hear people talk about step eight, there's some division as to whether we should put our own names on the list. I think women are particularly prone to harming themselves for settling for less than we want or deserve. There has certainly been a social conditioning of girls to be more sharing and caring, and I think that's a folly that's brought trouble in the past. Recovery has taught me about protecting my own space. I'm having to learn that the sky won't cave in on me for saying 'no'. Still, I have a tendency to get mobbed by guilt all the time. In the past, I'd cause an argument, or withdraw abruptly from people, to avoid saying what I really felt or thought. In part because I didn't know what I did think or feel half the time. At other times, I'd overcompensate trying to illogically repair some damage I'd done, without telling the person I was trying to make things right. A perverted form of people-pleasing to avoid simply saying, "I'm sorry, I was wrong, and I hurt you."

There was also the terror of someone saying, "You owe me because you did such and such, or you didn't do such and such." I hate being manipulated; it's been the cancer that has eroded many of the significant relationships I have ever had. Learning that I don't necessarily owe a person their happiness is a liberation in itself. It's okay for me to ask, it's okay for a person to decline, and vice-versa, is the definition of a balanced relationship.

There wasn't a morsel of food to be had in the town so for lunch I wandered the mile or so to the hotel and baked in the afternoon sunshine beside the hotel pond filled with yet to be eaten trout. I snacked on my hideously dry cereal bars. The kindly receptionist let me have as much coffee as I could imbibe but he was resolute there was no checking-in until four o'clock, "because of Covid." I spent the entire afternoon pondering how a disease became less virulent towards the evening. In the UK, The Prime Minister announced pubs were to reopen, and I was saddened when someone I knew from the fellowship plastered her social media with memes revelling in the news. How readily we can forget the damage of our addictions when the compulsion is back with a vengeance. It's always a tough lesson to remember that I am powerless over alcohol, and that it doesn't say who is doing the drinking. If she's lucky, she'll chalk up another list of regrets to apologise for, but if not, then what?

At five o'clock I hobbled back to the store and it was indeed open. I was doubly relieved to find the Amazon delivery man had arrived precisely at the same time. Sometimes hikers have to pay storekeepers to receive and hold packages, usually five or ten dollars, but the pricing system in the store was so befuddling, I'd no idea if I was charged or not. There was enough uninspiring hiker food to keep me replenished so I shlepped back to the hotel to repack it all.

Remarkably less impressive was taking delivery of size fourteen trousers, not initially aware this made them a UK size sixteen. In either country I was no longer a bloody size fourteen anyway. Ordinarily this would be welcome news, but I'd chosen this pair because they were bug repellent, and they were ridiculously priced for that reason. Thankfully they had a draw-string top, rather than a zip and button, so although I looked like a billowing-trousered clown, they would stay above my pelvis. They were dreadfully uncomfortable, the rucking around the waistband clawed into my hips, firmly squashed in by my now fully tightened backpack belt. A new form of torment to keep me distracted.

I managed to get a hitch for the one mile or so back to the trail, mildly nonplussed to find myself sharing it with none other than SatNav. He informed me he intended to resupply in Chester now that he'd talked to the man who owned the hotel he'd stayed at. They'd opened it especially for him, and by the looks of him, a good night had been had. Now he had to face an eight-mile uphill, and irked me that hungover or not, he soon vanished as I trundled upwards fresh as a daisy. A second car of four men also romped past me within a few hundred metres of getting going. I remained alone once again until the last third of the climb when I finally overtook a man in his seventies. I quickly forgot his name, but I was in awe to learn he'd walked the entire PCT in 2018. This year he and his mate, who'd fallen behind, were out doing reconnaissance on downed trees. He'd already moved ten with his long-handled shovel but was out to count the big trunks that needed specialist equipment ready for a party of volunteers to tackle. He said he was doing it in defiance of the PCTA who'd cancelled such endeavours because of Covid. He didn't need their permission to care about a trail he loved.

Bumping into him had kept me walking onwards and upwards, my ego refusing to stop and rest, when thirty years my senior was barely panting. We parted ways as the eight-miler flattened out momentarily before the second hill reared up. It was a four-miler sapping my motivation completely with its endless burdens and false summits. Now no one was there to judge, I found myself stopping too many times to count.

****

The Four Farters

If long-distance hiking is a journey of discovery, I never thought I'd find myself writing about toxic masculinity, but here we are. HAFE it is called - high altitude flatus expulsion, and it was undeniably the story of the week. Being a seasoned world-wide traveller, the reality of gas as a result of flying at altitude I was familiar with. It had never occurred to me that the same thing could happen at a significantly lower elevation. All one needs to do is ascend a few thousand feet in a few hours to around six thousand feet above sea-level, which is the daily norm on the PCT, and hey presto gas expands on the rebound. It also helps if one eats a lot of beans which is a popular American staple and then spends four nights camping with four men, only one of whom was vegan.

Leaving Sierra City, I'd stomped up twelve of the day's seventeen miles, honing in on the smell of smoke. I teetered into a campsite with a piddling stream nearby, plonking my belongings down beside a quartet of men encircling a campfire. They were quick to accommodate me, despite my feeling like I was encroaching. They readily introduced themselves: the eldest was The Hanging Judge who was spending the week with his adult son, Crocs, so called because that's how he was shod. Next to him was Knifeman, a man who carried many knives with various lengths of blades. Quite why, I never fathomed; he was the vegan. All the better to chop up his veg with, perhaps? Finally, a fellow PCT thru-hiker called Jim from Texas. He preferred not to have a trail name. Naturally he had the longest unkempt beard but was otherwise shy and retiring.

As dusk descended on another day, I wondered whether the phantom stag rumoured to cause night-time ruckuses would announce itself. The moment after we'd all turned in, the sounds of huffing and puffing crashed through the air as the deer seemingly rutted with any tree that it took offence to. All of us peered out of our tents, our headlamps scouring fruitlessly for the source of the racket. It remained elusive although it seemed only metres away, keeping us all awake for hours. This I know because neither snore nor burble was heard til well after midnight.

I was up and gone by six in the morning, leaving them to produce terrific emissions in differing rhythms. The bottom part of my legs, my ankles in other words, ached considerably from the previous day's exertions. My pack pulled hard on my shoulders. Aside from that, I felt I was in good nick. The views were limited, obscured by dense forest so the day became all about crushing miles. I'd planned on lunching at a popular camping spot, but then read about a rattlesnake living in the fire pit. It woke me up to the fact this wasn't only bear country after all.

In the afternoon, eight miles of the day were mostly absorbed in a trance. I sort of glided through time with ease. It was only the last mile which I could liken to grinding gears needing oil as I dragged body and soul to the spot I'd picked to rest that night. There I found the Four Farters already building a campfire and assembling their tents. I crammed myself in with them once again, like that annoying little sister, and prepared myself for another flatulent night. There was a beautifully relaxed ambience amongst the four men, laughter peppering the conversation uninhibited, as did their farts. Jim nodded when I remarked that I'd got myself into a zone in the afternoon, as often I'd only have an hour or so mid-morning. Usually, I was clock-watching and mile-counting all hours post-lunch, mindful of each throb, jolt or snag within my body.

The Hanging Judge had the deepest voice I had ever encountered on a man. He'd be a terrifying prospect for anyone finding themselves up against him in court. It was a source of disappointment to both Jim and I, when he told us he mostly dealt with parking violators. He had wads of duct tape wound around both feet, trying to prevent his soles detaching completely. Red raw skin peeked out from underneath his camp flip-flops, but he said nothing of it. I'd be wanting a full-page advert in *The Times* if I was walking on such damaged feet. He was just clearly content just to be hanging out with his son.

I used to find that curious. My own father loathed his only son: it was an open secret in the family. My mother had sat me down when I was very small, probably only six, and told me so. Who needs words to spell out the obvious anyway? She explained that was why she loved my brother more than me, after all, she had to compensate for his father hating him. My father was a workaholic, we never saw him from one day to the next unless it was incredibly special occasions, such as Christmas, when this forced family time brought even more ill-temperedness to an already angry home. We also got one week's holiday time a year with him, when his bad back would delay us setting off for wherever we were excited about going. Sometimes the pain would delay the trip for days so that would cancel the holiday, and the cure would be to return to work early.

But he was 'my' parent - the one who liked me, so it was fair that way, both siblings had a parent each. I was told so often that *my* parent was 'a good provider', who went out to work for three hundred sixty odd days a year, all hours of the day, and shouted a lot when he couldn't be there. Funnily enough though, I bore him little anger. I haven't seen him for decades, clueless as to his whereabouts. As I trundled along, I hadn't thought of him at all until I met The Hanging Judge. He simply doesn't exist in my psyche. But I still had to remind myself that fathers wanting and revelling in their children's lives *is* normal. I have spent a lifetime looking at male parents sideways - judging, assessing and fearing, wondering why they didn't have the courage to bugger off.

I suppose there are only two ways of learning: what you reason and what you are told. The deductive and the inductive if I wanted to be erudite about it all. I take responsibility for my flawed deductions, unearthing them and re-learning a better way of recalling

183

them. I've been shown how to be gentle to myself about having them, reasoning that young minds don't know it all. Sobriety has taught me that growing up and finding out things are not as you supposed can be enlightening and fascinating. I used to watch other children and their fathers laughing and playing together with resigned envy. I knew I didn't deserve a relationship like that because I wasn't a nice person; because I picked my nose; because I wasn't cute, because I reminded him of my mother. It never occurred to me that he had his own issues going on, and it manifested itself in workaholism. In some ways we are remarkably similar, except I hate working for a living, and he wasn't a particularly big drinker.

There's some relief to discovering things I used to believe no longer need to hold as much weight. Perhaps, I wasn't such a bad person, but I'd not half got my fair share of screwed-up thinking. That said, I can be significantly harder on those who gave me flawed instructions on managing life. I demanded, and sometimes still do, better of them. I suppose that's why alcoholism is a family disease: no one grows up unaffected by family dysfunction whether or not we go on to become alcoholic ourselves. That I became an alcoholic is 'understandable'; that other people are is 'unforgivable'. That takes a lot of straightening out.

I like watching 'earthlings' like The Hanging Judge and Crocs, all relaxed and casual. Croc nonchalantly mentioned that mum's homemade muesli was delicious. It was a heartwarming non-descript moment when his father readily agreed. They both wondered aloud how she was doing. I resolved to join Al-Anon, the sister fellowship for anyone affected by someone else' drinking on my return to the UK. I reasoned, watching them, it was time to soften, and reduce the abhorrent legacy of those fractured relationships. I'm a work in progress and it's been a full-time occupation just trying to get and stay sober, coming to terms with my own past. Maybe the time for venturing further afield was coming.

Rammed in all together with just millimetres of fabric between us, that night I slept the deepest and longest of my entire time on trail: a full nine hours. Jim was first up. I didn't want the night to end, nor the day to begin. Fifteen miles of downhill. I was right to dread it: at its steepest, only a third of the way down, I decided there was nothing for it but to cry. And to cry ugly. It was of no practical benefit, and painkillers offered little respite. There would be no trance to take me away from myself as I pummelled my way downward. Nor could the usual railings in my head deflect my conscience from the torture of my tibia, fibula and femur taking it in turns to batter my right knee cartilage.

As I neared the bottom of hell, I caught sight of a steep shortcut, believing it to link two of the 'zigs' of the switchback. It led down to a very secluded, and very charming campsite for one, complete with fire ring, grill and very grubby white towel, useful for drying oneself off following a dip in the adjacent river perhaps. Once again, unsurprisingly, I had taken myself away from the PCT, leaving me with the choice of a hideously steep climb of four hundred feet to return or to take to the river and rejoin at the bridge crossing the larger river further north. Naturally, I opted for a long splash along the embankment, slowly making my way towards a place where the trail and I could meld once again.

Not only was the going very sedate it was also tremendously slippery. I was absorbed by batches of vivid orange salamanders the length of my hand resting on pebbles just below the water's surface. I kicked myself later for not taking photographs, capturing their entrancing bog-eyed cuteness. I never saw anything similar elsewhere on the trail. I spooked a small harmless snake basking on the river rocks before running out of rocky shoreline. The overgrowth from a gaggle of trees pushed me across the placid river, now astonishingly deep: up to my chest, leaving me with nothing to do other than swim across it. Its graceful meandering body had no power to flush me away, but I'd forgotten my trousers were bug proof, not waterproof. My mobile phones, both with cracked screens, were given a thorough dowsing. I could only pray that my laptop and sleeping bag were sufficiently wrapped up, not that I'd been especially diligent about that since I'd left the Sierra. I squandered several hours of my day's journey. Worth it in many ways: the cool water had been a balm to my feet, ankles and knees, still raging away from the toil of the morning. I neared the point where the creek was to merge with a much more wide-ranging river. Only then did it occur to me that my stupidity was boundless: I did not know if this joining would happen from a great height, like a waterfall, or if the flow of the river would become copious, whisking me off to the Pacific in no time. By now, I'd calculated the PCT was probably forty feet above me, forcing me to haul my sodden self up a severe bank, thrashing through the dense undergrowth as I clung to branches, jamming my feet into loose ground. I heaved and scrambled and cussed my way through the bracken, plonking myself back on the smooth trail. There I promptly tripped over and ripped off almost all the fingernail of my third finger as I landed. The air tingled the usually protected skin beneath, setting my teeth on edge. I plastered it up as best I could, but the band-aids barely stuck to my sweaty skin in the humid lower elevation.

Despite the hours spent wading the river, by the time I had begun inching my way up the other side of the valley, I was disheartened to find I was out of drinking water. It was another three miles before I could fill up again. If recovery is a journey, discovering my levels of lunacy is seemingly without limits. Two hours later, taking time to filter water and bask on a large river boulder, I startled a man who mistook me for a bear. I was the fourth he'd seen that day, he muttered as he dodged by.

At the final third of a mile, halfway up yet another mountain, the aroma of camp smoke twitched my nose. Jim had arrived first, chasing off a bear, a real one this time. He set about building up the campfire, gathering small branches, and pulling fallen logs into place around it for others to sit. I, of course, was last to arrive, not expecting them to be there at all, but pleased again for the company. I squeezed my tent into the tiny site and joined them at the fire for dinner batting away at mosquitoes. I plopped myself down with a large groan and announced my day had been terrible because, "I'd broken a fingernail," only realising how ludicrously sissified I sounded when they all rolled around laughing. I held up my middle-digit now swathed in black KT tape as proof of injury.

For once, we all hung our food outside our tents, wary the bear would return. Crocs took mine and hid it behind a tree, too heavy to actually be hung because I'd flavoured a litre of water ready for the next day. Shattered, and still pestered by mosquitoes, we all took to our tents early. The following days groaning, moaning and farting started exceptionally early as the four men were keen to start their July 4th celebrations. I decided modesty was no longer required, emitting my flatulence along with the rest of them. It was just unfortunate it came out sounding like an advertising jingle.

****

186

What the bleedin' Jeff?

"Happy Fourth of July," one and all trilled back and forth. "If only we could celebrate with a cup of tea," was my wry contribution to the morning's sing-songs, the date of America's independence from Britain, following a disastrous tea party three years prior. Ordinarily a loud, rambunctious public holiday in the States, this year it was to be very muted, with many of its large celebrations cancelled, although small gatherings were deemed permissible.

It was also Aphelion day, when the Earth is furthest away from the sun. Not that one could tell, it was warming up rather nicely, even though we were at six thousand feet. I presumed it was something to do with lightyears and science and whatnot. Mind you, I always find it mystifying that daytime is already shortening before summer has barely introduced itself. In a mind-blowing kind of way, our days were still lengthening the further we eked our way north.

The five of us hadn't planned to regroup for a mid-morning break on a rocky outcrop, but the scenery had enraptured the lot of us, especially after days of being confined in never-ending woodland. During the day, I loved the cosiness of the boscage, with its attendant screeches amongst the ground dwellers and the chirruping of the birdsong above. Although, thinking about it, perhaps it wasn't so much the rare expanse of vista that had ensnared us, but rather the elevation and exposure giving us access to mobile internet, granting us brief contact with the outside world.

The news was that Canada was calling for its border with America to remain closed until the end of 2020. For those of us hikers hoping to cross the forty-ninth parallel, it would be a shame but just being out here and able to continue was blessing enough. Besides, September was a long way away, and there was no guarantee I'd make it that far. I put my phone away and stared gormlessly into the forested valleys, dragging on and on interminably. My wistful ponderings were periodically distracted by a loud popping emanating from a nearby mountain, each pop was followed by cavernous rumblings amid the vales. 'Odd to have daytime fireworks,' I mused to no one, but I couldn't see any telltale smoke, let alone fathom the legality of such things in the backcountry.

We'd been joined by Jeff, who'd already done ten miles to my paltry five that morning. He asked if I wanted to camp with him that night. It appealed given we were definitely in bear country. Bear ordure was ever-present: fresh and not so fresh. I only worried if it was steaming. We mutually agreed on a stopping point seventeen miles ahead, which was a tad ambitious for me, a real stretch to be more exact. Later on, my decision morphed into, "What the bleedin' Jeff was I thinking?" which is how I try to swear in polite company. I still needed to swear, particularly so when my legs rebelled at the twentieth mile of the day.

As we all rounded the corner, crossing a dirt track, we greeted men with guns sitting atop a large truck firing rounds at illuminous clay pigeons, bits shattering to the ground miles below. There were rifles and beer cans strewn everywhere, and a queue of people lining up to fire at the void. I declined both opportunities and made do with some bottled water and a chat with the local pastor; the best indication yet that my hellraising days were over. There was no food on offer, but there was a feast waiting in the town if I'd liked a ride down there. I declined that too and bid farewell to the Four Farters who were off to indulge in the celebrations at Buck's Lake. I'd miss them but the entire quartet would be breaking up as planned anyway: The Hanging Judge returning to civilisation, courtrooms and clean sheets.

My knee was feeling much more robust until I nearly lost an entire leg a few hours later. I barely missed landing my foot on a baby rattlesnake, avoiding it by a half-inch. It had coiled into a tiny pancake flat on the trail. I'd only noticed it when it rapidly withdrew to strike. Picturing its stink eye gave me cold sweats for days after. A baby rattler is rumoured to be just as fatal as an adult, although I suspect not. I was simply glad to not be a human experiment to disprove the hypothesis because it declined to lunge.

Jeff strode up behind me for the last mile and a half, keeping me enthralled and he delayed, as I dithered and dallied over the craggy path. He was quite the chatty man, telling me how he'd graduated college, got a job, never taken more than ten days holiday a year, worked his entire career, brought up his daughter, divorced her mother, saved for retirement and, when his employers were bought out by a large conglomerate, retired. Now he had time on his hands he was hiking the PCT. And as for hobbies? Well, of course, he was into ultramarathons. At fifty-eight, he was still extraordinarily fit. I couldn't decide what I found more baffling, working the same job for thirty-two years, or running ultramarathons. Not just marathons, but one- or two-hundred-mile-long races. I didn't dare tell him my CV was more shot to pieces than those clay pigeons and I'd only ceased smoking in December. The thought of running has always brought me out in hives.

We camped up that night with a husband-and-wife team who themselves do manifold marathons. She'd run in forty-eight of the fifty US states I overheard her telling Jeff. In the summer, they went thru-hiking. They'd also completed the Appalachian Trail and the Continental Divide Trail, but this was their preferred route. Unfathomably, they were doing it for the fourth time, and averaged thirty to forty miles per day. They'd probably squeeze in most of the return journey before winter fell. I was knackered just listening to the conversation, still perplexed as to why I was doing this at all, and even more bewildered as to how on earth they bore this much pain day in, day out. Most bizarre of all, in AA, these people are sometimes called 'the normals'.

The next morning, they'd all vacated the camp by five-thirty, making me comparatively slovenly leaving just after six. My target was to get to the hamlet of Belden, a place smaller than my former village, housing just twenty-two people. It boasted an average family size of two and a third, bemusing me hugely. Was the second person in the household particularly overweight, or the third person especially short?

The plan was to arrive for the opening of the town's only restaurant at eleven o'clock. It already surpassed my former home village by having an amenity. I fully intended to exploit it, knowing I'd need it to fuel me up the next hill. Post-lunch was to be an ascent of nearly five thousand feet over fourteen miles. I was determined not to stop before I reached the top; no matter how long it took; no matter how tempting the campsites were; no matter how much my legs screamed in revolt. Even if America's largest bear migrated from Alaska and blocked my path, I was going to barge my way past it and summit: I was that determined. It mattered because if I got to the brow, to the spot described as, "awesome unless there's lightning around," it meant I'd officially made it to the Cascades, the second of the two major mountain ranges of the PCT, saying farewell, or sort of good riddance, to the thirteen-hundred-mile-long path through the Sierra Nevada. Quite why I was thrilled to be saying goodbye to the granite-ridden Sierras and hello to the igneous Cascades was beyond me. These mountains are the most tectonically active mountains in North America. In less fancy words, the entire place was riven with bloody active volcanoes. Whereas one could presume it was ice that was out to kill before, now I could fear death by fire.

Somewhat predictably I got lost leaving the single track that took me out of the town. I left just a little after two in the afternoon when it was broiling. I drank over seven litres of water in the first four hours. Regardless, I tore up the hill at one with my trekking poles. I no longer noticed their existence, dangling off my wrists when I stood still, firmly gripped when on the move. I used them to draw me up steep inclines, like a Nordic skier, and balance me as I tottered over snaggy rocks. "Suitable for horses, my arse!" I found myself saying over and over as the ground reared up and down, but of course, mostly up. I also observed how much less often I was having to stop and pause to 'take in the view' whilst furiously hyperventilating.

I'd guessed sundown would be around about a quarter to nine but hoped the previous night's blazing moon hadn't been the full one because I'd more than likely need it to ease my way along the mountainside. Just over seven hours after settling my bill at the restaurant, I could be found sitting, physically replete, beside the Clingfilm Castle slurping on a decaffeinated coffee, waiting for my dinner to cook, on the crown of the mountain. My tent was a darkening silhouette against the fading light of the purple and orange sky, as the sun dropped below the tree line, then vanished altogether. I crawled into my tent and settled under my rancid sleeping bag as the shimmering moon blasted its beam of light through the fabric practically blinding me. I prayed the rustle in the bushes was a mere mouse, and the cracking of branches was nothing other than deer.

****

Chapter nine

Half-way through and somewhat underwhelmed

I shared a trough of water with Stryder, a pretty little bay horse, both of us hydrating as much as possible, readying ourselves for another stiflingly hot day. Stryder didn't have to go through the laborious process of filtering his intake. He was there to transport his owner, and various bits of kit, along the trail as well as to help shunt away the winter falls. A mischievous devil, he was keen to roll around in the dirt the minute his owner's attention was diverted. I painfully squeezed a couple of litres of water through the slow filtration system, watching the man dart back and forth, grabbing Stryder's reins to stop him mid-bow to the ground. He'd chide him affectionately, politely requesting Stryder refrain, then return to his truck to gather together more tools. Stryder would huff, ostensibly nibble at some grass, all the while watching patiently for the man's back to turn, then he'd be off sniffing at the dust, rotating, readying himself to lunge groundward.

I was benefiting not just from the bit of levity, but more so from the labour and investment of yet another solo volunteer. Unpaid and uncredited, these two were planning on spending two days clearing away energy-sapping blowdowns obstructing the way of many a hiker. I often wondered why people volunteered for stuff. It made no sense to me, I was always too hungover on a weekend to give up my time, which I viewed as highly precious in any case. Why should I care for strangers, their problems weren't mine, and besides, I had enough of my own to last my lifespan?

It was only after I got into recovery that I discovered the feelgood factor of giving time. I always thought of charity as a matter of stuffing a random number of coins into a rattled charity box. I read somewhere that if one wants a quick fix for low confidence and depression, then become a charity worker. It creates a sense of purpose that a job might not necessarily fulfil. I found it a cure for my chronic imposter syndrome. I was free to do the best I could. It took away my lofty expectations of myself. In my own grandiose way, I figured I was paying back what was freely given to me by partaking in AA's telephone service. I had reasoned I was paying it forward, but then I discovered it gave me a sense of self-respect, helping my self-esteem no end. All I had to do was talk with

191

faceless strangers on the phone. Years ago, I could barely look a person in the eye, but now I could tell them how things were so vastly different, and I wasn't working from a script, it was the truth.

I suspect I got more from the experience than I ever gave away. I'd only stopped when I'd flown to America. The set-up was such, I could even do it when I was on holiday, because all I needed was my phone, and a reference book of local numbers and meetings. Here in the wilderness, it was simply not possible to carry on with it. It was only six hours a week, and a busy night might be eight or nine calls. Most weeks, there were only one or two. I got to hear despair, just like I must have sounded, as the bewildered asked repeatedly for instructions on how they could stop drinking for a while. They weren't alcoholic, of course, but they just couldn't stop returning to the booze, and needed some tips. "Choose orange juice instead of beer at your Christmas do,' I told one gentleman facetiously when he explained that once he'd picked up the first beer, he couldn't predict what would happen next. He choked laughing, declining the option of going to a meeting.

Some were suicidal, others pissed and belligerent. There were the ones who told me they'd been to university, or were too wealthy, or were too senior in their company so they couldn't possibly be alkie. People would explain they couldn't go to meetings because their father, brother, sister was a household name or a politician, or because a neighbour or someone from work might recognise them, but usually it was because they weren't *that bad*. Occasionally, they called so they could tell their nagging spouse they'd rung us, and we'd confirmed they weren't alcoholic. No one can diagnose an alcoholic, it is the only disease that is one hundred percent, and nothing less, self-diagnosed. One can't even be a hypochondriac about it.

I'd listen to women sobbing telling me that I couldn't understand the shame of it, and how they feared social services would intervene and take away their children if they went to their doctor. Men who were terrified they were about to lose their jobs, their wives, their homes, because they couldn't get their shit together. Sometimes people would confess some of their antics, the stuff that horrifies the well, but is normalised for the drunk, stuff like drink-driving and violence and all that.

I fielded my fair share of angry spouses, parents and grown children who wanted to know how to prevent their loved ones from slowly killing themselves. All I could do was give them Al-Anon's number and wish them luck. I lost count of how many drunks rang me to tell me there was no God, and I used to say I didn't believe in the God they didn't believe in either. Being sober meant I didn't feel any great need to discuss the merits of religion with an indistinguishable, and very slurry, stranger. I'd explain, as nicely as I could, I wasn't a chatline for the pissed and stultified, and they'd react badly to that no matter how kindly I was. Most would not remember calling the next day anyway.

It reminded me of my own awful drunk behaviour, and if nothing else, each call made a compelling argument for sobriety. I have no doubt I was just as atrocious when intoxicated. As much as I'd like to think I was more sophisticated than that, my own hazy recollections confirm I was not. I wasn't that nice passed out person quietly stupefying in the corner, far from it. In fact, it was my raucous behaviour that ultimately meant I stopped drinking in bars, and confined myself to the house, where I couldn't make a prat of myself, or worse.

The funniest calls, though, were always those who'd asked for AA's number from directory enquiries, causing confusion as we determined whether they'd had a nervous breakdown or a vehicular one. Sometimes you could tell from the off, they wanted the other recovery service because I'd say, 'My name is Person, and I'm an alcoholic', they'd reply, "I'm so sorry," and clatter the phone down.

When I walked along, I preferred to spend hours thinking about other's drinking than my own for obvious reasons. I still like the podcasts to go into great detail about the 'drinking years'. They're called drunkalogues, some people love them, others loathe them. I think they are important though so that any listener can relate to the speaker, providing that invaluable but silent acknowledgement that we've done similar things or felt similar moods. The relief that I haven't done that...but then I can add an inaudible 'yet'. It is hard at first to listen for the similarities and not the differences, but as time goes by, finding things in common with others, rather than exploring ways of setting myself apart gets easier.

Some speakers were gravely serious. As I trudged through more forest, I'd audibly gasp at some of the stories. This day's share was a lass who in her early twenties had killed the passenger, her boyfriend, whilst driving her car under the influence. When people share their horror stories, it would be foolish of me to say, 'that would never happen to me' and 'I could never do that.' The reality is that addiction is not synonymous with choice. Maybe once, but not now. I sometimes want to tell people never to say to someone "Well, you'd be fine to drink now you've been sober for so long." It's a complete fallacy. I was glad my reality is that, whilst I've been a dick, I didn't have to try and make amends on that scale. The speaker had found a way to live with herself, and to live in sobriety and be re-accepted by society, but it was important to her to remind herself where the drink had taken her. It was a powerful morning's contemplation.

Other speakers revel in the ludicrous behaviour of the inebriated. I could laugh out loud at funny alco-logic - those tales, which might horrify a non-drinker, are only silly now they are in the past, although some were probably hilarious at the time. For any bystander or victim of a drunk, I imagine it's terribly offensive that we find humour in such places. My only defence is we are not a glum lot, and that sobriety is to be enjoyed rather than endured. I realise that holds everyone to ransom with the implied threat that if we're forbidden from laughing at our antics, we might drink again. Not so, but laughter is a medicine too. The best stories, of course, talk about finding redemption.

The section was largely drying up again, and reliable water would only be found off trail. I resented having to come off the PCT to find the source, usually down a ravine, with a nasty crawl back up again. Sometimes I could leave my pack and poles at the top, juggling four bottles whilst navigating steep and craggy side-trails on wobbly lactic-acid filled legs. Although it was a life-sustaining liquid, even I found it weird that once upon a time I was willing to go to any lengths to obtain more booze, and yet thought going a half-mile off piste to get a few litres of water in the backcountry an outrage!

A food stocktake that morning, and a quick review of what was coming up ahead, had me concluding I could bypass Chester and carry on to Burney Falls. I was low on electricity in my power bank though. There was a stream of restaurants along this section, like the one I'd just passed, and all were now open and inviting visitors. They might be amenable to a hiker needing a power boost. With Drakesbad and Old Station ahead of me, and both within striking distance of the trail, I conceded that there was a payoff between time spent eating versus calories gained, but they were to be traded against stints finishing well into the evening. I was by now finding I could do two or three more miles than my minimum of twenty a day, but each hour spent dining effectively costs two miles, and rarely did I stop for only an hour.

I was flabbergasted to find myself at the midpoint marker, which was nothing more exciting than a wooden post. It indicated emigration to be one thousand, three hundred and twenty-five miles away in either direction. I held a sort of ambivalence about the accomplishment. Was the trail half done, or half undone? Later I discovered the midpoint post isn't actually at the midpoint. Perhaps it was once, but it certainly wasn't now. The PCT has been tinkered with over the years, and various diversions exist annually to account for floods, fires, landslides, near-extinct species and collapsed bridges.

Nonetheless, I sat on the stone wall, which was more a collection of large stones, arranged over the years in a slightly haphazard manner permitting a moment's reflection. I kept it brief before battling my way into a tightly clasped metal storage container to sign the trail register. The whiff of skunk blasted out when I finally prised the jaws of the box apart. A good fist of marijuana rolled around below the notebook. I read that Amsterdam had been through two days prior, and SatNav was on the same day as me, but no one else. Beside the post, there was also a cooler, but it was long-since abandoned. I checked Guthook and saw it was a half-mile walk to the next camping spot. I decided that twenty-three miles was plenty for the day. I really couldn't be arsed to complete the rest of the nine-mile descent of Butt Mountain.

****

Injuring self and others

When caught with one's pants down, and there's nothing for it but to front it out. I knew as well as anybody one is supposed to go two hundred feet off trail, but sustained exercise also gives one a yearning for constipation. Sometimes, though, the slant of the mountain conspires against one's principles. I'd spotted a thick-trunked blowdown adjacent to the trail, which would hide all but my head and decided to risk it, especially as ordinarily I could go hours, if not a full day, in between encounters of the human kind. Saying hello to Jeff as he arrived around the corner was awkward to say the least. I could only accept it as karma for not following the *Leave No Trace* rules.

"Isn't it good to be halfway?" I piped up with that self-conscious high-pitch of the truly embarrassed, pulling up my trousers in a painful attempt to get my dignity back. Jeff, barely able to make eye-contact, stiltedly enquired whether or not I'd be continuing into Lassen National Park. The rules stipulate one must carry a bear can if one intends on staying within its boundaries. As the PCT only runs through it for nineteen miles, it's feasible to cross it in a day. I was well positioned, the border being twenty-two miles from my starting point, to actually abide by the rules. Besides, I was already thinking I'd probably broken enough for one day as it was, and I didn't wish to risk any further cosmic retribution.

My conscience has a way of sneaking up on me and reminding me to do the 'right thing', but sometimes I need a nudge, hopefully of the gentle kind, albeit sometimes a sledgehammer might be a better tool. I accept I am no one's idea of a saint but I'm working on it. I'd recently heard a speaker say that it took three hundred years post-death before beatification could take place. I found that a bit demoralising to say the least, but I intend to persevere regardless. I'm not altogether certain that's factual in any case.

A fast and fit FirTree also had a way of sneaking up on me. I nearly leapt out of my rucksack when he muttered, "Good morning," as he hurtled by. Today, he wanted to hurtle by three more times. The guy was seriously stealth, not once did I hear an intake of breath nor a foot crunching on the ground behind me. I only used one ear pod from my headphones as I hiked. It was not only good practice to avoid impeding a faster hiker, but also to ensure I remained partially alert as to what was about to kill me. Not once did I have a clue, when or how I'd overtaken FirTree. He'd just skulk up behind me, say "hi!" and I'd loudly beseech the Lord, convinced I was about to take my first steps into canonisation. Other times, I'd hear footprints or feel a sensation of someone lingering behind me. I'd pull to the side to find no-one there.

Later that afternoon, I joined Jeff and FirTree as they collected water, enjoying a late-afternoon snack and chat. I had just plonked myself on a small log when a loud crack pierced the woodland. Shortly after a rotting tree announced its demise, smacking the ground a few feet from us. I was awfully glad I'd toileted that morning, by now I was sick to death of nearly shitting myself.

The two of them were of the rule-abiding variety as I snaked my way to the campsite about a half mile off the trail on the outskirts of the park. We huddled together, near to a mosquito-infested spring, on the few patches of bare ground available. The area was thick with long, damp grass, and moss hugged the tree trunks, its shaggy tendrils dripping between branches. Earlier in the week I'd met a Southbounder who'd revelled in telling me that she'd woken up to bear scat blocking the exit of her tent. There had been several recent comments on Guthook mentioning a curious bear that didn't particularly 'shoo' when it was ordered to.

Lassen Volcanic National Park, according to its website, is home to steaming fumaroles and meadows freckled with wildflowers. I'd no idea what a fumarole was until I side-tracked off to one of the PCT's 'must-sees' called 'Terminal Geyser'. Sounding like a psychotic Essex boy, Guthook notes informed me Terminal Geyser was not a geyser at all. Perplexingly, it failed to mention what it actually was. Hikers are guided down a good distance to what looks akin to a cloud machine, faintly smelling of rotting eggs. Behind the steam, there is alleged to be a hole in the ground from which boiling sulphured water trickles out. The warning signs dotted along the route cautioned hikers not to put a foot wrong, lest we suffer severe burns, likely if the brittle ground gave way. Going beyond a certain point was completely forbidden. Once again, I had no problem following these rules.

I detoured to pass by Boiling Springs Lake, a cauldron of viridescent hot water, a good tenth of a mile wide. It wasn't quite at the simmer. I spent a little time there, then trundled on keen to make it to Drakesbad Resort for breakfast. It had advertised restricted opening, although several hikers had alluded to it being a worthwhile deviation, even if one had to wait awhile. Some had complained of poor service, but I received the best of it all: a full breakfast of several pancakes, yoghurt, fresh fruit, a mountain of scrambled eggs, a half-plate of diced potatoes, cinnamon buns and some bread on the side just in case and by the way, did I need to plug anything in for recharging?

There was only one server. She'd spent nearly twenty minutes on the phone being berated by a woman furious at being refused a booking for the forthcoming Friday. The server doing her best to explain it was a result of restricted seating, and prioritising staying guests. They had too few staff available in this covid-bound year to deal with too many large reservations. I felt that familiar cringe at seeing old behaviour reflecting back at me. Today I'd been at my patient, smiley best, and in return I was given what their paying guests had not been able to consume. That mountain of 'scraps' came free of charge and I could have wept at the generosity of it all.

I ploughed only to be plunged into the most hideous of landscapes: hundreds and thousands of dead and decaying charred trees, some standing, others littering the ground for as far as the eye could see. The previously lush forest was nothing but scorched skeletal remains, the floor mostly blackened and the trail dry and dusty. There'd been a substantial wildfire, spreading across thirty-thousand acres eight years prior, but the regeneration was so terribly slow that I wondered if this was a result of a more recently planned swaling. A land strategy to prevent much larger out of control wildfires striking out the whole area, causing carnage for the wildlife inhabiting it. It had an eerie vibe and I wanted to escape the region as rapidly as my legs would allow.

My bladder started to twinge, nagging me to release its contents over and over again, despite not having much to release. I could see for miles around me, enabling me to ascertain whether or not someone was susceptible to a full mooning. I feared a urinary tract infection. My pee was clear enough, so I knew I wasn't dehydrated. I'd picked up some electrolytes in a hiker box a while back and I'd recently started adding them to my drinking bottle. Perhaps a reaction to that? Regardless, I could do little about it, the nearest doctor would be in Burney Falls. A visit to the doctor was an inconvenience I didn't want. I threw down a handful of dried cranberries and hoped for the best, chugging at as much water as I could. I felt ill-at-ease even camped up that night, surrounded as I was by death and decay. My tent was engulfed in a swarm of flies only adding to the sense of decomposition.

****

The sociopath amongst us

I stood in the bathroom of yet another run-down, single storey American motel of the type typically depicted in psychological thrillers. Unlike the others, this one was memorable for having a huge airy bathroom, with clean modern tiles, and enough space to swing a rucksack. It was quite out of keeping when compared to the cramped bedroom, containing an aging fridge, microwave and television stuffed between the wall and the bed. Thankfully, though, there was a large coffee machine dominating the tabletop.

It wasn't a bathroom though, because it didn't have a bath. Even though most motels advertised a 'tub', what actually existed in most American hotels was an affront to an actual bath. One could barely submerge one's backside, let alone stretch out to allow hot water to relieve bound muscles. It was useful for washing a chihuahua I supposed but pointless for anything else.

I had adjusted to the waves of pain which ripped up my legs each time I stood up on my battered feet, my calves screeching out in revolt at being stretched upright again, but I longed to immerse myself in soothing hot water. I was resigned to the fact it may be many months before that dream would come true, most likely when I was back in the UK, where bathing is practically a national pastime.

Remarkably my agitating bladder had calmed down the instant I'd left the burn area. I presumed then it was psychosomatic but discarded the electrolytes just in case. A quick visit to Dr. Google suggested there was a link between so-called 'smart waters' and interstitial cystitis, something I'd suffered from since I was eight years old. Remarkably though, it had ceased as my drinking took off in my thirties. Once I stopped drinking, however, I'd developed urge and stress incontinence. It shattered what little dignity I had left in the first two years of recovery, almost forcing me to be a hermit. Several doctors and a few unpleasant internal investigations later, it

199

was put down to post-traumatic stress disorder. After a fight I managed to get some therapy, and things had improved a lot regarding the urge incontinence. Conquering 'The key in the door syndrome' meant I no longer unlocked my door and bladder simultaneously. A cough or sneeze remained a threat, but I could live with that, just like forty percent of women do. Standing in the bathroom, it occurred to me that even that wasn't happening anymore. I'd finally found a cure for women's incontinence - it's just unfortunate one has to walk over a hundred miles a week for months for it.

Taking my clothes off in the bathroom, contorting my limbs in ways they were no longer accustomed, was a torture. I examined my naked body in the large wide mirror above the sink. My weight loss was remarkable now and things were starting to look shapely. I retained my boobs, but the reduction of fat meant they looked a little saggy. My stomach had retracted a little, as had my backside, which was somewhat pleasing. My bingo wings and side saddles still defined my limbs. Slim I was not but narrowing definitely. I hoped my underarm hair was now considered fully grown, but who knew? I'd never grown it before.

Purple splodges lined my shoulders from the straps of my rucksack. Bruises abounded and I had a wide welt of rough skin across my lower back. My pubic hair had worn away at the sides. Further down, my legs were caked with dust up to my mid-thighs, though having waded through a river, I had a tide-line halfway up my shins. I ripped off the Kinesthetic Tape holding my right knee together, like peeling off a giant plaster, the skin underneath puckered, as did my eyes. I realised that my right leg was now scarred for life from the fall I'd had back in the first month.

My scarlet feet were horrifically sensitive, the briefest of touches had me flinching and yelping. I could no longer bring myself to rub or massage them. Sitting on the toilet, I tenderly took one heel and tried to draw my foot into focus. Blenching, I noticed another absent toenail, but the previously missing piggy had now fully regrown. Snipping away the tips of my smutty nails, my insides convulsed as I manhandled each toe to align with my clippers. I cut away part of a callus on the underside of my little toe. I used to be blessed with soft skin underfoot, but now both had ghostly-white thickenings aggregating here and there.

My teeth seemed fine and, if anything, whiter than usual. I'd guessed as a result of all the water I was drinking, but more likely because of the coffee and tea I wasn't drinking. I wondered how much permanent damage I was doing within my unsighted body. Without doubt, though, most alarming of all was the dust gathering in my eyebrows and above my lip. I'd been walking around looking like *Inspector Clouseau* for quite some time.

I never realised until I got to the ninth step, that part of making amends to oneself is to forge a better, more respectful relationship with one's own anatomy. I'd always loathed mine and alcoholism ensures one treats it with utter contempt. Alcohol, after all, is toxic and whilst the perils of smoking are well known, less well advertised is the damage that alcohol does to the physical form. Breast cancer is the most common cancer for women, and just three drinks a week increases the risk of that illness by fifteen percent. It interferes with almost every bodily system: making them sluggish and ineffective even when one rarely binges or has a 'few too many.' Alcohol is arguably more dangerous than smoking. As well as causing wrinkles, bad breath and body-odour, it strips away one's dignity and self-esteem, and that's before one even considers how it abducts and then obliterates the peace of mind of those around us. Yet, it's not yet common practice to put pictures of cirrhotic livers across bottles. Battered faces populate images of abusive relationships, but rarely is the link explicit between alcohol and violence, or worse, in my opinion, alcohol and psychological abuse. If anything, the role booze plays tends to be minimised. Not that any of that stops an addict, of course. I should know I am one, but I am starting to notice the inconsistencies between how alcohol, smoking and domestic abuse are depicted.

One of those teeth-grinding AA-isms, is that not only does AA stand for 'Altered Attitudes', but also 'Anti-Aging', and it's true, or at least until one becomes a thru-hiker. There's a remarkable difference in skin tone amongst teetotallers, when compared to those who drink a glass of wine a day. My hair thickened noticeably. Within a year of stopping drinking, it was the most luscious it had ever been, and all without the need for expensive potions. Now I was living a malnourished lifestyle once again, it hit home how important a good diet could be, not just to the physical well-being, but also the mental one. At this town stop, I gorged on boxes of fried vegetables

201

from the local Chinese restaurant, cramming as many in as I could, washing them down with real strawberry milkshakes and fresh cranberry juice as I tried my best to overcome my unbearable smugness.

Cleaned up and ready to get going again, I made my way to Burney's main road. My rucksack was now stuffed with ten days of food, plus more dried fruit and vegetables than usual. I resorted to affixing my tent once again outside of the pack. I stuck my thumb out optimistically for a ride. It wasn't long before a car pulled over and a man in his seventies got out and approached me in person. "Watch out for the man with a white pick-up, he's killed three women this year already," he muttered. "Right-o," I replied a little dumbfounded as he returned to his car, a silver hatch-back, and drove off. I didn't think to ask him how he knew. Soon after, two men picked me up in a plush jet-black pick-up so I knew I would be absolutely fine.

****

The regrets of the present

Leaving Burney, the UK headlines seemed optimistic that things were to start getting back to 'normal' albeit with heavy modifications on what normal would be, and how 'old normal' would be substituted with 'new normal'. In Bristol, a statue of a black woman, fist raised aloft, had been erected on an empty plinth and then removed by the council. It had been previously occupied by Edward Coulson, a man of many occupations: philanthropist, merchant, member of parliament and slave-trader. It had been ripped down and thrown into the sea in the recent protests, only to then be recovered and memorialised for entirely different reasons in a nearby museum.

People were being asked to return to work and crack on with recovering the lost economy, and yet worldwide the World Health Organisation stated the pandemic was expanding. Certainly, in America, the news suggested the crisis was worsening, and consequently Donald Trump's ratings were plummeting. To my reading, it seemed the world was getting angrier, segregating people into dichotomous camps, all the better to pit people against one another. To mask or not to mask? To take the knee or not? To return to the office or to carry on at home? On Facebook, there was more fighting for the right to be right. Across popular news sites I wondered where 'the people's voices' had gone in this era of experts, science and hard numbers, with an alarming absence of context. With little else to do, it seemed doom-scrolling had become the new national pastime.

I was used to wearing a mask in towns now. Colourful bandanas had become popular fashion necessities, allowing some individuality to creep into the bank-robbing look of the times. Others opted to wear what I considered to be the dis-used gussets of women's underwear. I'd simply pull down my snood, ordinarily used to prevent the wisps of hair from tickling my face. On the trail, a full-frontal face was still the norm, although mankind remained a rarity.

The solitude gave me a lot of thinking time, and subsequently a lot of crying time. An unresolved grief pouring out of me, the end of my marriage, the loss of all my future ambitions. The childhood pets I had and was subsequently forced to abandon each time we were dragged from one country to the next. The loss of friends and toys, and relationships. The sadness for the errors of my ways and the regrets I'd accumulated. Unlike self-pity, my sobs felt more cathartic and more natural, less gut wrenching than yonder years. I came to accept how I'd been frightened my entire life, riddled with insecurity and anxiety. I had masked it by lying, exaggerating, denying, minimising, gaslighting or generally avoiding facing up to the problem of being me.

I also started to see a clearer boundary where I ended, and someone else began. That just because I had behaved badly, didn't make another person Mother Teresa. That forgiveness is not a light switch that can be flicked off or on, but the end result of a much longer process. Willingness to forgive comes before the strength to actually complete the action, but quite often my inner axe-murderer will get the better of me.

It was the ninth step that asked me not to bask in my own victimhood to excuse the worst of my excesses. It doesn't permit me the right to weaponise myself by condemning someone else's behaviour, and it especially does not allow me to appease my own guilt by manipulating situations to distract someone's attention away from my own misdemeanours. Thinking about it, it's a hideous step making me accountable for the best and the worst of me. This is the step which requires one to make amends for past behaviour, and it was the one which fundamentally changed my relationship with fear. I don't know if I'll ever be done and dusted with this step, and that's probably a good thing, because it right-sizes me as much as it humanises me. Whether or not I am forgiven is not the point, it's about relieving myself of guilt. I'm not perfect, I make mistakes, I've had opinions that have hurt others' feelings thoughtlessly. I have overreacted to many things, particularly trivial matters, and under-reacted to others, usually out of fear of making a situation worse, stuffing my feelings deep inside, only to find out they bubble out another way.

As I settled into the first day of what I guessed would be a ten-day outing, I met just one day-hiker, an elderly man who launched into terrific detail about the condition of the trail for the next ten miles. I found the confidence to interrupt to say, "actually my feet hurt so I'm going to resume walking now," rather than hoping he'd read my mind and shut up. I'd made a pact with myself that I was never again going to stand nodding politely as someone droned on and on, like I had once in Moscow in minus thirty degrees centigrade as my ex-husband's work colleague had waxed lyrical on why I shouldn't be a vegetarian. I have decided, rightly or wrongly, I will never again allow anyone to mansplain, and I shall call them out on it with kindliness, in order to reduce my hatred of all things condescending. I trotted off with a 'nice to meet you' and went on my less than merry way not seeing another soul until Scraggy pitched up just after the sun had set the following day. He brought with him news of our fellow travellers: Amsterdam, SatNav, Jeff and Goblin amongst others. They were all now well ahead of me and still going strong.

The topography was clogged with ferns and other shrubbery. Moss dribbled across trees, the canopy above blocked out the worst of the day's heat. The dampness of the forest engulfed me, preventing sweat from wicking away. I'd committed to stretching my daily targets, but I hadn't bargained on cloying overgrowth. The trail was blotted out completely, delaying me as I bodily fought my way through, thrashing around with hiking poles, my feet could only scour for unsighted trip-hazards beneath me. Exhaustion forced me to rest up for the night short of my expectations.

I had developed a habit, a bad one, of hitting the trough of the mountain just as the day reached its scorching high. Later in the week, the temperatures would climb into triple digits for the first time. Hellish. I countered it by setting my alarm for four o'clock in the morning and the cooler starts helped considerably. I had just two months left, and I had not yet traversed the length of California. Refusing to panic about Oregon and Washington until I got there, I was nonetheless disappointed to have missed yet another self-imposed ambition: to complete the final two states in two months. Worrying, it is oft-said, won't protect me from the future - but it is a tough habit to break.

Night after night I camped alone. I could focus on the positives of having night-time privacy. I'd found ways of soothing myself, rather than waiting for the worst to happen, pondering potential night monsters only ever caused me sleep deprivation and day-time crankiness. A resident deer at Deer Creek stood within ten yards of the Castle the entire night watching me intently, unwilling to leave the area. I wondered how she'd mastered her fear of humans. The next day, fresh and well-slept, I chatted to her as I slurped on my morning coffee, and she slurped on my morning pee just a few feet away.

The following night, I'd ploughed on to a formal campsite run by the Forestry Service, yearning for the sounds of fellow man. I'd hoped too for a bin so I could offload some rubbish, an empty gas canister in particular. Eliminating a few small ounces had a disproportionate impact on my assessment of pack weight. It offered neither. The lonely latrine did supply toilet paper: a thrilling consolation prize given it was a precious commodity on trail. The mosquitoes were pretty fierce, so I forgave the place for not even having a picnic table. Another small gem was discovering some 'dried fruits' I'd bought were, in fact, sweets.

Proficient now at reading the ground underfoot, I guessed I was around a half day away from two hikers. Definitely a pair walking together, I'd adduced from the footprints I was stepping into. Two men for certain. Swelling with my own sense of sophistication, I felt capable; strong and knowledgeable. I'd always wanted to walk in endless woodland, and this portion of California delivered mile after mile, day after day. Each one offered nothing other than a single event demarking it from the day previous.

I stalled at a rattlesnake, dark green and well camouflaged on the trail dappled with sunlight. It snapped into its striking position blocking the path completely, compelling me down the steep bank. Then it asserted that it would be going that way rather than me. Content not to argue, I scrambled back onto the path. It slithered off hostile throughout. I observed it sliding down the vertiginous drop of the mountain. Never once losing direct sight of me, it failed to detect a small cliff and plopped off abruptly with quite the startled look in its eye.

Yet another day of uninterrupted rumination was finally broken when I spied a rucksack leaning against the trunk of a tree. Removing my own pack, I sat myself down on the bare ground of a well-used camping spot adjacent to an increasingly scarce stream and gathered together the component parts of lunch. "I'm just doing my business," a man cried out from a few feet away. Granted in the current terrain, with its high sides, and sharp downs, it was near impossible to find a spot off the trail to go but having a shit in a rare watering hole is a serious crime in hiking society. Once he was done, I could walk a little upstream to refill my water bottles. I decided not to antagonise him further. I probably maximised his shame by being polite and conversational. After I'd eaten, I left him to his silence and resumed my solitary saunter towards Seiad Valley, a place that I had no idea how to pronounce, and nor, it seemed, did Shitting Man.

I lost my much-despised hat. I had always hated wearing it, but it had sun-shielding flappy bits which mostly worked, and a peak to keep the sun off my pale face. In the thriving forest, I had barely needed to use it, so I stuffed it into my pocket, caring little about how greasy and gnarly my braided hair looked. The exposure meant no more hiking with my plaits dripping large globules of sweat down my chest and back. Of course, losing one's hat on the hottest day of the year was not my finest moment. I piled on extra sunscreen on my naked neck then ran dangerously low on that too.

A day later, I bumped into a father and son, jingling away with bells attached to their shirts. They were wild-eyed, stammering, "bears, lots and lots of bears!" They weren't sure if it had been many or one many times. I'd just spooked one too. In fact, I only saw its lumbering posterior as it raced up the hillside, keen to avoid me. This seemed to agitate the man still further, so I probably should not have told him about another vivid green rattlesnake I'd come across eight miles back.

Later on in the afternoon, I was confronted by another posterior, this of a woman. Unusually she'd opted to hike in a skirt, and unfathomably, she also preferred to go knickerless. As I rounded the corner, she was getting up from her sleeping mat, laid right alongside the trail, as if she'd just had a siesta. I received a thorough flashing of the type best reserved for one's gynaecologist.

That night, and very much to everyone's astonishment, I set up my tent with none other than Jeff, he of ultra-marathon running, and Amsterdam, with his exceedingly long legs and swift stride. We all laughed as I waddled into the camp, surprised at the unplanned rendezvous but pleased to have someone to celebrate the completion of one thousand, five hundred miles. They'd both resupplied at Castella, and my strategy of doing a long haul, with a heavy pack was paying off. Just one thousand, one hundred and a bit more miles to plod.

****

Faith and fears

Light crept in a good while after the day had broken formally, the treetops shrouding it out for a good hour or so post-sunrise. I commenced my day's hike with my headlight illuminating the ground before me. Jeff had already marched off. We'd arranged to camp together that evening. He was biding his time getting to Etna where he had a parcel waiting at the post office. There was little point rushing, he'd only arrive on a Sunday. He barely ever took a zero as it was, keen to do the thru-hike as fast as possible. "Goblin has shin splints, he's waiting it out for a week in Castella," he'd updated me the previous night. I learnt it was a common but incredibly painful affliction for long-distance runners, and difficult to recover from, often requiring weeks if not months of rest. Given he was so fit and fearless, I thought that was doubly sad. Injury, rather than fear, is the number one quasher of dreams after the half-way point. Goblin was the first I knew who had succumbed.

That evening, long before nightfall, I plonked my bone-weary body on a log, right next to Jeff filtering water, "Do you smell? I can't smell you." he remarked acknowledging my

207

appearance. I'd say I sat soaking up the first substantial wide-framed view on offer in many days, but in all honesty, I was more occupied by not having to walk another metre. I needed to cool down, the sun had burnt everything exposed: the tips of my fingers poking out of fingerless gloves, the tops of my ears, the parting in my hair. The rim beneath my hairline, where my bandana had slipped, was blistered. It was a remarkable vista, looking back, punctuated by the glacier-bound Mount Shasta. Like a giant pimple, the volcano juts up ten thousand feet from the flatlands encircling it. We should have been putting up our tents, and preparing dinner, but I just wanted the torment in my legs to subside.

"Not that I want to worry you, but the first sign of Corona is losing your sense of smell," I bantered back to him. It was a source of disappointment each and every morning that my olfaction was fully functioning. "The other indicators are feeling hot, tired and having a runny nose," I added. These symptoms we suffered almost all the time. Particularly so that morning when I'd dragged myself up a relentless hill, grinding out an ascent of five thousand feet, all but three hundred feet of it, had been compacted into a twelve-mile incline. It was above-average in the onerous stakes. Halfway up, I clocked an enticing clearing beside a cliff, offering a glorious look out across rarely seen blue skies. I thought it a marvellous place to have a snack, filter water and to stare vacantly into the distance awhile. I greeted a woman, clean and fresh-smelling, wearing a pretty floral dress. She occupied the end of a trimmed large log. I went to sit down a little further along, just as my rump was to connect, she shrieked at me to go away, muttering about 'social distancing.' I stepped back, but she hurried off, yelling, I presumed, for her husband and son, snapping about wanting to get away from the virus. I apologised for interrupting her, but even trying to say sorry terrified her.

The last ten miles were above the tree-line, flat and exposed, giving a welcome breeze to cool down with, but sheer fatigue dictated it was still an arduous afternoon's walk. We'd opted to camp after twenty-two miles on a barren, stony ridge. What the ground lacked in comfort, the view more than adequately compensated. We waited for Ivan to arrive, a younger woman in her twenties. She was a Southbounding thru-hiker, albeit one who'd opted to flip-flop to avoid much of Washington, which was still under heavy snow. It had been a high snowfall year up there and conditions were said to be particularly gruelling. She was still in her first fortnight, and looked outwardly healthy, until she moved, then her stiffness was blatant. I'd bumped into her resting up under one of the few trees remaining. She'd already chatted to Jeff. I walked with her to the intersection of two trails, where we both dumped our packs, taking ourselves off to find water a half mile away. I was no longer worried about someone rifling through my pack. She told me she was only managing ten miles a day, and she really wanted to break that barrier. As we gathered water, I could assure her ten miles was plenty for now, especially on hills such as these. It was the oddest thing finding oneself advising a newcomer as an anxiety-riddled imposter myself.

I'd let her know where Jeff and I planned to camp if she wanted to join us. It might spur her on an extra couple of miles if she needed the motivation. I then romped off, leaving her to crawl slowly along the dirt trail. An hour later, she emerged and collapsed on the same log Jeff and I sat upon. We lectured her with our own learnings. How it wasn't a race, but a huge feat of endurance, and to respect her legs accordingly. How the miles would come quicker and quicker if she stayed uninjured and fought the temptation to push hard early on. Our pleadings fell on deaf ears, just like they had on mine. I used to panic pondering how I was ever going to be able to do fourteen and a half miles a day, which was what I had to average to begin with. Now I was chipping away at my mandatory minimum: from a high of twenty miles per day, it was now down to nineteen and a half per day. I was managing that capably, mostly getting five or so extra in the bag to put towards a day off or two.

Jeff quizzed her on her kit, and we told her a bug head net was a no-brainer. Jeff approved of her having a puffy jacket, whereas I had sent mine on, and so I contradicted him. We both disagreed with her cold-soaking, stove-eschewing cooking system. Whether she wanted our insight or not, we were glad of having a newcomer to condescend. Eventually as dusk threatened, we crammed our three tents into a small patch that previous occupants had cleared of the mountain rubble. It was a reprieve to lie down and chat, rather than wobble around on a slender arse-numbing log.

They both slept soundly, yet I found myself unencumbered by sleep for long tranches of time. I moaned to Jeff as we readied ourselves for yet another slog. "What do you think will help?" Jeff enquired. "Probably about half a dozen valium," I yelled back. We wished Ivan luck as we packed up around her.

The terrain for the next few days was relatively benign, with meandering undulations, dipping in and out of forests, and winding through meadows. The summer was in full swing now: plants bloomed and stretched outwards, and water sources reduced to mere trickles. "It's like milking a bull," I complained to Jeff late one afternoon as it took an age to scoop up a small cup full of water before tipping into the narrow neck of a water bottle, then squeezing it through a filter into my drinks container.

We bimbled our way along the crests of the mountains, joined only by solitary bees whizzing around us like giant hula hoops. They were more distracting than threatening as they escorted us away from their flowering havens. To our right, Mount Shasta loomed, commandeering the side of one's eye, giving rise to a strange notion all we were doing was merely circumventing the volcano several times. It undoubtedly haunts the PCT, and rumours abound of paranormal activity. People talk of seeing Bigfoot, and according to some, aliens are inclined to pop by too. The most enigmatic occupants are thought to be the Lemurians, primates who survived when their previous lands sank. Taller than the average man, it is claimed they now skulk about a network of tunnels beneath the volcano, and swan around in white robes.

It is probably no coincidence that Mount Shasta has become a birthplace for several new spirituality movements. The largest was the 'I Am', which still dwindles on, although it has shrunk substantially since its high of one million adherents in the 1930s. The native Klamath tribes hold that it is home to Skell, a spirit of the Above World. Irrespective of one's beliefs, it emits a distinctive emotional aura, and at times it can be a foreboding one. It remains an active volcano, although not predicted to erupt in the near future. That must be a relief to those living in the nearby town of Weed, although they may be too stoned to care.

Having a hiking partner proved disrupting to my daily rhythm. Ordinarily, I tended only to stop when I needed to filter water or a toilet break. Occasionally, if there was a tempting flat rock, I'd rest up for five minutes or so, but I rarely dawdled. Jeff would stop frequently, whenever he had a yearning for a snack, and that happened religiously every two hours. I'd often catch him and

210

opt for a short rest myself. Only we were both conversant types so we would end up consuming quite a bit of time. It was doing terrible damage to my snack quota. My lunch was also taking a hammering - quite literally, the hamburger buns were disintegrating, and the cheese was more of a goo that oozed now that the daytime temperatures were scorching. A few times, I'd declared it, "absolutely fine," when I'd flicked off some germinating mould. I'd make the buns up first thing, but by noon, I was finding they'd already been eaten. I was still at least three days from Seiad Valley, and I started to worry it would be like Sierra City, with slim resupply pickings, forcing me to overcome my cynicism around instant mashed potatoes, the foodstuff of the devil.

There was, of course, the option of diverting to Etna, a town originally christened Rough and Ready. Not that long ago, it had renamed itself after its flour mill, which was named, of course, after a rather ferocious volcano in Sicily. I was reluctant to squander the head of steam I'd built up, but then the night before Jeff and I were due to part ways, my research revealed I had to choose between a seventeen-mile day, or twenty-five-mile day, on account of a water and flat ground shortage. Worst of all, an unusually gigantic hill stood between my current camp spot and the next possible one. Essentially it boiled down to a choice between crying now or crying later. That's how Etna became the arbitrating factor: selling itself outright by asserting it was the friendliest town on the PCT. With claims like that, who better to judge than I? If I really pushed myself, I could rush the twenty-three miles to the highway and do a zero on the Sunday. Jeff, who didn't do zeroes, converted his beliefs on that matter too.

Starting at three in the morning, I left Jeff to his slumber and inched my way down the steep descent towards the highway, refusing to break for even ten minutes. Lunch was confined to a twenty-minute stop at twelve o'clock. As I trudged on, the cooling woodland enveloped me once again. Behind me, I knew Jeff would be on the chase, and my precious ego demanded I stay ahead for as long as possible. From deep below, eerie mournful bellows reverberated around the valleys, a maelstrom of agonised moans all chiming in together. I could only liken it to the score underpinning a horror film, with the occasional ominous clanging of a bell

211

signifying the passing of time. It was only when I stopped to filter water from a cowpat-splatted spring that it all made sense.

****

Chapter ten

Just one day

Step ten is the stuff fridge magnets are made of, or the more modern Facebook memes. Behind the perky posit, of course, one might be vaguely aware it reflects an aspiration of the publisher, rather than reality. In true addict style, AA has an entire tiny booklet of them, known collectively as the 'Just for Today' card. Whenever I felt overwhelmed by fatigue, or the soreness in my legs became unbearable as the day ploughed on, or by the head demons inciting themselves into a frenzy, I would try to recite as many as I could, starting with the first.

Just for today, I will try to live through this day only and not tackle my whole life problem at once. I can do something for twelve hours that would appal me if I felt I had to keep it up for a lifetime.

And getting to the end of that, I would realise I had blanked out the rest of them. I carried the card with me but lodged within a Ziploc holding my electronics, deep inside my backpack. I could only peruse it each night as I typed out the day's events. It proved a slightly more sophisticated self-check than, "everybody fed, no one dead," assessment of my day's accomplishments.

Jeff delighted in telling everyone we passed that I had a laptop in my rucksack. Previously, I'd seen a photograph on a PCT Facebook group mocking a former hiker for doing precisely the same. I'd inwardly twitch. Granted it was a much sturdier laptop than mine, but I can be so thin-skinned it was an effort not to take it personally. I'd committed myself to writing a thousand words a day, and astonishingly I was sticking to it. The words were mostly to be discarded, but useful for monitoring where my thoughts were at. It was my form of a daily inventory, but in long form. Exceptionally long form.

Just for today, I will have a quiet half hour all by myself and relax. During this half hour, sometime, I will try and get a better perspective of my life.

The problem with long adventures is that it all mushes into random events and acts, with little context as days blend into the interminable, "I walked up, and then I walked down, and then I walked up again. For twenty-five jeffing miles. Now my legs hurt, and my head has not shut up all day." I'd kept blogs in the past, but they tended to be heavily edited into a jolly, "I'm having a good, but rather dangerous time of it. Glad you're not here!"

I was grumpy when Jeff caught me long before our four o'clock deadline. The predictable but seemingly ceaseless downhill to town tortured my impatient legs. In the distance, we could hear cars and bikes hurtling around the mountain road, though we were still several miles from it ourselves. Jeff confirmed the hotel could take me as well as him and, best of all, the manager would collect us for a nominal fee. Using a very thin stream of service, Jeff arranged for them to pick us up at five from the roadside. I'd conceded I wasn't going to make it by four, punishing myself mentally for the missed deadline.

Just for today, I will adjust myself to what is, and not try to adjust everything to my own desires. I will take my 'luck' as it comes and adjust myself to it.

The footpath beneath was rocky and uneven, rushing, I frequently tripped, barely avoiding the full face-splattering I feared. A tiny pebble found its way into my shoe, thwarting my haste. Many hikers swear by ankle gaiters to prevent picking up debris, but I'd opted against, having binned the calf-high ones Bex had gifted me, and had rarely been affected. I hankered for zeroes for many reasons, but this was my first Sunday off trail, allowing me to attend, via Zoom, one of my regular weekly meetings, constructed around the *Just For Today* card. We'd kick off the meeting by taking it in turn to read the 'Just For Todays'. Then, one by one, we'd pile in with whatever stood out for us that week. I always smiled at Old Marjorie tutting as someone read aloud, *"Just for today I will be happy, most folks are as happy as they make up their minds to be."* She'd compromised it by replacing the word 'happy' with 'satisfied.' She was always riled by the whole notion of choosing to be happy. I can't say I wildly disagreed with her.

Caked with dirt, every inch of us shambolic and overheated, Jeff and I slumped roadside, the dusty and rocky parking lot offered nothing in the form of seating nor shade from the unrelenting afternoon sun. It was just gone four-thirty, and by checking the time, it occurred to Jeff he had no text confirming our extraction back to civilisation. Stranded with no phone reception, there was little to do but be indecisive: the road now deserted. He apologised over and over, but it really wasn't necessary. We mulled over one of us

214

hitching into town, but then how would we get the message back that the car was or wasn't coming? It only mattered because the town's restaurant was due to close at seven. We sat there in quiet contemplation, with only streams of sweat racing down my back to distract my thoughts.

Just for today I will be agreeable, I will look as well as I can, dress becomingly, talk low, act courteously, criticise not one bit, not find fault with anything and not try to improve or regulate anybody except myself.

The hotel manager, Shannondoah, turned up on the button, informing us the restaurant was expecting us and just to be sure to have ordered by seven. We didn't need to rush - the owner would hold for us. She'd also be doing our laundry; we were merely to dump all our clothes in the basket provided and take it to the office door. "Oh, and by the way," she said, "we have the best hiker box you've ever seen." That was inarguable: well-organised and tidied into separate containers, it even had expensive women's razors, spare Ziplocks, chocolate bars and all sorts of lotions and potions, as well as a wide selection of DVDs. I wondered who the hell had thought to bring a DVD player with them!

It took just over a half hour to detangle my hair before I could dive in the shower and slather it in conditioner from the hiker box. The razor grappled at my underarm hair. I was taken by how draughty I felt after. I dressed myself in loaner clothes - a hotch-potch of mismatched, ill-fitting attire donated to the hotel just for us to use on zero days, permitting all of our clothes to be decontaminated. I then hobbled off to the restaurant. The chef, cum-waiter, scurried between the kitchen and dining room, no longer able to afford staff during Covid. He'd reduced his usually substantial menu to pizza and salads. 'The Greek salad, no olives', and the 'Vegetarian pizza, no olives, please', humanised me. Nothing was too much trouble for him. Ten minutes later, he came over to say he'd just received a telephone order for a vegetarian pizza, no olives. He asked if this was the norm for vegetarians. It was my honour to confirm that all pizzas were ruined by the presence of an olive, and that yes, if he ever updated his menu, he should eradicate them.

Just for today..., I will do somebody a good turn and not get found out. If anyone knows of it, it will not count. An edict, thankfully qualified later by *Just for today, I will have a programme. I may not follow it exactly, but I will have it.*

I find it difficult to decline a round of applause for acts of public service, but any future vegetarian visitors to Bob's Ranch House can thank me in writing for my dedication to the cause of eliminating olives from pizzas. Whoever had said Etna was the friendliest town had done them a disservice. They were also the happiest townsfolk I met, and it was infectious.

The next day I tuned in for the AA meeting, and wondered where Old Majorie had gone. She had died the previous week. I presumed her to be happy about her wish to be dead finally coming true but, I learned, despite being eighty-eight she'd been furious. With nearly fifty years of sobriety, she succeeded in the ultimate accolade for people like us: to die sober. My heart broke when I found out only ten people could attend her funeral. She deserved hundreds and would have had that in ordinary times. Hers was the third death that month, all from cancer and none from Covid, of someone I knew in the fellowship. I knew them because they'd opted to stick with recovery, no matter what.

Just for today, I will be unafraid, especially I will not be afraid to enjoy what is beautiful, and to believe that as I give to the world, so the world will give to me.

I took a second shower after the meeting, taking the time to shave my legs too. The hairs on the front of my legs had all but worn away. I fingered a large lump on the base of my spine, now grown to the size of a tangerine. I could only assume it was benign: the result of the near-constant pressure imposed by my rucksack. Trying to assess it in the mirror, I was taken by how dramatically I'd lost weight since my last inspection. My ribs stuck out, especially around my sternum, and were it not for a belly button, I think my shrivelled stomach would have become a loin cloth. My boobs were now delicate flaps of skin. My body was finally cleaving fat laid down in the 1980s from my rear, pleasing me no end.

I padded across the tiny town to the nearby supermarket. A cheerful cashier pointed me in the direction of sunscreen. Alas, the hat selection all came with alcohol motifs, bar one plain black one. I shoved it on my head, crushing down my unrestrained, frizzy auburn hair, now tempered with blonde streaks, and headed off for a second breakfast. As I queued up for a milkshake and more coffee, a man

216

tapped me on the shoulder to mention that, from behind, I looked like Cousin It from the Munsters. He assured me repeatedly he intended it as a compliment.

Just for today, I will try to strengthen my mind, I will learn something useful, I will not be a mental loafer, I will read something that requires effort, thought and concentration.

It took me bloody ages to find out that he meant Cousin Itt from the Addams Family, described by Wikipedia as a diminutive, hirsute being, composed entirely of floor length hair, wearing a black bowler hat and sunglasses.

Just for today, I will not show anyone that my feelings are hurt, they may be hurt but I will not show it. But I can always write about it and call him an arse.

****

Take the pain, be amazed

It is always darkest before dawn, so they say. It's also coldest too, which is why I sometimes wondered at the wisdom of getting up before five in the morning. I must have remained befogged for quite some time after my legs had started the daily grind. Despite anticipating a dearth of water sources, a consequence of walking along a ridgeline for many miles, I pottered off down a side trail with streams galore. If there had been a trail sign, I was oblivious to it, and some two hours later, my phone indicated I was precisely in the middle of nowhere. I could only conclude my maps had broken.

Time slows down when things are dawning in my head. In the thick of the dense wood, the centre of a vast green splodge on Google Maps, my panic zipped from cell to cell. Pausing to pray and waiting for a silence I could tune into, I was struck by sounds of tinkering and twittering, and the occasional shrieks, of a family playing deeper within the valley. I wasn't quite in the middle of nowhere after all. Reluctantly, I had to concede I'd gone wrong, and I'd be retracing my steps for at least a couple of hours. An hour later, to my astonishment, because this never ordinarily happened, Google Maps revealed a dotted line, indicating a sister trail I could return to the PCT on. In reality, not even a faint path existed for me to follow. I nearly tumbled into a dollop of bear scat as I scrambled between bushes, my hands red raw from scampering. Holes appeared between the tread of my shoes, roughened by the gravelly ground. Three and a half hours after I'd left camp that morning, I scampered back onto the trail, livid with myself. I had only reduced my quest to get to Canada by two miles.

Jeff had opted to embark on a full marathon as he left that morning, a distance well beyond my abilities. Including these pointless miles, I finally called time on my day after twenty-eight miles, proving me wrong yet again. There was no sign of Jeff. Instead, a man calling himself Compass inadvertently rubbed my nose in my folly. He'd pitched just off the trail at the head of a disused dirt road. Out of respect for his own time on trail, I tried and failed to pitch my tent on rubbly ground far from him, but the ground was impenetrable by my stakes. I'd bent one in the process of trying to bang it in with a rock. Tent choice is key, and one downside of going for a very lightweight single-lined tent is that there's an absence of frame, relying on my hiking poles to prop up either side. Without being able to pin it in, the tent was useless. Cowboy camping would have been a solution, but the mosquitoes remained the voracious vampires of the night. Bees still found me deliciously attractive. Compass accommodated me pitching right next to him, even picking up his framed tent to move it slightly across, giving it a good shake at the same time to repel the two bumblebees even keener to encroach on him. A large family of deer circled around us, and knowing how much they love human sweat, I cautioned him to bring his trekking poles inside. Jeff had already lost one of his cork-gripped handles to a marmot. I'd hate to imagine what damage a deer could do. As it was, this lot seemed content to play kiss-chase around our tents the entire night, tripping over my guidelines on more than one occasion.

An annoying trail phrase is to 'embrace the suck.' Most days had a bucket-load of it. It was not all meandering streams, coursing through vibrant green fields swaying with verbenas, chamomile and buttercups. All of which might be dutifully attended to by fluttering butterflies and hovering cerulean dragonflies, above which hawks, eagles and kingfishers soar. In more open lands, flying crickets rapid-clacked as they launched themselves metres high. *Clack, clack, clack*, like an old football rattle.

Leaving behind the rugged grey ridge top, I was glad to plough down back into my favourite, and cooler, alpine mountainside, with its oaks and conifers jostling for space. Beneath them lived the rich undergrowth of ferns mangled with spruce and shrub. I could lose myself absorbing the sounds of trunks battered from the hammering of unsighted woodpeckers, or the squeaking of squirrels and chipmunks as they frolicked away. Deep within the forest, I would mindlessly wander along only to happen upon a full facial assault of grassland and azure blue sky. It always perplexed me as to why meadows existed at all: why the trees hadn't just taken over, like they had everywhere else on the mountain.

Now in the height of summer, the fields were plush with dots of yellows, whites, reds and purples, all kinds of flowers crying up to the sun. The smell of wild chives, licorice and lilies would waft around before nose blindness eliminated them. My legs would whack against Indian paintbrush and tall lupins, and in turn they would smear their pollen across my bug-repellent trousers, enticing butterflies to dance around me. Others would congregate atop little pebbles sat in the streams. The immutable ones would force me to splash through the water, drowning my toes, making my shoes heavy. Some, I observed, loved life living in shit: any dropping or turd left behind by a coyote or bear, would be smothered by dainty purple and white basking lepidoptera. It was these ones that would ensure I would carefully place each foot down to avoid squashing them, but not for altruistic reasons.

At one meadow, I rested up where the tree-line finished and the grasses waved around in the cooling breeze. A particularly fuzzy bee took it upon itself to go for a little off-piste caper up my trouser leg. Unable to orientate myself to the frantic buzzing, it spitefully alerted me to its peril when I stood up. I banged out my own version of *'Knick Knack Paddywhack'* and in return, it gifted me its sting, leaving me with a saucer-wide burn. Contrary to what I'd been taught at school, bees do not die after their injection of irritation, they exist to sting and sting and sting some more, then give one more sting for luck. Only then, did this bee make a dignified exit of my right trouser leg, none harmed for its little adventure. Five large bumps sprang forth, the largest a saucer-wide burn at the top of my thigh, the smallest a round fifty-pence piece near my ankle. They itched and smouldered for days.

Dropping out of the alpine into Saied Valley is akin to arriving at the furnaces of hell. One is unable to avoid the long asphalt road hugging the bank around the Klamath river. The sound of the rushing watercourse which cuts through valley added a perverse torture to my dehydrating body. Enveloped by private land, the rivers offered no place to climb down to leech some of its water. The sanctuary of the town, an oasis of cold drinks and hot food, rests on the opposite embankment, all the while the bridge to connect the valleys sits three miles to the east.

Practically on my knees, I pried open the stiff door of the village grocery store and crept in, only to be requested I leave my pack on the sidewalk. It was well stocked for the hiking community. I picked up a new pair of socks, which oddly came with a free Slush Puppy, giving me brain freeze. I bought a second. I declined the invitation for a barbeque to head on to the Tavern for a homemade vegetarian burger and some coffee. With little by way of desserts, I discovered the orgasm that is a Root Beer Float, a four-hundred calorie glass of sugary delight. One is never enough, of course, I had a second as I sat out the mid-afternoon heat. I struggled to make conversation with my fellow hikers, one of whom was calling it a permanent day. I declined her kind offer to swap shoes.

I had a nine-and-a-half-mile brutal uphill dominating the afternoon, rendering me in no hurry to depart, despite knowing dusk could make my travels more complicated. The proprietor informed me that Jeff, the bloody lunatic, had left about ten minutes before my arrival at around one o'clock, just an hour before the day hit its horrific high. Two hours later, I began my own four and a half thousand-foot ascent of Kangaroo mountain. It kickstarts this range of many buttes - as the hills are commonly called around these parts, tickling my inner twelve-year-old. My ambition was to get to the top where I could replenish water from Kangaroo Spring, critical as the lower ground spring had run dry. Six hours after leaving the bar, in the dying of the day, I collapsed at the side of a murky pond. The dimming light revealed it was riddled with wriggling larvae as water skaters whizzed back and forth protecting their territory when I plunged in my water bottle. A few hundred metres beyond it were two tents. Relying now on my headlamp, I was able to squeeze in besides a small one-person tent. "Is that you, Jeff?" was how I ruined his slumber.

Dawn rudely broke once again. We bushwhacked through prolifically flowery meadows, then stuttered across a brief rocky section until the path carved its way through woodland with a difference. Giant firs, the highest I'd ever seen, stretched my neck as far back as my rucksack would permit. Beneath them, the forest was hollow: no undergrowth subsisted whatsoever, merely scatterings of deadened pine needles, dry snapped branches and the occasional fallen tree. Otherwise, it was sparse, empty and soundless. Splodges of barren land existed for no reason. Former meadows, I presumed, they were now nothing but naked swatches of ground as if someone had turned off nature's power. It would have made sense if it were a burn area, but the trees surrounding me were stoic and thriving.

Jeff was enthusiastic to call it quits earlier than planned but we were dismayed to find few sites suitable to pitch two tents. As the clock crept on, we happened upon a large clearing, previously well used, about a hundred metres off trail. Lumbering down to it, we hailed the occupants already residing there. They were swift to suggest they didn't want company, compelling us on. Too shattered to argue, we meekly tramped on. A half mile further down the trail, Jeff spied another gap in the woodland, kicking away dried cow pats in a vain attempt to clear two spots. By now, I had few standards, but sleeping amongst cow shit, crusty or otherwise, rapidly became one of them. A further half mile later, my eyes battling against the fatigue, I gave in to my limits and we assembled our tents on the prickly ground part-adjacent to a remote dirt road. Far from ideal, we could only hope no traffic would come. A single line of faint tyre tread persisted on the dirt track from who knows when. The view, however, was expansive and heart-stirring, overlooking pitching hills of blues and greens. I couldn't have been more apathetic.

As I put away the remainder of my dinner, the wind picked up, rattling the sides of my tent. Elsewhere the ominous ringing of cowbells clamoured. Jeff's loud, "Uh-oh!" meant he too envisaged a thorough stampeding at some point in the night. They were my final thoughts as I passed out with exhaustion, long before the sun crashed down on another day.

****

The wrongs of work, rest and play

I suspected I remained motionless throughout the night, not stirring at all right up until I registered Jeff's, "Wakey, wakey PI!" Once I did move, my hips screamed out their pain. They truly hurt, they couldn't or wouldn't lie on that matter. Packing up was an excruciating affair. I wobbled off, leaving Jeff to catch up. We'd agreed to converge in Oregon later in the morning, but it wasn't long before he scuttled past me.

Oregon! I, a slob of the first order, had teetered, tottered, stumbled, shlepped, staggered and crawled across the third longest state in America, on a trail which ducked, dived and by design, did its utmost to avoid an efficient route from one hill to the next. As I limped around the corner, a stark wooden sign indicated Canada was a mere nine hundred and fifty-eight miles further north. Moments later, the two men who'd shooed us away the night before ambled into the tiny clearing. They'd wanted to apologise in person. Jeff informed them we'd walked nearly seventeen hundred miles, and this was our first experience of rudeness. In a country as vast as America, space was still highly-contested.

Clearly neither of them had cats, because that kind of atrocious territorial behaviour is quite the norm. Try getting into a double bed with a cat already lying across it, and one becomes accustomed to impertinence on a whole other level. I still yearned to wake up to my cat's bum in my face, which is what used to constitute a good morning. A friend sent regular pictures of him sleeping in a strange repose, but it didn't quash that urge I had upon waking to reach out to stroke a warm, vibrating body that wasn't there.

Apologies accepted, photos snapped, register signed, there was little else to do but lumber on for yet another quarter of a century of miles.

"How would you improve the PCT, PI?" Jeff enquired as we roamed through the first few pretty miles of Oregon.

"I'd give Washington to the Canadians, Jeff," I replied, and in one fell swoop, I reduced the PCT by five hundred and five miles. Walking across two more states was mind-boggling. Being so bodily tired, and with such on-going aches and pains, I fantasized endlessly about slobbing around yet another nondescript hotel room as my shoes disintegrated by the hour. My blue-socked foot peeped out and occasionally jammed into a miscreant stone or branch waylaid trailside. A detour to Ashland beckoned nearly thirty miles ahead.

We spent a lot of time identifying cultural differences as we mooched along together. Jeff hadn't even a passport, true to stereotype, but when one lives in a country the size of America, it isn't necessarily small-mindedness that keeps people there, but rather the sheer number of places and climes to wonder at. That, plus little by way of vacation time available. Having a 'few days off' from work is frowned upon, and Jeff rarely used his holiday allowance, as is the American way.

When one lives on a tiny island which rains a lot, demanding the urge to warm up is practically considered a human right by most people I know. Time off from work is also sacrosanct, but I had certainly experienced the pressure of presenteeism in my own career. In my first year of sobriety, I'd stupidly changed jobs, as many are wont to do. My new manager was obsessed with bars and enforced social time to make us, in his view, all the better, more effective, more harmonious colleagues. He seemed to require us all to drink late into the night. I hadn't told him I was trying to live a sober life, thinking it was none of his business. Going to yet another jeffing pub to drink yet another insipid fizzy fruit juice simply had zero appeal a few months in. It came to a head when I'd refused at nine in the evening, following thirteen hours of meetings, to go and be social. Notwithstanding that the following day, I'd be getting up at four in the morning to catch a train to London to do a job that wasn't strictly my responsibility: he'd already sacked my counterpart whose job it had been. I suspected I was facing the same result, but he had to keep me on for a bit. After eight hard months, I couldn't reconcile myself any longer with the company culture. Ironically it is a company which preaches to students the importance of balancing work, rest and play. I quit. I had enough money sloshing around, I could truly put recovery first, to eke out a living from writing and consulting. Career suicide looking back, but I doubted I'd have stayed sober for much longer.

The following day we lurched into Callahan's restaurant; an upmarket eatery attached to a plush resort. The waiter cocked up our order, declining to charge us to make amends. Only I learnt the waiter would have to pay for it out of his own wages as penance. I tipped him the same value as I ate. Jeff explained that it was the norm in the US to dock wages for human errors, but it seemed all kinds of wrong to me. We said our goodbyes as Jeff, in typical fashion, was shunning rest days. Getting into town in between lunches allowed me a few moments to peruse market stalls full of arts and crafts, and other souvenirs I'd love to buy but wouldn't and couldn't.

The sidewalks were bustling with tables and chairs, many occupied. People revelled in their re-acquired freedoms. In the UK, excited chatter began to ripple around as the government suggested that August be spent 'eating out to help out,' pledging various discounts to induce Britons to partake in a more sociable summer, and to help kickstart the economy, as well as, of course, adding pounds to the growing obesity industry. As is my contrary way, after days outside, the option of relaxing indoors was now a luxury I could not resist. Life was resuming at long last for many. Dotted around the streets stood stands of hand sanitisers and signs reminding us six feet apart is better than six feet under, but the scent of rebirth hung in the air.

Walking without a pack was now nearly more uncomfortable than walking with one. I consoled myself with two fresh strawberry milkshakes as pre-lunch drinks, with a side-serving of coffee. I bimbled down the main drag once again, just missing an act of vandalism. A restaurant's glass facades had been smashed to smithereens. Several police cars were in attendance as the store worker swept up the shards, but there was no real agitation to gawk at.

Weaving around the policemen, I popped into an outdoors shop with a small offering of lightweight running shoes. I'd also needed new tips on one of my hiking poles, much relieved the staff was happy to fix that for me, offering me free wi-fi whilst I waited and showing me to a sofa to collapse on. I loaded up my shopping basket with various specialist ready-meals costing a small fortune. They are packed with dehydrated vegetables, making them vaguely more appetising than ramen noodles and plasticky dried macaroni cheese. There was a launderette a mile and a half away from my hotel: I hadn't thought to check the distance. It helped break in my new shoes: not being brand-tied, I risked blisters by always chopping and changing, though I was rarely afflicted anymore.

Taking two days to rest up in Ashland had on paper seemed a marvellous idea. Regrettably the room above mine was occupied by a pair of shaggers, who moaned and groaned, and rhythmically bashed the bed at midnight and again at six in the morning. I'd treated myself to a slightly more upmarket hotel for a few extra dollars per night, but it didn't buy any superior sound insulation. My two-night stay was catastrophic for my minimum mileage per day. I now had twenty-two and a half miles to crush out daily and no more days off if I wanted to make it to Canada.

Oregon, the rumour factory has it, is flat. By now hikers are fit and trail-savvy, and so it's touted to be reasonable to complete around thirty miles a day. I couldn't envisage managing anything close to that. Worst of all, was the boredom that seeped in mid-afternoon. The hours and miles seemingly expanded from around two o'clock onwards as I tried to maximise the daytime hours, all the while combating a diminishing pace and pain threshold.

I was dropped back at the trailhead by a twenty-something trail angel who'd already notched up the Appalachian Trail. She had been forced to quit the PCT with a hip injury having completed five hundred miles. It had taken eight months, and several operations, before she could walk unaided. She was young too. It was a salutary reminder of how fragile our bodies can be.

I struggle to wrangle the tensions between work, rest and play. Finding the right balance between competing necessities is the challenge of recovery, and it isn't a one-size fits all remedy, but unique to the sufferer. Whenever I have fun, I feel guilty, whenever I work in offices, I resent it, and rest - well insomnia is all part of being middle-aged and menopausal, no? Sleeping in the wilderness wasn't helping one jot. Especially not when lightning struck, setting alight the first wildfire of the season, which was now roaring across the dry forests just a few miles south of Ashland.

The next day, the sky grimy, acrid smoke lingered, hazing out the vistas. The state of Oregon had already announced a ban on all recreational fires, a month earlier than typical, but they couldn't command the weather systems. Back on trail, thunder cracked back and forth. I dodged any actual rainfall, but I could not completely avoid vast tranches of damp foliage. Once again, the PCT became a vacated destination.

225

****

The levelling of the hierarchy

After several consecutive nights alone, I was always thrilled if a fellow hiker turned up to share a campsite with me. I'd feel oddly spurned if they were continuing on with their hikes. Sometimes, I'd intrude on others camped up. Then as I dined, I'd surreptitiously appraise their gear from afar trying to ascertain information about them - ostensibly, I supposed, to form an opinion about my fellow 'woodspeople'.

One night, a loud, excitable and much-welcomed primary school teacher provided the entertainment as she set about experimenting with her new tarp. It struck me as the most pointless kind of shelter, a six-inch gap between the fabric and the ground ensured every critter could visit - even the monsters of the night. If that were not bad enough, her ground sheet spread out beyond the boundary of the fabric: any rainfall would undoubtedly trickle its way inside, shaping any slumbering occupant into an island.

The following night, an identical tent to mine had been much more sloppily erected. I silently denounced it as a rather floppy affair by my tauter standards. Two women shared a two-person tent, I pondered how they didn't stifle one another. Many of these so-called two-person tents are stretching the truth a considerable tad. More suitable for one and a half at best in my esteemed opinion. Mine, as Jeff would say, was quite a substantial piece of real estate, but at least I had room to lose stuff.

I had unwittingly joined the secret hiking pastime of judging, although in true alkie style, I don't judge, I condemn. I perceived an invisible hierarchy to hiking, and in Oregon I became particularly aware that I was within its confines. I'd become used to people stepping aside so I could pass without hindrance, whether or not I technically had the 'right of way'. I'd started taking it for granted, and a few times, I was quite obstructive. My defence, your honour, was that I had become incurious to my surroundings that I forgot my manners as I trudged mile after meandering mile. It was easy to see why thru-hikers might give off an air of entitlement to other users of the trail.

I passed by two men and a donkey, then a married couple, one on a mule. The size of the beast, as well as its hooves, starkly

226

reminded me that it was my turn to step away from the path, irrespective of the incline. I enquired if it was okay to take photos, and then with a yes, I tried to stroke it. It turned out the mule hated PCT hikers. Mind you, given the smell of me, I could understand everything giving me a wide berth. Later, a trio of people sprung apart when I rounded a corner as if I'd caught them doing something truly atrocious. It transpired they had been standing less than two metres apart. They confessed quite readily. Now standing in a neat line, I remarked they looked like they were about to greet royalty. Two curtseys and a deep bow, I felt suitably revered and promised not to tell anyone.

Adding to my general gripiness, the water carries were getting longer and longer. I felt burdened and resentful with the additional weight. One's pack tends to lighten up as each five hundred miles are discharged. In theory one realises what one can live without, but also as possessions break, they are replaced by things which weigh less, if not done without completely. Notionally this was true, but no one had yet adequately explained the phenomena of it feeling like the pack gets heavier the more mileage one has under one's belt.

I couldn't understand why water remained in such short supply, given that this section seemed more rainforest than desert, until I detoured and discovered it was all being stored at Crater Lake. It is the deepest lake in the United States, albeit it's actually a sunken volcano from which not a single stream leaks from its sides - a fact that I found both reassuring, and frustrating as I had to climb the damned side, of course in the heat of the midday sun.

My hauling of self and backpack up this gigantic egg cup was rewarded with America's worst pizza, clearly reheated from frozen in the state-run restaurant. There were no free refills on the coffee, and a second cup required a re-queuing. This struck me as about as anti-American as one could get. Disproving the AA adage that no one likes change, it's more accurate to say I don't like change that I don't like. Yet, when I returned to the UK, I knew I would quickly re-adapt to paying for individual coffee once again. I conceded in my best food-critic snark that the brownie was nice, as was the ice-cream that it came with. I bagged up some of the cloying pizza for later and headed outside towards the rim of the volcano, where I consoled myself with a visit to the other eatery, this one a cafe. I bought myself a full fat coke and a cup of mixed tropical fruit for a considerable chunk of change. Whimsically, I then added a large cornetto to combat the inexorable summer heat. I waddled outside to sit and appreciate the crater from a man-made wall. A bright day had scores of visitors admiring the cobalt waters encircling two rock formations: Wizards Island and Phantom Ship. My first big lick of the Cornetto swept the ice-cream off its cone, and I could watch on forlornly as it barrelled down the inside of the crater, leaving me holding a miserably dry, thin wafer to crunch on. Lunch then decided to make its presence felt; I dashed across the parking lot to the mercifully open toilets and reduced my body weight substantially.

I joined two older men at a spacious campsite that night, one of them opting to sleep in a hammock. It intrigued me: how would one roll over in the night, especially if one hates sleeping on their back? I was also curious as to how one protects oneself from the never-ending onslaught of savage mosquitoes. He assured me it was far superior to an inch-thick air-blown sleeping pad when one's bones started to creak. In turn, they asked me why thru-hikers didn't slow down to enjoy the views; why we had this cumbersome gait, with eyes cast downwards as we plodded along. We ought to look up and out, they informed me. They asked me how long I had left, and I replied I had to be gone by the twelfth of September because of my visa. "You'll never make that!" they exclaimed. I knew it was tight, but I was getting nearly a marathon a day done, keeping my hopes alive. "Oregon's just a long green tunnel, go to Washington - it's far better," they attested. "There's nothing to see in Oregon," the other emphasized as the sun set over the rim of the awe-inspiring Crater Lake.

I'd anticipated I'd be gently floating down towards sea-level, and the Bridge of the Gods, a giant staple attaching Washington to Oregon. A day later I huffed past a sign that said, 'Oregon's highest point.' "Oregon is flat," is the biggest myth on the PCT. Aside from the crater, which is technically not on the PCT, there are still a great many pointless ups and downs. That it is not quite as steep as northern California is more than compensated by having an abundance of ankle-shattering, joint-breaking, teeth-gritting lava fields for hikers to traverse. They are huge, rubbly, rock-strewn sections of blackened, and sometimes reddened, paths of hell. Divine

228

to look at, just like a hungry tiger might be, up close they are pretty enraging entities to come into contact with. I simply called them lava turds only to be corrected and told they were talus and scree. Regardless of what matter it is, there was no trail to speak of, just miles of uneven, rough fragments which impeded any speed, and brought any soft-souled, sofa-surfing, poorly-shod person, such as I, to dismal tears. The forested areas which separated the hardened lava flows were made insufferable by the plagues of mosquitoes, forcing walkers to wear bug-nets over their heads, invoking a humid claustrophobia. Occasionally, day hikers could be spied wearing them with a mask underneath. I suspected they also carried cylinders of oxygen in their small packs.

Scraggy bounded by, this time with news that another women hiker I vaguely knew had quit the trail with shin splints, just like Goblin. It never ceased to amaze me I was still plodding on at all, and even more astounded when I lunched with two younger, fitter men in their twenties. They'd skipped a few hundred miles, having fallen behind schedule. When they lit up a bong, things became more transparent for all of us in different ways.

"How many miles are you doing today?" Was an oft-cited conversation opener yet loaded question. The added weight of bravado crept into the rhetoric of the thru-hiking community here more so than anywhere else. That could equally be a figment of my terribly sensitive imagination. I was still short of managing thirty miles a day, yet I refused to permit myself any respite from traipsing at least thirteen hours at a time. I cajoled myself just a little bit further each day but to no great avail. I'd set a target each day, break the day into sections and race against time to complete it, telling the foliage and terrain how much I despised it when it impaired my flow. I was nowhere near what people were saying was the norm for Oregon. Those prone to competition boasted of thirty-five to forty miles per day. It could be late afternoon, and they'd mentioned they were just going to pop out another twenty miles and then call it for the night. Others talked of whether they were going to challenge the sixty-two mile in twenty-four hours record, set in by Dixie, a female thru-hiking YouTuber. It used to be, "when did you start?" would ignite the cringe. Now the further I pushed along the trail, the less this question piqued my defensive disposition. On one level, though, it merely indicated that I had simply traded one worry for another, just like when I lose weight, I transfer any residual self-loathing onto another body part. Clearly, the joys of being dysfunctional are limitless.

I extended the next day's mileage by striving for a so-called proper 'campground'. It had sounded alluring simply because it had a pit latrine. Having limped in, I was miffed to find it out of order. A simple hole in the ground, covered by a white plastic toilet seat, with no flushing capabilities at any time, wasn't 'working'. The place, however, was thronging with people, making ablutions somewhat problematic.

The weekend residents are less inclined to follow the etiquette of 'hiker midnight': the cessation of noise either at dusk or eight or nine o'clock: no one really seems to quite know. Oddly, I found appeasement amidst the sounds of strangers. With America opening up again, and decent weather, there were fresh interlopers into the wilderness. As I closed in on trailheads, I'd encounter day hikers blasting music aloud from their phones pinned to the straps of their daypacks. It sort of distracted me, but one could see why it is deemed nuisance behaviour, especially if there were two or three in a group, each one belting out a different track. I failed miserably playing 'name that song' but then I am rubbish at popular culture at the best of times.

Another trifling matter adversely impacting my sense of joie de vivre was the return of condensation inside my tent. When my sleeping bag was a soggy mess at the footwell, I'd have to squander time drying it out as soon as the day warmed up and a sunny spot could be basked in, thwarting my day's ambitions to push hard. Perhaps though, my lagging frustration was born out of the reality I was only just beginning the second half of my daily odyssey. The romance of the trek, if there had ever been any, turned into a dead bed. If one is to survive the middle bit, perhaps a heart of stone is all that is required.

The word *but* seemed to crop up frequently in conversation. Oregon is flat *but* there's a lot of mosquitoes. The Sierra is hard work, *but* you don't have to carry water. This campsite is fantastic *but* there's a lot of wind. It reminded me of the first time I'd heard someone say, "Don't be a moped," mimicking a rapid fire of '*but, but, but, but*'. But the further I travelled, the more I had the means to compare. Oregon is wonderful, but it's stuck between Washington and California, and there's something about not being nearly there yet that eats into morale. For me, it was just a delusion that the miles were easier, and big distances were readily possible. I suspected this mindset was compelling the ending of many a thru-hike amongst my fellows perhaps more so than injury. Too many thru-hikes now fraught, like mine, with compensating for too many zeros, or too much partying early on. If one hasn't quit before the Sierra, then this is the section of trail that seemed most probable to piss on one's chips.

Oregon was rendered little fun for all the time and distance pressures, not because of a lack of scenery or wonder. I was miserable pushing so hard, inducing a feeling of deprivation. One day, I'd chosen a shelter twenty-five miles into the future to be my reward, my *objet de motivation*. But then Shelter Cove happened, and before I knew it, I reasoned I could try for a resupply there. It meant I could skip Chemult, which had been my intended re-supply. Going to the Cove would forsake a night in a hotel. Still, I knew if I went into a town, I might as well have two because otherwise I wouldn't be able to say howdy to my friends back home. I really should go to an AA meeting, my guilt monkey would chime in. It was like being an active drunk again, telling myself I'm only popping into the shops to buy bread, only to find myself returning with a bottle of Bacardi, a can of coke, and a random colander.

But I really wanted to get to Washington, so I would have to stay as close to the trail as I could, and that would mean I ought to resupply at the expensive, but limited stores that populate the private campgrounds. People whined so much about the prices in these out of the way places, but what one was really buying was time. So that was how I accidentally found myself diverting to Shelter Cove. Truth be told, I was enticed by its ice-cream and burgers, coffee and picnic tables, and proper flushing toilets. Undoubtedly, it was a seductive money pit of loveliness. I tried awfully hard to muster up the energy in the heat of the afternoon to leave; to do the remaining eight miles, but then Dr Doolittle and Photo arrived, followed shortly after by Crocs. I had been hunting down the two German-speakers since they went into the Sierra two days before me, but I'd not crossed paths with them since. I learnt they'd been sewing in and out of the PCT post-Sierra, alleviating the pressure of the distances, and they seemed to be much happier for it. He was struggling with a recurring heel injury. Her previous crew-cut had grown starkly upright. I listened intently as they told me all about their experiences on the trail whilst imbibing a near-full jar of Nutella, kindly abandoned in one of the hiker boxes. "You're looking very skinny," Photo observed as I scraped the last of the hazelnut chocolate from the glass bottle.

Having been lured into spending the night there, which was hardly a mental battle of epic proportions, I put my tent up alongside the other members of the PCT hiking community. Then I grabbed a three-minute shower for two bucks missing out on two lads hawking pizza. The shower was a treat, coming as it did with industrial grade liquid soap in a huge container that took up much of the shower floor. I put on my wretched clothes immediately after.

My evening ended by pissing off another hiker who was using three of the six power sockets, her unwieldy plugs had blocked the access to the remaining three points, preventing the rest of us from charging our own stuff. I genuinely believed one of her battery packs was full, but she was clear: I was very wrong about that. She was equally clear she wasn't accepting my apology, and my attempts to do so made her more incendiary. I wanted to yell but I saved myself the bother. Besides we had a YouTuber in our midst, one of those who insisted on editing his videos loudly at night, and she was camped right next to him.

I reflected that evening that I might have only done sixteen miles to get to Shelter Cove, but I had passed the nineteen-hundred-mile marker. But that just meant there was still a bloody long way to go.

****

After the promises

Comparisons are said to be the thief of joy, and without doubt the full-time occupation of some committee members in my head. In Oregon, I discovered that this was not a strict truism. Using the barely-there internet at Shelter Cove, I discovered that my 'training schedule', although I was not actually training for anything, was more rigorous than Mo Farah's preparation for the London Olympics. Of course, I opted to remain conveniently oblivious to the fact he was running twice per day, whereas I was merely plodding along. Still, I was now fixed on a minimum of a marathon each and every day, and this blew my mind.

The wildlife was by now truly alive and plentiful, momentarily distracting me from tortured thoughts, and ever more tortured body parts. I received the filthiest of looks from a pine martin as it scuttled behind a log. I celebrated my one hundred and fortieth day on the PCT by playing a game of hide and seek with an indeterminate rodent as I rested upon a congregation of rocks overhanging a valley. Small clans of deer pootled about the place. Woodpeckers drilled manically above. Marmots would meep back and forth, and chipmunks darted left and right, while the squirrels, some nearly jet black, charged up the nearest trunk to play peekaboo from one side or other. I saw signs of bear: scratchings on bark, flattened nests and soft scat but nothing in the flesh.

The woodland was once again endless, trunks dressed in mossy jackets and downed trees in various states of decomposition batted about the ground. Unseen workers had recently cleared the trail - the telltale patches of fresh chainsaw dust scattered across the path. The smell of cut wood served to remind me that the trail was a man-made joy, even if the hiking wasn't always so. I shlepped past pond after pond, many cuddled by crusts of drying algae, others were adorned with lily pads. They billowed out the latest mosquito hatchlings. My head net dulled my habitat. Inexplicably my forehead remained a mass grave of their successful assaults, as did the tops of my fingers poking out from fingerless gloves. I had obtained more toothpaste at the store at Shelter Cove, slathering my hands and head with it. Scratching at their bites was the equivalent to mental ruminating: an enjoyable, but ultimately indulgent sabotaging of time.

Alcoholics are expert ruminators I was told. Whilst the rest of the world was growing up, and getting on with it, we were asking plaintively 'why?' It certainly occupied a few hours each day, but I was no nearer to discovering why I was doing this, nor in fact, what if anything I was getting out of it. And yet, conversely, curiosity is said to be a superpower. A questioning mind is thought to be a sign of intellect. Yet another speaker stated alcoholics are of above-average intelligence, the following speaker pointed out that only alcoholics say this, one never hears Al-Anons lauding our superior thought processes, let alone anyone else. When I look at the wreckage of my trashed life, my lost career, my lack of property, my failed marriage, my poor bank balance, my abysmal pension, I don't feel particularly clever.

I couldn't see much by way of change in my sense of wellbeing, and what I was gaining in physical fitness, I was losing in dexterity. The woman at the Shelter Cove shop had observed thru-hikers find using pens a real challenge. It was true: my handwriting, never particularly neat, had regressed to a childlike scrawl whenever I signed in at trail registers. I wondered how after a long-distance hike how one re-assimilates having done something so epic. Depression was bound to follow in all probability. Would I just end up back on the pills again? Another brick in the wall, with all the pointlessness of a hole in a doughnut.

Adventure, followed by wallowing sadness it is over, has plagued my whole life. I've done so many extraordinary things, and this most likely would be the last one. Age and poverty would mean I had no choice but to accept I have had more than my fair share of fun. This stark reality of my situation distressed me more than anything. As a child, it was not my choice to be dragged from country to country, but as an adult it was, and over time each escapade had to get bigger and better than the last, an addiction in itself. Now the music was stopping, and I was feeling the pressure of having to find a chair to sit on before they were all taken.

I ambled through the rugged Three Sisters Wilderness, the jewel of which is a glorious waterfall cascading down, framed within a cliff festooned with verdant conifers. Did it ever run dry? I stopped merely to photograph its irrefutable beauty, refusing the opportunity to linger as the site was already occupied by a couple enjoying quite the formidable picnic. Besides, I was in a groove. I followed the path through the bedazzling Obsidian Limited Entry area in remote Oregon. It is a highly-controlled zone and few are permitted to wander around it in order to preserve its fragility. The glittery pitch volcanic rock litters the trail, with large, sparkly blackened lumps embedded into the surroundings. The area is slightly other-worldly catching the sun's rays slicing through the canopy to rebound around my feet. Reverers of crystal believe obsidian absorbs negative energy and forces the observer to wake up to one's true self. In the first few years of sobriety, I had carried two small pieces of polished rose quartz to rub together when I was feeling impatient or anxious. Like a stress ball, but less imposing in one's back pocket. Then I realised I looked like I was just fiddling with an arse cheek to any casual bystander and had fallen out of the habit.

The future terrified me. I had no idea how I was going to begin to put it all back together. I am quick to make plans, and then ever quicker to abandon them. I raised my own cortisol level by dreading the long-term, and all the subsequent losses I was still to experience. My cat was already nine years old; I couldn't get a job; I was going to end up homeless, albeit properly homeless, not just between homes as I hoped. I was going to end up working in another dead-end job; to subsist to simply pay the bills so that people at the top of a tree can enjoy a lovely, healthy pension. And I knew if I kept carrying on thinking this way, I'd end up communist, and that would be tragic too. I really don't suit the colour red. Then, only then would I put on a podcast to remind myself it's all going to be okay, as long as I follow a few simple steps. Sometimes, I'd resort to reciting aloud *The Promises* as I wandered along to soothe my querulous mind.

If we are painstaking about this stage of our development, we will be amazed before we are halfway through. We are going to know a new freedom and a new happiness. We will not regret the past, nor wish to shut the door on it. We will comprehend the word serenity and we will know peace. No matter how far down the scale we have gone, we will see how our experience can benefit others. That feeling of uselessness and self-pity will disappear. Self-seeking will slip away. Our whole attitude and outlook upon life will change. Fear of people and of economic security will leave us. We will intuitively know how to handle situations which used to baffle us. We will suddenly realise that God is doing for us what we could not do for ourselves. Are these extravagant promises? We think not. They are being fulfilled among us; they will always materialise if we work for them.

As mantras go, it was beyond superfluous, but it placated, nonetheless. I had shifted my daily listenings to after lunch now, which was encroaching earlier into the morning. By eleven o'clock my keen eye would start to assess fallen logs: were they wide enough and high enough to offer easement? Calling it lunch was a misnomer in any case because I would have already walked for five or six hours by that point, sustained by my first breakfast of two French pastries and a second breakfast of two large bars of chocolate. I'd finally succumbed to buying the three-hundred calorie bundles of unadulterated pleasure, and ate two at a time, licking the melted chocolate from the wrapper with the fervency of a slobbering Labrador. I probably left streaks of dark smear around my chin and cheeks, but vanity was a different religion these days.

Lunch remained two dry cheese sandwiches. The humidity meant I could no longer make the buns more palatable with a few dollops of mayonnaise. Instead, I fluffed them up with a handful of dried cranberries and rinsed away the eggy aftertaste with another chocolate bar. Despite promising myself I'd try to keep to a reasonable diet throughout my hike, healthier snacks were no longer having any impact on the ever-gnawing hunger. All cereal bars had come to taste the same: dry cardboard crumbs with conscience-appeasing bits of indecipherable fruit or nut.

Not concentrating on an audiobook or an AA share until the afternoon, accorded time to explore the mornings in a different way, when I was more alert and unbothered by the monotony of traipsing up and down dale. It dawned on me that something peculiar was starting to happen: I'd find myself free of thought. Not zoned out, but free of any committee member chuntering away. For the first time in the history of ever, I had actually worn the mental demons out. My head morphed into a library with a strictly enforced policy of silence. In banishing them, there was not a murmuring for entire chunks of time, sometimes hours. When I suddenly discovered I was mid-afternoon, the revelry would fire up again as the tedium of the trek kicked in. Then it would quickly return to carnage up there once again.

The downside of this revolution of my mindset was it made it bloody difficult to think of things to type about. In my diary, I noted I'd spilled my dinner's pesto sauce all down my front, which hardly made for a riveting read later on. There was nothing new in that anyway, me and food spillage have a long and convoluted relationship, although I still retain the habit of being terribly careful with drinks. I could only conclude I finally understood serenity. It is literally peace of mind. A voiceless existence so I could just be, rather than do. It was not surreal happiness like I had presumed it was, nor the burbling of excitement one can feel for other reasons. That's optimism and hope. This was just a nothingness, an existence free of anxiety, not necessarily free of pain or noise, but just an absence of bothersome thoughts, or false pretenses. It was nothing more than a gentle appreciation of not feeling overwhelmed or overburdened. It was quite unlike any sense I had previously discerned.

Of course, like conditions on the trail, soon enough it would cease its casual meander, and the next level of hell would present itself. In Oregon, this was always going to be abominable lava turds to scramble, straining tendons in my feet and ankles, and impeding my progress considerably. The uncertain footing made the hiking arduous. The weather had deteriorated, and the rumbling of thunder stalked me as I lumbered downhill. Small droplets of rain became larger and more intrusive, splattering all over me as I embarked on yet another section filled with dead and dying trees. The higher I ventured, the more the landscape turned skeletal, bare and grey, before all semblance of life was eradicated, leaving nothing but miles and miles of mounds of ragged blackened rock. Underfoot there was nothing by way of dirt, sand or ground to smooth out the way. Just pockmarked chunks of dark rubble. Each step was now accompanied by the crunching and grinding of rough rock being bashed around as I followed a faint line curving around gigantic lumps of bedrock. Overhead, cracks of lightning spat out of an enraged sky and left me pondering, "Ye Gods, what have I done to upset thee now?"

****

Chapter eleven

Unquellable forces

Crocs, he of the croc-shod foot, was again my camp-mate for the night. He was waiting at the trailhead for a friend to turn up the following day. It was one of the few places to rest in a long section of much despised volcanic rock. Demoralisingly, he'd worked out there was another four miles of continuous lava fields to navigate the following day, whereas I'd wrongly estimated two. I never realised how bad I was at simple maths until I started hiking the PCT. On the plus side, I was relieved to split the last litre from the water cache with him. Water supplies were hard to find in these parts: I'd already passed one collection of empty plastic containers on the way to this one. I could manage without, but extra water meant an extra cup of coffee both at dinner and at breakfast. I was taking my wins when I could find them.

"The difference between an alcoholic and a non-alcoholic is that non-alcoholics change their behaviour to meet their goals, and alcoholics change their goals to meet their behaviour." It's a line from the *Big Book of Alcoholics Anonymous*, but I'd not realised that until the day's podcast. Not that I hadn't read that line, but that it hadn't lodged in my brain as originating in a chapter from the 'back of the book', which is how anything written in the last seventy percent is referenced.

Step eleven, which is outlined in the first third of the book, suggests recovering alcoholics seek *through prayer and meditation our conscious contact with God as we understood Him, praying only for knowledge of his will for us and the power to carry that out*. It is the reminder that my true purpose in life is not to lie around planning to get drunk, recovering from the drunk, and living in a funk, but rather quite the opposite. Life is for living, and enjoying, and partaking, and giving and receiving. To be a part of something, and just not a problem for someone else to deal with. Sobriety is about keeping one's mind open to possibilities, and to keep doing whatever is needed to ensure one doesn't slowly slide back into the clutches of active addiction. At the same time, step eleven reminds me to ward against not having a future so tightly bound in perfect ideology, that anything short of attaining it, results in incomprehensible demoralisation.

"Have you been enjoying swimming in the lakes and ponds?" Croc enquired as I battled against a stiff breeze to pitch the tent. I felt I simply didn't have time to stop anymore. Earlier in the day, I'd refilled my water bottles alongside a man floating in one of the lakes. It felt all kinds of peculiar as if I was interrupting his bath. Assuring me it was refreshing; all I could bring to mind was leeches. I knew I still had 'swimming in the lake' on my to-do list but there always seemed to be a reason to not do it. Time was, and is, so often my own personal Judas, and leeches seemed a wonderfully new innovation of matters to fear.

It was also convenient for me that Elk Lake Resort and Big Lake Youth Camp remained closed, ostensibly because of Covid, even though restrictions had long since been lifted. I was glad of their choices to limit any conscious contact with coffee and sparing me yet another diversion that I could not have otherwise resisted. My quiet half hours were dedicated to when my phone would bleep with rare and random bouts of reception. A discordant mixture of pings, bongs and trills would fire up, usually as I neared the head of a hill, and then I would look for a suitable arse landing place: a flattish rock or decaying log on which I could park myself to catch up with the outside world. Sometimes I'd make do with the ground itself.

I was hunting down Jeff, who I believed to be a few miles ahead of me. We'd text one another the mile location of our previous night's camping spot to be picked up who only knows when. I truly felt like I'd arrived when I got to tap out, "I'm in 1984!" because it was a year I could remember what I was doing, given I was ten years old, full of childhood plans and ambitions that involved lots of animals and a happy home on a farm, being all mucky and free.

If prayers are asking, and meditation is listening, then The Bridge of the Gods, to my mind, functions to sort out the injured from the walking near-dead. Facebook posts were all too often announcing retirement plans: people for whom the pain had become a notch too unbearable to suffer. Reports of repetitive strain injuries were commonplace; hikers were losing the war between mind and matter. Loneliness had felled another. Each hike is so unique, and each one's expectations are so different. I had come to accept loneliness as part of the story, my all too familiar foe.

Further north, a Norwegian man overtook the Swedes, who'd previously been the trailblazers through the Sierra. He was now heading towards Canada, perhaps a week out, doing something like thirty-five miles to forty miles a day. He was likely to be the first to finish. On the second to last chance of phone reception in Washington, he typed out a post begging for a lift to take him straight from the uppermost trailhead to the airport so he could return to his Scandinavian home on the day his visa expired. He was inundated with offers but he would not know that for a few more days. Then, and only then, would he be able to make the decision to continue to the remote border, or quit to give himself enough time to get to Seattle. Elsewhere, Southbounders were still asking one another about the snow conditions in Washington.

I said goodbye to Crocs, I presumed for the last time, and headed off to breach the four miles of lava hell remaining. As soon as I passed it, fog rolled in, whiting out all the views, including the much-welcomed resumption of vibrant fir trees. Rain lashed down with increasing tempo and the wind blew up stretching quickly into a gale. Lightning again flashed before my eyes. I'd count the time between the roar of thunder and the next strike: it was honing in on me. I put on my new anorak and hunkered deep within it, hindering me further as my glasses steamed up. Bobbles of water also stuck fast to my lenses distorting my vision, so much so I blotted out passing the two-thousand-mile marker. Although a simple arrangement of stones, like all the others had been, I completely missed this monumental moment of my thru-hike in my haste.

I stopped at an unexpected and unmapped cache of water. It didn't require filtering. Quaffing some of it, I contemplated the significance of having walked a full two thousand miles. I was now, whatever way I reasoned it, no longer in my last one thousand miles. There was just the rest of Oregon, and then the whole of Washington to go. A mere six hundred and fifty-something mile dawdle to Canada, and just one month and one week to complete it in.

The cooler temperatures and abysmal conditions forced me onwards and upwards. As I hobbled towards the end of yet another marathon, I was dismayed to find I was deep within a burn zone. The storm continued to lobby hard. Despite my exhaustion, I didn't dare risk pitching up a tent between the stalks of tall, blackened wood, fearing they might topple. It left me no choice but to wobble on another four miles towards the top of a sheer mountain side where a small tightly-packed forested area clung on for dear life. A sixth of a

240

mile beyond lay a lake, with good camping sites but I suspected from the pictures on Guthook it might be just more charred woodland. I spied a tiny clearing, just about suitable to take my tent, albeit mildly angled and root-bound. Nonetheless, I deemed it acceptable mostly because the night was falling fast. Dismally, the wind and rain had not abated. I hoped the covering from the canopy high up would spare me a truly disagreeable night. Alas, the atrocious storm howled on. I was distracted by the sound of water dribbling down the outside of my tent. Like an ornamental living room fountain trickling away, supposedly to bring calm and peace, I find such noises only activate the urge to pee.

The following day, sleep-deprived, I packed away my soggy tent, and reacquainted myself with my waterlogged trousers and damp fleece. I'd taken all my drenched clothes off before bed in order to help me warm up. With no spares, dressing made for a tough start. Overnight, I had discovered a new form of angst: being disturbed by a bear would be awful but being disturbed by a bear butt-naked far, far worse. I clearly harboured a perception that death is more appetising if one is wearing underwear! I blame all those mothers who told their daughters to make sure their bras and knickers matched just in case they had an accident. Cockypop! I've met a few paramedics and not one has confirmed they've refused to treat a patient because their pants didn't pass muster, let alone colour-coordinate to their bras. Still, wearing knickers, like sleeping in a tent, works to give one a sense of security when sleeping in the wilderness.

****

The accumulation of regrets

With the burn zone and lava fields behind me, the sun also beamed back through the woodland, speckling the ground. The trail was once again a source of graceful beauty and life as it curled its way around Mount Jefferson. I certainly wasn't as elegant as my surroundings: my muscles had seized from the previous day's thirty-one-and-a-half-mile exertion. On the one hand, I was delighted to have smashed the thirty-mile barrier, but on the other, my body was paying a huge penalty.

Jeff's text popped in late morning. I'd camped a mere six-tenths of a mile behind him the previous night. I texted back I'd be doing another marathon that day, giving me something to push for as I tramped my way further north. By mid-afternoon I was overtaken by Beetroot, last seen in the first one hundred and fifty miles. He was swarthy now, stick thin, frazzled, practically unrecognisable from the clean-shaven, boy-next-door twenty-something model of modern man over four months prior. In fact, it was he who broke the tension of him squinting at me, squinting at him with a simple, "Do I know you?"

He'd been part of a foursome but they'd long since split into two, and more recently he and his hiking partner, HeadGirl, had gone their separate ways. "I stopped being so hard on myself when I started walking alone. It's easier to set my own targets, and not feel like I'm letting anyone down if I want to stop two miles ahead of where we'd previously agreed." I understood that and then did what all alkies are prone to doing: focus on the differences. He was American, whereas HeadGirl, like me, was European, making our end-dates non-negotiable. Beetroot mentioned that she was sick of hiking already and just wanted it over and done with, whereas for the two of us there was no rush back to a job or a home. She wouldn't quit, he explained, but the romance of hiking day after day had long since eroded. His own sense of wellbeing had improved now he'd taken on his own hike. I bid him adieu, or rather he just ploughed on ahead with a speed I had no hope of matching, but the encounter left me with that inner knowing, that somehow, I was still managing this. I didn't know how or why - this was not me. I will give in before I start. I fantasize a lot, consuming my low reserves of energy. I talk a good job and walk away as soon as it gets tough. I am readily distracted. "Perseverance is not a marathon, but a series of short races," someone had once quoted me. But I hated racing, I was rubbish at it.

The strain between miles and smiles was broken by the existence of Olallie Lake and I joined Beetroot once again as we'd both opted to resupply there. Lacking any kind of restaurant, it still offered a great supply of hiker junk food, and even stocked cheese and frozen bread. Three large and heavily caffeinated coffees later, Beetroot met the most animated and energetic version of me on the trail, a notch up from sloth-like. After a two and a half-hour sojourn,

I bid him adieu to recommence my mandatory marathon. The coffees propelled me the remaining nineteen miles, and I was near drunk with delight when I happened upon huckleberries. I'd spied little purplish and blue beads here and there, but I was reluctant to be a human experiment until I happened upon a family picking away at the scrubby plants. I joined in with them. The berries were tart, but sweet, nicer than the similar-looking blueberry, which I'd always found watery. Huckleberries thrive upwards of five and a half thousand feet, the man had said, and were a North American delicacy. They grow singly, requiring one to delve in and separate rigid foliage in order to pluck the tiny fruit.

As dusk commenced, I limped into my pre-determined camp spot truly beaten but thrilled to find two other PCT thru-hikers, Weekend and Dentist, in attendance as well as three novice section hikers. They'd already lit up a campfire and were in awe at having some 'professionals' in their midst. Curious as to whether we'd seen rattlesnakes and bears, we revelled in telling them in grand detail all of our brushes with the wildlife as their eyes widened in part fear, part envy. Dentist was due to leave America in the first week of September and had opted to pay the four-hundred-and-fifty-dollar extension fee, with no idea yet whether or not it would be approved, risking several precious days off trail to be interviewed. Time she could ill-afford.

The resupply situation in Washington was now the latest thing for us thru-hikers to obsess over. I wondered whether it really was that problematic or was just a manifestation of boredom and absence of stuff to fret about. Before I set off on this adventure, plenty of people had planned and published their itineraries from start to finish, with elaborate colour-coordinated spreadsheets, complete with symbols and detailed instructions. I wondered what had become of them. I'd worked it out as I managed each sub-section, estimating how long I could bear to be out in the wilderness between stops and how much mileage I'd be able to cover, and plan accordingly. But Washington seemed to be similar to the Sierra, with a glut of closed resorts, and substantial distances to cover to access towns. That familiar foe anxiety began to seep in, festering in my insecurity born of not knowing the region, and not ever feeling like a competent hiker.

Weekend had opted to cowboy camp, which was also on my to-do list though I bowed out on this opportunity to sleep rough, given the mosquitoes still waxed and waned. I was particularly glad I'd shirked the opportunity when our resident cowboy camper shrieked in the middle of the night: a mouse had scampered across her face. In previous years, these plagues of opportunistic cretins would stealthily occupy popular campsites, waiting patiently for nightfall so they could gnaw through tent fabrics to get at the inhabitant's food stashes. It is rumoured many a cowboy camper has found one tunnelling down deep into a sleeping bag. The dearth of hiking this year, with our careless scattering of crumbs, had effectively hindered the breeding season.

What should have been the easiest marathon of Oregon was everything but. I could only describe myself as 'trail sick', overwhelmed by a lagging sensation when putting one foot in front of the next. Everything had become too cumbersome. I never found any sense of flow to my day, no matter what I tried. I couldn't find any semblance of peace in my mind beyond how exhausted I was, how devoid of energy and how each footstep caused me to wince. I supposed this was hitting the metaphorical wall. I'd put it down initially to poor sleep, but there was a tinge of depression-like sluggishness that I couldn't shake off either. I fell foul of berating myself for not enjoying the easier, soft-treading trail, the mild inclines, the cheerfulness of passing day-hikers. The fresh, warm day supplemented with a gentle breeze. It all should have made for idyllic walking conditions, but I could appreciate none of it. I was so utterly replete of drive. Barely maintaining a steady one and a half mile an hour, I'd grind to a halt almost every half hour to just sit and not move. It seemed particularly callous to be in the section where most set their longest day on trail. Whatever momentum had enabled me to grind out one long day after another had vanished. I was putting myself back under that irrepressible weight of expectation, and it was strangling me.

It had been over two weeks since my last zero, a day of decompression from the relentless challenges of just plodding on. I was annoyed at myself for spending too long having rest days and too many zeroes early on my hike, recovering from injuries, or waiting out other people's agendas. I found myself resenting them for having their choices, especially now they had long-since abandoned their own thru-hikes. I was back in the blame game, playing my silent Stradivarius. Like the speaker of the day, I might not have had a pot to piss in, but I could easily manifest a swimming pool of self-pity in which to thrash around in. I didn't even want to listen to the podcasts. Two weeks without a day off, meant two weeks without going to a proper meeting, and I knew deep down I was as dry drunk as I could be. Those old familiar feelings of restlessness, irritability and discontentedness had a stranglehold on my behaviour.

I came across Weekday, who suggested I perhaps take a day or two off trail. I was just under three days away from the Bridge of the Gods, my next intended zero. Government Camp was closer but previous comments inferred hikers were unwelcomed there. When I checked Guthook for clarification, everything suddenly vanished bar the maps. Weekday, who'd hiked with a group for a few days, had observed all the Android users were missing either pictures or notes, or both in recent days. I would need to reload the entire software to get it working again. I dumped my brooding all over Weekday who reminded me that this was my hike, and if I needed time off trail, then I needed time off trail. I could recharge my batteries, and no one would care that I might miss a mile here or there. In this instance, I'd be missing forty miles. Besides which, she informed me, the trail down to the Columbia River was a brute and swerving it might ensure I actually got to the end rather than fall apart completely.

I find it is often this way: that good advice is never generated in my own head, my ego is a guaranteed way of totally messing everything up. "ASK" is one of those annoying AA acronyms - it's the 'Arse Saving Kit' many alkies prefer not to make use of. The trick is to tell someone how you feel, then do exactly what is suggested, resisting any temptation to go off on a vain poll of 'What would you do' to a multitude of fellow 'experts', only to do whatever regardless. In AA, I've sometimes heard people say that God comes in human skin: the right people are in the right place at the right time, and I have no idea why or how beyond happenstance.

Any other recovering alcoholic would recognise immediately that I was living in the borders of four states: hungry, angry, lonely and tired, which are the clarion call for the four horsemen of the apocalypse to saddle up and prepare to charge. If my demons were to win this battle, history dictates the next four feelings would be terror, bewilderment, frustration and despair; and despite knowing this on a theoretical level, I, like most addicts, have a mind that convinces me this time would be different. "I don't know if I'm an alcoholic because I have a short memory, or if I have a short memory because I'm an alcoholic," a friend of mine was apt to say. Sadly, he was already out there drinking again despite that pearl of wisdom.

I sent up a prayer, asking what to do next, and yet again the Trail Gods intervened. At the end of the day, I staggered into a private campground about a half mile off the PCT, and one I discovered required a booking. A sign placed at the entrance announced it was already full. Nonetheless, I limped up to an old-fashioned hand-driven water pump, baffled as to what to do next and very disinclined to redo the half mile to return to the trail. An elder couple approached the pump seconds later. I enquired of them whether there was a communal campground within the vicinity. In response they let me know they had booked two private spaces but only needed the one - and did I want the spare? I spooked their adult children by pitching up at the wrong site. I soon erected my tent, then hobbled off to use the latrine. In my absence, they delivered a massive stash of sweets, breads and cakes, leaving them on the large picnic table for my return. It cheered the soul no end, and their timely act of generosity meant I knew I would be battling on for a while yet.

First, I needed to get my head back in the game. The next day, I took myself off at Highway 35. My only regret, which I didn't realise for another week, was that I missed something I had been very excited about: a quick visit to Timberline Lodge, where *The Shining* had been filmed. I have never actually seen the psychological thriller, starring Jack Nicholson, telling the story of a writer and alcoholic who resided there briefly one summer only to be tormented by a power he did not understand. As it was, the Lodge had very restricted opening hours. Indeed, looking back, perhaps I would have bypassed it altogether in my relentless march north had I arrived at an inconvenient hour.

In its place, I hitched a lift from a fascinating woman who was a professional hemp dealer of twenty-odd years standing. Not remotely flash, she lived largely in the woods, off-grid and delivered drugs day after day, night after night, here and there, living the life of her dreams. For her, business in the pandemic was booming and she hadn't had a day off since March, whereas all her customers had had way too many of them. She was off to Washington to say goodbye to her father who was dying of Covid-related complications. I learnt from the industry insider that legalising cannabis in America had, in her view, made society worse not better. Deregulation for her meant she was having to work twice as hard to earn half as much. She felt that using mood-altering substances for anything other than acute pain benefited no-one and she wished it had become a prescribed medicine rather than a recreational drug. Despite my sore hips, my cracked lips, the bruises along my increasingly thin-skinned back, and the non-stop tendonitis in my calves and ankles, she offered me no freebie samples, and nor did I ask. For that, as well as her generously lifting me to the Bridge of the Gods, I remain profoundly grateful.

****

The Inuits are coming

Cascade Locks, on the banks of the Columbia River, is a drab little industrial town, with worn out signage and half-working neon lights flashing for attention. It's the lowest place on the PCT, practically at sea level, perhaps not only physically, but also for many a thru-hiker as morale hits rock bottom. Cheryl Strayed also terminated here, planned, rather than defeated, having got the healing she was looking for in her one-thousand-mile odyssey. I booked into a shabby hotel not far from the trail, near the flatteringly named Bridge of the Gods. The bridge itself is a man-made, unimpressive steel structure spanning across the broad Columbia river, joining Oregon to Washington. Despite its less than attractive appearance, it is a far superior alternative to wading the wide, brown, fast-flowing watercourse.

The hotel was equally as run-down as the town, and very much in need of a good lick of paint. The building required an entire renovation if not a full demolition. The room, small and dingy, came with wi-fi and coffee, which is what grabbed my attention first. My UK WhatsApp pinged immediately after I powered it up and there sat a text screaming, "Call me urgently." It was sent four days prior. I rang just as morning was about to break in the UK and spoke to a fellow, who talked and talked and talked, leaving me none the wiser as to what the emergency was. Eventually he enquired, "and how are you?"

During the mornings podcast, I'd chuckled at the speaker telling a story of how he'd just come out from a double heart by-pass surgery, only for a sponsee to ring demanding his attention because his car had a flat tyre, and he didn't think he could handle the stress of it. In the background, the room erupted with laughter: the collective recognition of our tendency to talk endlessly about ourselves, oblivious to the fact that our matters may be intruding on their day, or the timing may be just a little out of whack with someone else's priorities. It's something we all learn when we become sponsors ourselves. There's a knack to listening well, and resisting the urge to fix, or dismiss, especially with a hyper-sensitive newcomer. I suspect more often than not, we were all once in the same hyperbolic over-dramatic headspace. I've been shown how it is better to let someone debrief until they're ready to take onboard what needs to happen next and that normally means allowing them to calm down, and then suggesting they hit the pause button, by going off and saying a few prayers.

"Bad." I replied now that it was my time to talk, feeling mentally and physically broken, terrified I didn't have another five hundred and five miles in me. I was just about to wind up into a long diatribe of how awful I felt when he cut across with, "Well, you know what your problem is, you're not grateful enough. You need to write a gratitude list every day, that's the key." I lost it. Apoplectic would be more accurate, and I terminated the call as fast as I could. Something, though, was clearly afoot. An obvious clue is going on about how glorious life is now they've decided to quit AA, as if AA was the problem preventing them getting on with their lives in the first place. "How quick we can be to pull away from the life AA has given us," I heard it said on a podcast and it had stuck but the truth is we don't know what happens when we stop going to AA. Some do cope but I don't know whether I would. I suppose that's the point.

One of the blessings of the pandemic is that AA is still everywhere and on demand. I rang someone else in the fellowship and bored them with how awful my trip was, and how terrible I felt, and I had no idea what part of her day I was interrupting, nonetheless I was grateful for her time. She suggested going to the Women's International Meeting which was twenty-four hours a day, seven days a week on Zoom and text across the details. It meant I wouldn't have to wait until early evening to get a hefty dose reminding me of my priorities in life.

Gratitude is an emotion in my experience, and not just written down in bullet points. Although that's a practice that, ordinarily, I would do every night. I found it concentrated my mind at the end of the day, training it to look for the good in life: something I'm not naturally disposed to doing. In a few months, I'd forget this day of demoralisation, at least become indifferent to the feelings suffocating me, but it would add up to another sober day, which, of course, contributes to the ongoing count of positive sobriety. Whilst hiking, I no longer wrote down the gains of sobriety each day, I'd replaced the practice by verbalising them as I walked along. That said, I hadn't been feeling the corresponding sense of gratitude for a while.

That all changed the instant I discovered my hotel room had a deep, old-fashioned enamel bath, with gushing hot water on demand. A long shower rid me of the worst of Oregon's dirt and dust, before I filled the bath to the brink and submerged myself totally from head to toe for the first time since I'd arrived in America. It was such a novel and welcoming experience, and completely unexpected, that I couldn't resist a second one just six hours later. I can't say that it repaired the damaged, worn muscles bound tightly to jaded joints but it restored something deep within.

On the toilet seat, my laptop belted out the Women's International Zoom Meeting. I, of course, had my camera off but the familiarity of my clan brought further rehabilitation. There were over two hundred women at that meeting, with all kinds of accents, speaking a common language. It worked its magic on my dire mental welfare. For anyone who has no strong conception of a God, being a drunk amongst drunks is a form of kinship. We are especially empowered when we are sober drunks. Shame has no place in our meetings, nor is there stigma, we simply congregate to get well and stay well for a brief moment in time before we all melt away to our so-called 'normal' lives. Each one of us has a God of our own understanding, and at this meeting God was a she.

A meeting is on the surface just one fellow talking about the stuff of nightmares in order to help themselves, and perhaps, just perhaps, benefit someone else. Strangers, some faceless like me, converge online as one woman after another talked about childhood sexual abuse, and the long-term damage of being someone's else source of gratification. Each speaker talked of the damage done, and then how they got rid of the guilt and shame that is the residue of such an abhorrent encounter. That is the stuff of gratitude - being rid of someone else's sickness. I loved it when a woman reminded me that gratitude isn't a shopping list but a change in attitude. I don't have to go to AA for my drinking anymore. In AA, I learnt that I don't "have to" do much at all. I don't have to use the phrase 'have to' ever again. I can replace it with 'get to'. Because I'm an alcoholic, I get to lie in a bath, listen to the most amazing women talk of empowering themselves and leading lives unimaginable to them years previously, when they believed they were once a piece of shit, and behaved like it too. That is undeniably a power greater than anything else I can think of. It is certainly far more impactful than someone telling me 'there's always someone worse off than you' which strikes me as barely-disguised condemnation for actually having a feeling and voicing it.

I slept well that night, having spent hours simply listening to women talking about recovery, and I popped into a UK meeting the following day. Someone told the Eskimo joke, and I apologise for using a now-offensive term, but the joke works whether one uses Eskimo or Inuit.

There are two guys sitting together in a bar in the remote Alaskan wilderness. They are old friends, but one is a priest and the other is an atheist. They argue frequently about the existence of God. The atheist retells a story of being lost in the thick, ice-bound tundra during a particularly heavy blizzard. Freezing in the sub-zero temperatures, he fell to his knees to pray, and in doing so he beseeched God to rescue him and prevent his slow death from hyperthermia.

"It didn't work," said the Atheist.

"So how did you make it out alive?" asked the Priest.

"Oh, two Inuits turned up and I followed them out."

As I readied to leave Oregon and start my final leg of Washington, I breakfasted at a restaurant adjacent to the Bridge of the Gods, signing in with a phone number that would be rendered obsolete within a few days. A stranger on another table paid my bill when I ordered a round of pancakes having hovered up the omelette and hash brown in record time. Despite the generous American portion, my insides tore it apart within seconds. Then Jeff arrived, still reeking of the wild existence he was living and introduced me to his partner, Laura, with whom he resides in Washington. Her face mask concealed her smile, but her eyes were vivid and exciting. In line with Oregon's strictly-enforced social distancing requirements she stood six feet apart from my table, whereas Jeff plonked himself down opposite me.

Straight away they informed me they would be making sure I got to Seattle airport after my hike was over. More to the point, Laura and their friends were going to be following Jeff as he ventured through the final state, bringing him his resupplies. If I stuck with Jeff, they could do the same for me, Laura suggested. This was the lifting of a huge burden. The Canadian border remained resolutely closed. It was clear this wasn't changing any time soon and it blocked my return home via Vancouver as I'd planned. I booked an entirely new flight from Seattle to Heathrow on the twelfth of September, but now Virgin had filed for Chapter Eleven bankruptcy, which was momentarily horrifying, until I learnt that they could still trade but it left things uncertain. Flying from Seattle added another thirty miles hiking to the five hundred and five miles still left to complete as I'd have to return to Hart's Pass to be collected. If I could keep up with Jeff then all my shopping problems would be solved, relieving some pressure considerably. Because of skipping to Bridge of the Gods, Jeff was effectively one day behind me. We agreed to meet at White's Pass if he hadn't caught me before.

They said their farewells for now and headed off so that Jeff could wash, launder and reconnect with Laura after nearly one hundred days on the PCT. I put my first tentative footstep on the metal lattice bridge peering through the holes to the brown water being channelled to the Pacific far below. I jostled for space against the cars rushing at me. It always took a while to adjust to the fast-moving world after days in the backcountry and being cooped up in a hotel room didn't do much to reacclimatise one.

The trail resumed up the steep-sided, and aptly named, Table Mountain, which flattened off only once one has pushed and pulled oneself up the three-thousand-foot ascent. Washingtonians I'd previously met spoke of this climb with a shudder, but fuelled well, it really wasn't quite the mammoth feat of endurance I'd anticipated. Despite a late start, I cranked out a nineteen-mile day. As dusk approached, I walked alongside a small tributary, and happened upon a reasonably flat patch of dirt which beckoned me to stay the night. As the sun began its final descent, I heard the scrapings of footsteps. Seconds later, in front of me stood French Guy. "Oh, my God - PI! I can't believe it's you. I need company tonight - can I stay here?" There was just enough space for him to cowboy camp adjacent to my tent. "This trek is now a race," he said, "it started as an adventure, but now it's a race to do it before the visa. Because in France, I now have to get a negative Covid test which will take three days to get the results. Of course, I don't know how to do this from the trail, so I think I have to run to the border, and then come back in time. My visa expires on the third of September."

Ever since I'd first met him, he was pulling big numbers in his daily hike. I was astonished to even see him again. "I took a week to go to a wedding," he murmured, "It was a lot of fun, but not so much now." He was having a torrid time. Fed up with being in pain, being alone and having to push so hard. He no longer took time to chat to others, besides which he was sick of answering the same questions over and over. He envied the Southbounders - all healthy, and muscular. He was keen to go home now. He wanted to get married and start up his photography business again, but he also had acute wanderlust, and yearned to cycle across Japan. He'd eaten in Cascade Locks and then pushed, no time to rest, but coming down to the Columbia River had been so indescribably agonising, he was barely able to do more than a mile an hour. He had a long stride, and would readily be described as athletic, although these days he had more of a distance-runner's physique than a sprinter's. As the real midnight came and went, we finally ceased our chatter. "You know, PI, just telling you how awful I have felt for a few days, how much I want to quit, but not quit, you know, I feel so much better already."

****

There is such a thing as a dumb question

"What time is it?" I heard French Guy shuffling around. The birdsong was well and truly in full throttle. Starting my day after eight o'clock in the morning seemed a travesty, but undoubtedly the

252

consequence of prattling late into the night. I said goodbye to French Guy, twice: once as I left camp, and then an hour later as he zoomed by, his ability to fast hike now seemingly restored. I spent the rest of the day trying to mentally calculate his daily mileage, average mileage and where he would likely spend the night. Little maths tests just to keep my mind off the many and varied mental and physical challenges confronting me.

Changing shoes had brought about an acute pain where the toes and the feet connected on my right foot, leaving me to wonder how on earth I was going to complete ten miles, let alone the twenty-something ambitions I had. I wondered if foot bones had individual names, because I couldn't think of a single one. The agony of pressing down was causing a mild but detectable limp, which in turn bruised my hip joint, and strained my knees. Each morning descended into a ritual of asking myself what was actually working. How much did various parts of me hurt? What didn't hurt? And why the hell was I doing this in the first place? That latter question is the most commonly asked question. "Idiocy," had become my stock-in-trade answer. I had no idea, and I couldn't face telling multiple times a day how a friend had watched *Wild*, and then died. Not because she'd watched Wild, but because of cancer. And no, it wasn't some carpe diem response to grief. And no, I wasn't doing it for charity, but still after nearly two thousand, two hundred miles, it startled me that I still didn't have a neat, plausible realisation.

"Are you thru-hiking?" is the typical way one breaks the ice with fellow travellers. On this particular day, it was asked by a thirty-something male as we crossed paths mid-morning, mid-trail. "Yes!" To which he asked, "Are you Australian?" Sometimes to entertain myself I would hold entire conversations with a discernible, but very dodgy, Australian twang. I did actually have an Aussie accent once upon a time, but then elocution lessons pummelled it out of me. On this occasion, I admitted to my Britishness. "Ah, in that case, do you want crisps?" Food of the Gods! *Walkers* are better known as *Lays* globally. Same logo, different name. Unfortunately, different flavours too, and I struggled to get excited by Limon, Habanero or Dill Pickle but the universally acceptable Original Flavour Doritos delighted me greatly. I'd met the legend that is GoldTech. Each year he trawls back and forth sections of the PCT, giving out a treat to any Northbounding thru-hiker he crosses paths with. He knows full well

253

that hiker hunger is second-worse in terms of the physical discomfort now faced by thru-hikers. If proof was ever needed that long-distance hikers are not marauding animals, each hiker has always accepted GoldTech's single and generous token without mugging him for the remainder of the giant sack of treats he carries about him.

There were plenty of other questions I answered quite repetitively. "Do you carry a gun?" was one of those random and particularly daft ones to ask a thru-hiker. I imagine if we did, by Washington, day hikers would be negotiating their freedom in exchange for a half-dozen Snickers.

In the afternoon, it was my turn to break the silence with the query, "Are you thru-hiking?" to a healthy-looking Southbounder lolloping toward me. "Yes, and I know I'm late!" he snapped back as he bounced by. If he was sick of the question after five hundred miles, I hate to think how demented he'd be after two thousand, two hundred miles. It's definitely a good thing long-distance hikers don't carry guns. That said, I frequently heard the sound of shots cracking across the valleys, practically daily, leaving me with nothing else to do but hope and pray they were being pointed in the other direction.

Being asked questions was just about the only distraction most days. The views were largely irrelevant given it was thick woodland in every direction. Aside from questions from the occasional day hiker, days remained quite laborious. A plethora of garter snakes rapid-firing off the trail would give me a timely jolt of adrenaline here and there. Another day, I was mesmerized by two small, bright pink, pudgy snakes all curled up beside a rotting log. They both eyed me warily, I assumed at their most vulnerable as they had just shed their skins. Later, when I asked Google why they were so pink, I discovered it was probably because they were northern rubber boas, which explains why they didn't shoot off, or kill me.

It was always painful to stop and chat, but occasionally the diversion was welcome. Many day hikers were curious creatures, and I was always baffled by them asking, "Where have you come from?" By now I had taken to replying with a very exacting, "Oh, mile two one nine oh point nine," or something equally befuddling to them as if they all spoke thru-hiker lingo. A section-hiker had whipped on his face mask as I'd dragged myself up a particularly sharp hill. "You thru?" he muffled. "Uh-huh!" was all I could muster in response as I gasped at thin air. "You British?" was his next question. I was astonished he'd worked that out from two barely-there syllables. So, I stopped and nattered to him, although quite honestly, I'd have stopped mid-way up anyway had he not been there.

Earlier in the day, my spirits soared when a friend messaged to say her breast cancer treatment had been successful. I don't think I would have coped with losing two very close friends in one year, both in their early fifties. We'd gotten divorced at the same time, and spent many a night pondering why and how, taking it in turns trying to piece together a definitive story of why our marriages had both rapidly imploded, leaving us stunned, impuissant and devastated. Both of us had staggered around punch-drunk for the first year, and largely drunk each evening for that matter. We bonded over any flavour of wine we could get our hands on and schemed about ways of getting revenge on our dearly departeds. Someone had once said, "you mourn the marriage, not the man," and I found that to be true - most certainly when it came to appraising our spouse's characters, we could only come to damning conclusions. "What on earth did you see in that twat?" was asked more than once.

In getting divorced, I found more friends than I could cope with, but the hurt of a failed marriage had never dissolved, although it became less profound over time. I had fifteen years of memories to unpack, and the hardest part was that he featured in the vast majority of them. Once he exited stage right, it left me wondering whether any of my previous life had been authentic. His presence in my reminiscences sprayed a sourness around them but walking so far on my own had enabled me to reclaim them. I no longer said 'we', but rather 'I'. I did this and that, and with that he was simply erased from my story-telling. I once quad-biked around the UK: the first woman to do so. When I used to say 'we' people often asked if I rode pillion and it irked me. Now I just say 'I' as if he hadn't been a part of it at all.

"Are you doing it alone?" is oft-asked. I'd quip back, "No, I have about sixteen imaginary friends, albeit most are of the frenemy variety. I think I've lost two or three on the way though." But asking about my solo existence was now a welcomed question. Time has passed and I've shifted away from feeling like a sad, abandoned divorcee. I'd married him when I was an intrepid, curious and naive young woman. He left just as the brakes of turning forty slammed on. I felt very robbed of my life story, and walking alone for all these miles, was reintroducing me to that very same adventurous, gung-ho, devil-may-care itinerant of yonder year. I was delighted to meet her again. I had realised just how much a marriage can bury a person and it had taken me all these years before I could accept his leaving had been for the best for both of us.

"How many miles do you do a day?" That is another opener. I'd let go of any idea of continuing with a daily marathon, but I was still managing around twenty-four miles a day. I stuck fast to other routines, though, like trying to enjoy my mornings, and using the harder afternoons to do my daily listenings, prayers and meditations. The latter were more of an ambulatory pondering about what I needed from the universe, and what the universe needed from me and where the hell was my 'Road to Damascus' moment which would solve all my future problems.

I spooked yet another mule, this one more horse-shaped with enormous upright ears. It made me think of scooby-doo on drugs. I was taking to carrying larger and larger reserves of water, filtering several litres at a time from tadpole-riddled ponds and lakes, now evaporating in the height of summer. I'd plunge in my old mineral water bottle, being careful not to stir up the sediment too much in the shallow waters, and even more conscientious not to suck in an undesirable visitor. Many times, I'd wade in, my feet submerging in claggy mud so I could get sufficient depth. Its cooling effects would provide much needed relief on my taut toes, which no longer had conventional feelings. The rivers had begun thinning out as well. I began to pre-filter water through my sweat-soaked PCT bandana. Each year, over six thousand American dollars are raised via GoFundMe to print these so they can be given as useful, and free, souvenirs to all aspiring thru-hikers as we pass through Kennedy Meadows. I hadn't wanted to use mine, preferring to keep it as a flag of my accomplishment for years to come, but I'd taken to wearing it under my black cap to keep the sun and the horse flies off my neck. The latter had recently introduced themselves as the latest injectors of misery.

One exhausting afternoon my capacity only just saw me through a bone-dry patch, and I was relieved to kneel before a tiny algae-filled pond. As I waved away the water-skaters and tadpoles, a dog dived in splashing around in ecstasy, ostensibly chasing frogs. It ran amok stirring up the sediment. Moments later, his owner turned up warning me giardia was rife in Washington.

It was not unusual for people to warn me of impending doom by way of making conversation. Some would bang on about conditions ahead, often stressing there was a four-, six- or eight-mile gap between water sources, which was not remotely challenging to my mind. Others would stress how steep the next hill would be, even though I wasn't at one of those 'notable' spots where that kind of information was useful. It was an odd thing listening to someone believing they were being helpful, yet in reality they were doing little except showing off how much they knew, adding nothing to my day's hike but a minor delay. I supposed, if anything, it made me aware I was now well-versed in meeting conditions as they presented themselves. They weren't to know I would have a day's plan outlined in my head, relying on Guthook to make me familiar with the terrain and its resources.

I met an older man a few hundred metres after I'd traversed a deep river rushing up to my thighs. It was a little tricky but left me with an energetic sense of being more *Action Man* than *Barbie Doll*; my drenched trousers were sopping as I stood before him. I told the oncomer that I'd found a good spot about fifty feet upstream from where the trail actually crossed. He told me the river he'd just crossed had been quite the palaver too, so I was bemused to find two sturdy logs to make use of. Proper river wading was now a rarity, and I made a mental note to jettison the heavy waterproof socks at the next available bin. My backpack, despite only having a few days of food within, felt more and more as if I was carrying an obelisk around. I could only put it down to having recovered my puffy pants and jacket from the Post Office at Cascade Locks.

The most welcome of all hikers were the ones coming towards me first thing each morning. They would have cleared the trail of the cobwebs which first tickled, then clogged up one's face. The thin strands of stickiness weaved from tree branch to tree branch each evening and were rarely obvious to the naked eye, unless the spider was loitering directly at eye-level. Instead, one skulked forward with little option but to wave one's hiking poles ahead, a deranged jamboree leader, until it was too exerting. My trekking poles were tacky to the touch as I lengthened them each evening to fit the demands of my tent. I could only hope I didn't pick up any wandering arachnids between dissembling and erecting the Castle each day.

The one hiker I expected to meet was Jeff who was supposed to be hunting me down, tagging me before I got to White's Pass, but I spent my one hundred and fiftieth night alone on trail, metres away from the tree trunk likely to have killed Finn "Colours" Bastian a year earlier. He'd been struck by a falling rotten tree as he crossed a small wooden bridge. It was that random. His was the first thru-hiker death by tree recorded, amazingly, because the area is swamped with dead, decaying and broken trunks. It's astonishing to think cars have killed more people on the PCT than anything else. The twenty-nine-year-old German's memorial was said to be set a little back from the trail, but I couldn't find it. Nonetheless, I said a small prayer for him and his loved ones. It was a spooky night, but the camp was an upmarket one, coming with several choices of log seating and flat spots. I ate dinner watching a small mouse dash out of a hole, strip a leaf of a nearby fledging tree and dart back again. Ten or twelve sprints was all it took for the sapling to be confined to death too.

****

Seconds and inches

The day's podcast introduced me to a new phrase, "Seconds and inches." All recovery stories are recaps of miraculous escapes or happenings, often interpreted as coincidences, synchronicities or divine interventions. One, of course, can simply put them down to plain bad luck or fate, but there's no denying that being a drunk is having a past that is littered with near-misses and fortunate happenings. The phrase was also a timely reminder of how precious seemingly inconsequential encounters are.

The area was riddled with side trails and here the PCT meandered adjunct to a major highway. Hiking on a Monday and closer to society than usual, I was still surprised the backcountry was so awash with people getting out for some fresh air and exercise. Ordinarily I presumed they'd be cooped up working. Closer to trailheads, I noticed how more and more groups passed by with almost everyone wearing a mask. Some would hold their breath as they jumped aside, and my not-so-cheery "good mornings" might only receive an "um-hum" in return. Others would turn their backs on me to let me go on uninterrupted.

The pandemic had isolated us all in odd ways, forcing what would previously have been deemed anti-social behaviour to become an acceptable norm. The outside world would only have a vague notion that the pandemic must surely end but no one knew yet when. I read that infection rates in Europe were surging once again, defeating the hitherto optimistic hope that the warmer weather would have killed off the virus by the end of summer. There was a sense of people getting fed up with a partial existence, the novelty of lockdowns and limitations wearing off. There was only so much baking one could do before the effects of cake took hold. I was now well into the second half of August and I remained steadfastly focused on my goal. For the first time, I dared to believe that I might make it to Canada, and I had begun to enjoy myself again. Knowing when something ends can make anything much more bearable.

The change of view helped too as I penetrated deeper into Washington. Inclines and declines were once again becoming more of the focus than miles and time. Ascending the mountains of this state, the trail dragged me above the tree-line, treating my eyes to sprawling mountain ranges, like rippled waves of green oceans. I pondered whether any of those in the backdrop belonged to Canada. Around me, three snow-capped volcanoes stood to attention, stoic and proud. Mount Rainier, the highest point of the Cascades, is the iconic feature of Washington: an active volcano enveloped in stark white glaciers. Despite the tumultuous terrain, I'd somehow increased my average speed. One morning I'd completed eight miles in three hours, it was only the insatiable demands of my stomach that had me pressing pause. I'd rolled my sleeves up, quite literally, and left myself with sunburnt and mosquito-bitten lumpy arms as I blasted my way along.

The following day, there remained nineteen miles between me and White's Pass with its small gas station laying a half mile down the main highway. It was rumoured to make one of the best pizzas on the PCT, wide-rimmed, home-made and piping hot from a dedicated pizza oven. I'd have to get there by six o'clock in the evening. This struck me as perfectly doable, even though I needed to navigate the Knife's Edge. It was, as expected, a pretty straightforward, except for the dodgy bits, walk along the slender ridge of a mountain. In parts some of the very gravelly path had eroded: one bad foot placement would see me glissade painfully down the scree of the mountain wall. Further along there were still long strips of snow where one slip could plunge me hundreds of feet into a barely thawed lake. The height of it offered the most spectacular but distracting views. It was a wonder I made it across at all given my propensity to trip over invisible objects.

By half past ten, I'd cleared the ridge and began to barrel down the mountain towards the pass. I still had a full fourteen miles to go, plus the half-mile road walk on top of it. Between me and it, there was a small hill of one thousand feet to conquer too. I was only a few miles out from the highway when I was heralded by three mask wearers with a muffled "PI?" These were Jeff's friends I gleaned. These people, who I wouldn't recognise in a police line-out, certainly knew a lot about me. They also wondered if I knew where he was. I was astonished he had still not overtaken me and guessed from his last text he was trailing by several miles. They informed me they were my trail angels and would be providing my supplies too! It's hard to extricate oneself from the kindness of strangers, but the pull of hot pizza did the trick. I lumbered off and raced towards the service station for five o'clock. My mind was thrilled by how much time and distance I had managed to cover, although my legs reminded me as they shook with adrenaline and over-exertion.

Alas, the pizza oven was already cooled and cleaned down. To my right, the last order of the day sat in its box awaiting collection. I could smell the oozing cheese and I guessed pepperoni. The attendant offered to microwave a ready meal or oven-bake a frozen pizza from their freezer if I wanted one. I did my best to graciously accept, and I hoped I had masked my own crushing disappointment: another benefit of the face-coverings. I resupplied for the next stint, it was a pretty well-stocked shop, and I drowned down as much bitter coffee as I could in one hour. Then I went off to pitch my tent in the stony car park. Another thru-hiker, Bird, who I'd not previously met, had already set up base there, and I was reassured by the presence of a companion for the night. It was a popular gas station, and I doubted I would have slept a wink had I been on my own.

A few hours later, Jeff arrived, his face was a battered bloody mess. "Those damned rocks, they jumped up and got me," he said by way of explanation. He was lucky to still have all his teeth. He said he'd done the 'math', I resisted correcting him, and claimed we could finish at the latest by the seventh of September. I told him I felt the tenth would be preferable. He was ready to be done with it, whereas I wanted the task to fully expand to fit the time. I didn't see the point in flogging myself so hard to get to the end, only to sit in a hotel for a week before flying out to face a world I was not yet ready to rejoin. Perhaps, we wouldn't be hiking the rest of Washington after all. It was a conversation for another time as his friends whisked him off to I know not where.

I made full use of one of the picnic tables and chatted with Bird, mired in his own need for absolution. I read the web, posted pictures on my blog on the slow but free service. It all kept me up much later than usual. At midnight a helicopter floated close to the ground directly above me, and I feared my tent, with me in it, would be sucked up by its backdraft. In the wee hours, a couple had a row next to the gas pumps. Cars and trucks flew by and in between the surges in traffic, I listened to my fellow PCT hiker snore relentlessly. I didn't dare put my ear plugs in so close to town, like I would have if I was embedded in the forest. At first light, I packed up, and when Bird woke himself, he announced he hadn't slept a wink all night, but much to my amazement, he'd heard me snoring.

I plodded back along the highway and Jeff caught up with me late-morning. We walked much of the afternoon together and explored once again the differences between our two countries. All too often, I'd have to describe what I'd thought was shared vocabulary or because our pronunciations differed. I refused outright to say 'rout' instead of route though. Over lunch, we agreed on a twenty-two-mile day, so I was surprised when at twenty miles he called it time. We crammed our two tents into a spot that ordinarily would only take one.

The weather was ever damp and threatening, but the site scored points for being close to water. I was showered with condensation when I rose in the middle of night, forgetting that I couldn't actually get out of my tent without giving Jeff, snoring mildly in his tent, a good kicking. There was nothing for it but to perfect the art of peeing in a Ziploc without peeing myself. Practice finally paid off.

There was a banality to walking mile after mile exploring the Cascades, dipping down into lake-filled valleys, then rising up once again to peer over a mass of conifer clinging tightly to the valley walls, with small holes of vivid green meadows standing out like worn patches of an old carpet. The area was tear-inducingly beautiful, but I was now so over-exposed to it, I could become far more excited by the idea of a pit latrine in a car-park.

Jeff mentioned that two of his friends might be residing at a nearby trailhead in their campervan, and I looked forward to using a convenience. We stood on an overpass at around ten in the morning. Without mobile phone reception, we couldn't inform his pals of our presence. It looked like another round of disappointment was in store. Then we spotted a tall man sauntering along perfectly normally, without a trace of a hobble, on the ragged edge of the highway towards the bridge. They were there, waiting with a ton of fruit and hummus, avocado, bagels and hot American coffee. They were vegan themselves, and apologetic for the synthetic milk they supplied. It was lush. We stayed around an hour and took advantage of their clean water supplies before heading out once again. I doubted they'd ever seen anyone hoover up melon quite like I did that day. Not only is it my favourite fruit, but after so long without the zing and crunch of raw nature, each cube was its own cascade of unadulterated joy.

Although we'd already overcome one big climb, the second of the day was aptly called Sourdough Pass. It was a breeze with the sustenance of caffeine and vitamins. Another lunch was had sitting on some rocks on the side of a cliff just off trail, soaking up the gorge deep below. From there, we mooched back into another burn zone, then sometimes forest, and sometimes craggy rock. Mostly, though the trail was sandy underfoot, giving a drag to each step. That extra meal, despite the time spent stopping, propelled us to the twenty-third mile of the day.

Packs dumped, we explored various sites. A bare path at a trail junction was littered with scrunched up toilet paper, but all around us the forest remained tightly bound. Jeff thought we could cram ourselves into a small swatch of ground about a quarter of a mile back from the junction. Packless, we bandied along a side trail into a large clearing to determine if better spots could be found. We perused the site of an ancient plane crash. It was nothing more than a single-engined mangled frame with its large propeller still attached at the nose. Likely a civilian plane, there was nothing left of the fuselage, although a few scraps of thin metal could be spotted scattered about the nearby woodland. What happened to the plane and its occupant remains a mystery. My expectations were it would at least be recognisably aviatory, so I hobbled dejected back to the gnarly strip for the night.

We set an ambitious target of twenty-four miles for the following day. The weather carved it up into three sections for us. It had started dry for the first eight miles, whereupon I landed upon a gorgeous winter cabin topping the head of a long meadow. I treated myself to a hot coffee and sat on the porch inhaling two pieces of lemon drizzle cake and a snickers bar, soaking up the sunshine and the charming peace of the summertime meadow. Two chickadees frolicked on the metal steps centimetres away from my toes, hoping for a few dropped titbits. I'd not seen such birds before, and they reminded me of hyper-active but half-sized train station pigeons.

I went on my merry way, and soon after the fog swirled in, making the mossy woodland eerie and confined. I interrupted Jeff having lunch. I'd just had mine not even fifty metres away from him. He caught up with me shortly after and we pootled along together for quite some time, despite him commencing the conversation with, "Even as slow as you are..." I feigned umbrage for the rest of the day, between our mutual giggles at his faux pas, but a melodramatic flouncing wasn't actually possible in any case. We separated after a few hours when I stopped for a toilet break which he called a 'restroom' break. There's no rest when one has to dig through a ton of rootbound ground in a hurry.

Eight miles later, the fog was dampened down by pelting rain. Late afternoon, I approached Jeff, huddled up inside an oversized anorak on a large log, a shivering denizen of the forest. "I wanted to know what you thought about stopping here," his teeth chattered. Yet again, there was one muddy spot we could cram into. I said, "Go for it!" Lost in translation, he looked utterly crestfallen, as if I'd ordered him to yomp on to our previously-agreed destination. We'd done twenty miles and that was plenty given the conditions. We raced to erect our tents and get ourselves into drier clothing. When it comes to getting comfortable, I beat him hands down.

Jeff confessed he was learning tricks from me. He'd noted that I had the most efficient way of setting up for the night. The knack, I had learnt, was to throw one's entire rucksack inside one's tent first, get dinner on the boil, then leave it to rehydrate. Only after cooking has begun, does one need to sort out one's belongings. He agreed a watched pot is a torturous way of preparing supper, a term thankfully we didn't need to debate. Until he met me, who is, by very nature, incredibly efficient (for which one should read lazy) he was stuck in the routine of unpacking each item, and flinging it into his tent bit by bit, after which he'd have to shunt stuff around so he himself could clamber in. He'd only be able to start on the proceedings that is the last meal of the day once he'd finally got himself organised in his tent.

He also discovered the benefit of having a hot meal each night was greatly enhanced if one boiled enough water for a hot drink too. Prior to this, he'd been very miserly about using his gas, almost to the point of obsession, permitting himself to only briefly warm up already cold-soaked meals. Now he was willing to boil water first, pouring some off into a cup. He'd then use the rest to properly heat his dinner. Jeff called his hot drink 'tea,' but I corrected him on that. Brightly-coloured water is simply not tea, whether or not one pronounces herbs, with or without an 'h'. Another routine we'd quickly established was enquiring of one another's meal plans. On this particular night, I had opted for ramen noodles because of their salty simplicity, followed by ten Oreos for 'pudding'. This utterly baffled Jeff given they are a biscuit and not a custard-based dessert.

Once everything was imbibed, we'd set about agreeing the next day's agenda. Then I'd type and he'd do a crossword in the fading light. Sometimes he'd ask for my input, but I more often than not was hopeless. I blamed it on the fact we are two countries separated by a common language. Jeff observed that daybreak was taking longer and longer to arrive, and suggested we start hiking a half hour later than usual. It was pointless starting in the dark wearing a headlamp for thirty minutes, draining scarce battery power, he concluded. I saw nothing to debate. I slept, for the first time since the Sierra, in my puffy trousers and jacket, and had the most congenial night for months. Until then, I hadn't appreciated how much being skin and bone makes air mattresses so much more unpleasant. The added padding had me doubly glad of the extra time to lie in, feeling all snug and warm, and safe and sound.

****

Chapter twelve

Sometimes quickly, mostly slowly

The mountains were vivid, imposing granite structures stretching skywards, though for much of the morning I was oblivious as I waded through deep woodland getting thoroughly drenched. The spray off the plants made sure no part of me escaped saturation. By mid-morning the day had cleared, the damp ebbed away, leaving a delicious petrichor. Above the treetops the sunshine splayed across the wilderness.

I disrupted several ptarmigans, or partridges as I thought they were. They waddled around the undergrowth, some with tiny baby chicks scooting back and forth. They would lurch out of the shrubs, squawking their offence at my presence. One mother noisily flapped an energetic jive, screeching out her dance at my feet. She hoped to give time for her three little babies to scamper safely into the thicket. Of course, the chicks sort of raced around being chick-like. If I was in the market for lunch, it wouldn't be her offspring I'd be interested in.

The trees were now knobbly with mushrooms, some the size of frisbees. Elsewhere bright red, white and brown fungi poked up from rare patches of dark soil. Whether they were edible I knew not. I wasn't willing to risk a hallucinogenic experience nor anything worse. Around me plants fought for tiny specks of light beneath the treetops.

I glimpsed berries galore. Thimbleberries are a sort of raspberry, slightly juicier but less tart, but they definitely justified a pause. Rarer still were the salmonberries, yellow-looking raspberries, and much more delicious. Then there was the tiny ground dwelling wild strawberry, also well worth a rummage for. Oregon grapes, easily mistaken for blueberries, had a hard little stone inside them, and certainly didn't quite compete with the exquisite, and abundant huckleberry. The best of those were found on exposed hillsides, where the bold sunlight enhanced their sweetness.

We'd meet pickers, groups of up to twenty people, from Thailand and Cambodia, who were cheerful and inquisitive. One woman told us they would get around seven or eight dollars a pound, but it would take hours to get such a small amount, and they were concerned about the other pickers securing better sites. Jeff thought it unlikely all would have permission to live in the States, but their harvest would sell for a premium in the shops. Theirs was undoubtedly a hard graft, by the time we'd set up camp that night, they'd be on their way back to who knows where, no doubt just as tired but with a few buckets of berries for their efforts.

At other times, coming into contact with others was less welcomed. Space was at a premium at Mirror Lake, a favoured campground. It was so mobbed by visitors, it forced Jeff and I to stagger on far further than we'd anticipated. I'd convert it manually to gratitude later when I added the extra miles to my daily tally. Masses of weekenders poured in long after dark, heightening my senses.

In the morning, Jeff rushed off, leaving me to amble down to Snoqualmie Pass alone. I remained none the wiser as to why my legs jarred, and the miles lengthened on such days. It would be my last proper night in a hotel until the end of my trek. Snoqualmie was more of an out-of-season ski resort rather than a thriving town. The multitude of chalets and swiss-style holiday homes were constructed in an orderly fashion around the town's grid. I crept through a vacant garden to the town's only motel, not arriving until well after eleven o'clock. I bumped into Laura at check-in, she was negotiating an extension for her room for a few hours. Jeff was showered but insufficiently organised to get going again. Outside his two male friends, who were to accompany him for the next few days, waited with clean packs and even cleaner clothes. They were brimming with enthusiasm for the trek ahead. All three opted to dress head to toe in beige. The three beige men. Only the shape of their hats distinguished them.

I intended to spend a single night in the hotel, making use of the local convenience store for the next two stints, so it would be my turn to do the hunting. Jeff had reasoned that without 'trail legs' they'd be unlikely to manage more than fifteen miles a day. He fervently hoped they'd do more. As I rang my cat carer to see how my little boy was, the waiter informed me that my breakfast was paid for but by whom he would not reveal. I ordered a second breakfast as soon as I finished the call - my cat was adorable and cute, she'd told me, which could only mean he was plotting something. Shortly after, fat pancakes topped with strawberries, cream and maple syrup arrived and I scoffed the bloody lot in less time it took to make. Within an hour, I was ravenous again.

Briefly I saw HeadGirl from Warner Springs, the young German woman that had once hiked with the Beetroot, Dr. Doolittle and Photo. She was now with someone I didn't know. It was nice to connect. Inexplicably, until this moment I had concluded I was doing this all so languidly. Jeff would introduce me to everyone 'This is PI, and it's her one hundred and fifty-eighth day on trail,' and inwardly I would wince even though it wasn't intended as a put down. Meeting HeadGirl finally convinced me that I really wasn't that tortoise-like after all, my perception of myself is what was wonky. Jeff had just passed his one hundred and thirtieth day. His friends called him, "Non-Stop," and I cruelly jested that was because he non-stop farted, a result of not strictly adhering to a celiac diet as he ordinarily would. The three beige men ambled off just as I began demolishing lunch. Not able to check in until three I shopped and gave my excess to Laura to take to Steven's Pass. I handed her the rest of my shopping list which was sufficient to get me to Canada from there. She refused to take even a dime for it.

Once in my room, I sorted through my belongings and donated my toenail clippers, my waterproof socks, my small pot of Vaseline and my antiseptic ointment to the hiker box. Fractions of ounces, I doubted they weighed even a quarter of a pound altogether, but they seemed surplus to requirements now. I collected my new shoes from reception, identical I thought to the ones I'd just discarded, not daring to risk changing anything on this last, but crucial section. I was still two-hundred and sixty miles from the border, and we still had to walk back another thirty miles once we'd tagged it. I'd be absolutely fine with breaking an ankle in the 'non-section' and being helicoptered out, but not a metre before. In fact, I felt breaking an ankle in the bonus thirty miles was quite the inspiring idea.

The task for the next four days though, was to cover seventy-one miles, arriving at precisely twelve o'clock and not a minute later, at the closed Ski Resort at Steven's Pass. Before he left, amiable Jeff had mentioned my expected time of arrival so frequently, I warned him I would rename him 'Drill Sergeant' if he said it one more time. It seemed perfectly reasonable on paper. I forgot that only maps are made of paper, not trails. The first day I managed a paltry fourteen miles, four short of what I'd intended. In part, in fact I lie, in whole, this was because just as I was about to check out, I'd noticed my laptop was nearly out of power. Not only was it my diary, but its battery was my reserve power bank for my phone. Given it was now to keep me cogent for up to three weeks, there was nothing for it but to sit and will it back to full health in record time. It took over an hour. Watching a pot coming to a boil would have been far more fascinating.

Those fourteen miles were nothing but punishingly brutal large stones and climbs. I read that to form this part of the PCT, engineers had blasted dynamite into the mountainside to create the tight walkway, known locally as *The Catwalk*. I certainly didn't saunter up and down it but rather despaired at the chunks of rubble tipping my feet this way and that, tottering about like a child wearing their mother's high heels for the first time. When I was not concentrating on my newly-shod feet, I would battle to force oxygen into my depleted lungs. For sanity, I'd estimate how many footsteps it would take to get from tree to tree, or from the start of one rock field to the next, then concentrate on the counting. I'd often lose count of the counts, which only added to the complication. My pep talk whenever I was finding the going less 'walk in the woods' and more 'torments of the trail' was to say to myself 'At least it's not a Hauser Creek day.' It was in reference to that first trifling but hellish, eight-hundred-foot ascent that taught me that this would be a journey of altitude and attitude, and that overweight and overburdened, I had made more than one mistake of epic proportions. It would initially have me devising ways of crawling back home, changing my name and starting again in a whole new county.

Despite my physical misery, this area was the undisputed jewel of Washington as we skirted through the Alpine Lakes Wilderness. It is rugged but magical. Fat chunky marmots, these much greyer and whiter than I'd previously admired, squealed all over the place. Best I could, I kept an eye out for white, shaggy mountain goats but saw nothing except deer munching away, utterly unperturbed by this sweating, cursing, panting and rather knackered Englishwoman. I sounded no less fit than when I started nearly five months prior, but I had clearly transformed because a man suddenly blocked my way and said, "You're a thru-hiker and I know you, but I don't recognise you." I told him I was PI. I couldn't believe I was talking to someone I had met from the very first stint, although I had absolutely no memory of the man at all. He'd injured his ankle not long after I'd camped with him at Hauser Creek. It had taken all summer to repair, so he was hiking Washington heading south to finish the rest of the PCT another time. He recorded every thru-hiker he'd met since the Northern Monument. I was number thirty-three. Jeff was number thirty-two and he was, the man thought, about ten miles ahead. That came as welcome news.

I pushed hard the next day, traversing rickety bridges and hopping across shallow waterfalls and streams. I camped with a fellow Brit, who was now a Texan, and we talked all things Essex, a county I know little about, making it a potential for my next geographical should I ever need one again. An oncoming hiker had mentioned Jeff had most likely aimed for a site at Deep Lake, which would place him just six miles ahead of me. This was the stuff of motivation. We'd previously agreed that he'd leave an arrangement of sticks or stones, or scorch into the ground, a 'P' and an 'I' at a spot close to where they'd overnighted to help me understand the gap, but I saw no clues when I passed by.

Overhead a fighter jet screamed across the sky, the sound roaring around one valley, as the machine thrust through another. I gasped my way up yet another mountain, then another and another. In twelve and a half hours of scrabbling up and down, I had still only managed twenty-one miles. Enquiring from people heading toward me, I re-guessed that genial Jeff was eight miles ahead, so his friends were clearly keeping up with his ambitions. It was either that or this usually mild-mannered man had truly morphed into a drill sergeant, screaming at them, "There's no such thing as pain!" as he barracked his comrades up yet another hill.

There is no pleasure in playing catch up and I wearied of racing. I counted out fourteen miles before the clock struck twelve on the last full day before Steven's Pass. This pleased me. Very little did that morning. My feet by now were indescribably painful, particularly the right one. I knew it to be nerve-damage more than anything else, although my right bunion was rubbing too and occasionally the left one joined in sympathetically. My left ankle twinged as if I'd over-extended somewhere. My toes had atrophied completely. I screamed silently for the next few hours and sniffled when others were not around.

Late in the afternoon, I met an oncomer who gave me the bad news: they were covering the exact same distances as I: twenty-one miles a day, and they estimated they'd be arriving at Steven's Pass a full two hours ahead of schedule. I, on the other hand, would be two hours late if I rose and got going at daybreak. I had no way of letting Jeff know, neither by using the trail telegraph of sending messages via faster hikers nor by text, so it was all I could do to get up, yet again, at four in the morning to compensate.

****

Carrier pigeons

The day's podcast was one of those 'fire and brimstone' types - using fear and anger to warn us to get into step with the AA programme 'or else'. It was a bit too full on for my liking. There was a lot of 'you' and 'have to' to the rhetoric, and strictly enforced 'dos' and 'don'ts'. I had not yet marked five years of continuous recovery, the line one crosses to join the winning 'fifteen percenters'. That's the proportion of alcoholics predicted to make it that far. That number is not recovering alcoholics in AA, that's alcoholics who had to use rehab to get detoxed. It had initially astonished me to learn that only fifteen percent of treatment centre attendees go on to make five years of sobriety, with or without on-going programmes of support. This chimes with AA's own stats that around fifteen percent of regular attendees are over ten years sober.

The speaker gave a lot of justification around being 'recovered' rather than 'recovering' which grinds my gears. "Whatever keeps them sober," a good friend of mine will frequently interject, when I start opining on how I think AA should be done. Like the day's speaker, I'm quick to have an opinion, but considerably slower about doing my own recovery work. Nonetheless, it gave me something to bristle over as I ploughed on with the task of trying not to be late for Jeff and his friends.

I had never really thought about why I was so punctual. I have a real thing about being on time and sticking to my commitments. At the end of my drinking career, I was starting to not turn up when I said I would but these days anyone could set their watch by me, I truly loathe tardiness. I wondered whether it was a boarding school syndrome thing as a shrink might say. My first one was like a kennel for Pavlov's dogs - there was a bell for everything. Wake up bell, go to breakfast bell, line up for school bell, bells to signal the beginning and end of each lesson, bells for dinner, for supper and a bell to usher us into bed. A sort of mechanised existence, I really did start salivating at the striking of meal-time bells.

My sponsor is also a graduate of the boarding school system and he's quite chilled about time. He's not one of those likely to slam the phone down if I'm a minute late calling. I'd only discovered that was a thing by listening to podcasts. Granted alcoholics are reliably unreliable, and in that respect, my obsession with time-keeping is an anomaly. The fact that I can warp that unusual characteristic into proving I'm not a drunk, proves I still have a drunk's way of thinking, or 'Alco-logic' as some would say.

The second boarding school saw us dispersed all over its huge grounds, rendering bells pointless. To accommodate us all we had staggered dining room times that changed each term. We used watches and clocks like normal people, and got a thorough verbal bollocking for transgressions, or the occasional 'time-out' in the form of detention or litter picking. I think I preferred the latter approach.

Alarmingly, the speaker had joked about having a new pigeon. I thought I'd misheard at first because it's not a phrase I'd ever encountered before. Yet, it was clearly fashionable at some point to talk about pigeons because seemingly the entire audience knew what he was referring to. In my jaunt across America, I'd listened to hundreds of hours of digitised AA speaker tapes, and this was the first time anyone had talked about pigeons. It occurred to me, as I filtered water at a little brook, that I had never seen nor heard a single pigeon on this entire trip. I thought these 'flying rats' as they are sometimes derogatorily called, were ubiquitous world-wide. It transpires, just like people, they prefer to live in towns and cities with readily accessed take-aways and other conveniences. Who knew?

However, this speaker wasn't talking about birds, but in reference to having a new sponsee and showing them how to work the steps. In this man's philosophy it seemed more about micro-managing another person's life, and he threatened all sorts of sanctions if he didn't comply. The phrase 'pigeon' reminded me of

272

the old fagging system in boarding schools, a younger pupil at the mercy of the elder's beckoning. I hear the practice is obsolete now - and not a moment before time. The second boarding school was rampant with systemic bullying, particularly for the boys. My volatile personality kept others wary of me, like all character defects, they do have their uses, but being in recovery reminds me that these occasions are few and far between. I'm glad the phrase 'pigeon' is not an acceptable term within the circles of the recovery groups I favour.

The twelfth step is about how we carry the message to the still suffering alcoholic. It hadn't occurred to me before that the alcoholic isn't necessarily drinking, they may be dry and suffering - living toxic, co-dependent, anxiety-festered existences with few notions of contentment or joy. The man's oratory was worth listening to just for that insightful observation, although he himself was particularly offended by the advice, "Take what you need from AA and leave the rest."

By the time I had finished the podcast, I had less than two hundred miles of the PCT to walk and another twelve miles to go until I rejoined Jeff. I put on another podcast, selecting one that was more history-based, and educational. I figured I might be faster if I spent less energy arguing with invisible AA speakers, some of whom are probably long since dead. I'd spent much of my first few years of recovery believing that I wasn't doing AA properly. This was in part because some people talk very emphatically about how they think 'you' should do recovery, but also because I was afflicted with a terrible sense of imposter syndrome. The two clash horribly, and I react appallingly. I have several quotes from the *Big Book* bounce around my head and one I like to trot out to our more bombastic members is, "we realize we only know a little." It comes from the concluding paragraph of the chapter '*A Vision for You*'. As I wandered along, with my belongings strapped to my back, my fingernails thick with dirt, the stench of my body odour lingering long after I'd left the vicinity, I finally accepted I was living a life beyond my wildest dreams, just as promised. Still, it amazes me that a book that was published in 1939, when Bill was also in his fifth year of recovery, and Bob in his fourth, continues to sell at a rate of one million copies per year. AA has now sold over forty million books. It remains the most misogynistic, God-bothering and

273

antiquated book I have ever had the misfortune of reading, but it is also the one that has had the most profound impact on my life.

I smile when I hear those with twenty years plus of sobriety say, "I've been sober a few days." I'm more confident about the things I've done well, and the mistakes I've made and I'm happy to talk about both of them. I still have no idea how it all works though. I've changed my views on God over time and now think the God part is essential, however, one wishes to interpret those words. Whatever I am doing is working and that succinctly is, "Go to meetings, work a programme, and do it one day at a time." I've no other way of knowing how to do it because I have simply never tried any other way of getting sober. I didn't do rehab. I haven't tried going to a doctor. I have no wish to go and try 'controlled drinking', counting pebbles from one pocket to another to limit my intake; nor do I wish to keep a drinking diary to shame me into drinking responsibly. I have never been able to control my drinking, and I have never wanted to. I have never given up drinking, I just don't drink today. If I want to drink, I'll drink the day after tomorrow, because tomorrow I've got responsibilities and plans to tend to. But I keep with AA because it's about self-development for me now. It filled a gap within me. It's an effective antidote to my self-doubt, which so often manifests as arrogance, and gives me a guide for living and being. I don't do it perfectly. I am not a saint.

I confess I have read a ton of self-help books over the years trying to work me out, or work others out. They have typically a two-stage approach to describing the problem, and then outlining how it can be fixed. I suspect I'm not the only one who particularly enjoys the first half of the book, the bits where they explain why and how one has ended up an emotional basket-case, only to lose interest in the second-half, the bit where it shows me what to do about it. I might try a few of the ideas for a few weeks, and then abandon them altogether. And yet, here I am still sober with no ambitions to drink.

I had moments when I was hiking away, and I felt so utterly alive and privileged to be out there, I could not begin to convey this sensation to another human being. A recovery addict would define it as being rocketed into the fourth dimension - a place where the mental, physical and spiritual states within a person harmonise. If my feet hadn't hurt so much, this would probably have happened more frequently.

So, this is just a journey of putting one foot in front of the other and taking each day as it comes. Sometimes it simply became about breaking it down in minutes and metres. The only difference between recovery and thru-hiking, as I see it, is that thru-hiking involves a great deal more physical agony, and a lot less booze - but then I was lucky I didn't get liver failure or pancreatitis, I suppose. If I made it to the border, this walk across America would undeniably be the second-best thing I have ever done.

It was my phone bursting into an abundance of bleeps and bongs, which announced my impending arrival back into the conventional world. I messaged Jeff to say I was going to be two hours late, my early start had helped, but I still retained all the speed of a wounded carrier pigeon. As I dropped down into Steven's Pass, I called him for directions on where to go but his phone rang out, as did Laura's. I hit redial several times before Laura responded. Waiting for me were Jeff, Laura, Joe, Ray and Leslie, also knocking around were Jeff's daughter, her husband and his granddaughter. They had all brought coolers filled to the brim with food. They set about pulling together the tables from the deserted ski resort so we could all picnic six feet apart. There was cold pizza, fresh fruit, hot coffee, iced tea, brownies, bean salad, green salad, and pasta salad. Everything was offered and everything was inhaled. They didn't mind one bit that I was late.

I hung my tent out to dry between servings and unwrapped the shopping that Laura had brought me, before repacking them into my rucksack. All the while, Leslie watched on. "All your trail food is white carbs!" she exclaimed. "Calories. It's all about calories now. I have the rest of my life to eat good, healthy, proper food but right now I just need as much sugar and carb as I can feasibly get into me, and it must all weigh as little as possible. Besides, I have handfuls of fresh berries on tap and a wodge of cheese each day, so it's not quite all carbs. But just you wait!" I smiled at Leslie.

Leslie and her husband, Ray, had been on their way to Campo when the email dropped in from the PCTA asking everyone to postpone their thru-hike. They'd debated on what to do, and in the end opted to wait a few weeks to see where the land lay. They were hurt when the PCTA then said that anyone who hadn't departed on their start date had rendered their permits obsolete. Having delayed their start, the PCTA could cancel them. It looked cynical because the PCTA didn't have the authority to cancel them under other conditions. The PCTA had also closed the portal which prevented anyone from printing out the permission slip to walk, impeding those who still had valid start dates. This act had gone down very badly and left a sour taste in the mouths of many a wannabe thru-hiker, especially now hiking was encouraged by the PCTA for everyone else. Despite the hugely different decisions we'd made, Ray and Leslie showed no sign of envy or contempt for Jeff nor I for doing it differently.

I made a remark about not being an experienced hiker, "Well, you are now!" both Ray and Leslie chimed practically in unison at me. They'd read all the popular books on thru-hiking and watched the YouTube videos just like I had. They'd researched and researched some more. They planned and re-planned their hike. It hit me like a sledge-hammer: whilst I might not know it all, I was capable of talking about thru-hiking with a modicum of authority born out of experience.

It was with great reluctance that Jeff and I said our farewells a few hours after I arrived. Laura, Joe, Ray and Leslie would also be waiting for us at Rainy Pass, so we'd been seeing them all again soon enough. In the interim, Joe and Ray needed a good shower and some decent food. Jeff had really marched them hard, and he was as impressed as I was disappointed, they'd kept up with him!

We rejoined our narrow path, now covered in pine needles, making it wonderfully gentle underfoot. "How do you think the trail has changed you?" Jeff drawled as we set off for the next meander through the tightly packed woodland towards yet another campsite deep within the forest.

"That's a good question, Jeff." I fell quiet to contemplate it. "Leslie asked me, but I don't think the trail's changed me at all," Jeff uttered.

"Me neither, Jeff," I replied. "Me neither."

****

Same old pair of glasses

Jeff and I agreed we were going to aim for eighteen or nineteen miles a day. It was less than either of us had initially wanted, but it permitted us to stop more frequently, filtering water and snacking at dribbly springs, resting weary legs on broad fallen trees. For the most part we were back in the forest, with its plush overgrowth, living life slightly dimmed, and our clothing permanently damp. The trail was lacking love and attention, and I frequently found myself fighting off groping branches, shaking their morning dew all over me. Colossal trees blocked our path, some with trunks the thickness of a car, spread across the trail. Sometimes we could crawl under them without taking our rucksacks off, but often getting around them was an adventure traipsing down and back up the mountainside through the thicket.

We complained to one another that there was nothing new or inspiring about this state. We wondered whether it was simply overegged by biased Washingtonians, but then in all likelihood it was because we'd already seen phenomenally-oversized boulders, massive meadowlands, craggy mountains, azure lakes galore, and every kind of forest dweller one hoped to encounter, and a few we wished we hadn't. We could compare Washington to the Sierra for alpine beauty, and Oregon to Washington for forest freshness and ease of walking. The elevations of six or seven thousand feet weren't any different to what we'd marched up and down in the northern Californian desert. We both carried a feeling of being underwhelmed and over-promised. At times, I found Washington State confounding, and at other times topsy-turvy. Often there were bridges where no bridges were needed, and no bridges when wide icy streams intersected with the trail. Most cumbersome were the broken bridges, V-shaped, one had to climb onto them, tread carefully down the rotting boards to the centre, hop over the water, and scrabble up the other side, before climbing off the structure to carry on one's merry way. They were a peculiar type of palaver.

I concluded the true gem of Washington was its toilets. Here and there, little signs pointed out this unexpected feature of the wilderness. Hikers can leave their packs and poles at the entrance to a small side trail to indicate its occupied status. Within a third of a mile or so one could spy a wooden box with a lid, mounted upon another box, under which a sizable hole had been dug many feet deep. One could sit comfortably a while, study the nearby foliage, ponder the meaning of life, and lose body weight al fresco. Nowhere else on the trail had such facilities been so readily abundant.

Typically, toilets were the dubious, fly-ridden luxury of a trailhead, fully enclosed within hot tin-roofed shacks. In this section, these outdoor potties appeared every ten miles or so. No more fighting foliage to dig a cat hole before aiming then missing.

Other sources of entertainment included sneaking past separate groups of hunters crouched down in camouflage pointing rifles ahead of them. Over lunch, Jeff asked if they bothered me but given they hadn't even acknowledged my existence until I yelled a cheery, and slightly naughty, "Hello!" I didn't really rate their stealth. Apparently, they were hunting bears, which was odd because I hadn't seen any indication of any for weeks. No scat, no prints, no marks on trees. I was relieved for the bear getting the hell out of dodge. That said I fervently hoped the rifled men knew that the PCT weaved around the place each time I heard a volley of gunshot.

I passed the two thousand, five-hundred-mile mark, although there didn't seem to be any reference to it. I felt it should have blown my mind, but I was now accustomed to checking off over a hundred miles once or twice a week. Besides, I'd already come to the conclusion this hike was never going to end. I was keen to have the past behind me already. "This is the heaviest our packs will ever be again," Jeff observed one afternoon as I groaned when reconnecting it with my back. His words gave me some hosanna. Like how miles stretched on, and pains increased in agony on a town day, the same phenomena seemed to be creeping into the final days we were on trail. Even the days seemed longer despite the daylight shortening.

Shortly after, we promptly conceded we'd been utterly wrong in condemning Washington as dull and glum. The valleys suddenly became awe-inspiring, jaw-dropping, vast and stunning, leaving me much short on suitable adjectives to describe the feast before my eyes. Rivers were gentle flows, allowing luxuriant vivid moss to cuddle each rock and stone, other-worldly like a scene from a fantasy film about Hobbits. The maple trees were starting to turn a burning red, and larch trees a mustard yellow. Flecks of snow remained on the higher peaks from the previous winter, and the lakes we passed were bluer than blue, clearer than clear. Ponds nestled in faraway gorges, some iridescent green with algae. After we had been spat out of the forest, we ambled through miles and miles of meadowland still blooming away. All the while, the huge Glacier Peak loomed over us. It was one jigsaw puzzle-esque beauty after another with marmots lumbering about the place, indifferent deer chomping away, and pollen-fat bees buzzing loudly. I was particularly grateful the bees left me alone. They remain lacking in cuteness in my opinion and more to be feared than bears in my experience.

The weather was due to turn and the first of the big autumnal storms was expected to creep in at any moment. Jeff had taken to stopping and asking the few random wanderers we met for a weather update, whereas I could manage a terribly British, "Lovely day, isn't it!" It would only occur to me what I should have asked them five minutes after we'd parted ways.

I'd been warned there were no places suitable for tents four miles either side of Milk Creek. The climb up the mountain on the north side was frequently referred to as 'hell'. It was a steep series of switchbacks, muddy, with incommodious rocks unsighted beneath coarse overgrown shrubs. It was all people seemed to talk about. "This is why you never miss a leg day at the gym," one poster the year previous had quipped in the comments on Guthook. This year there were so few of us to dampen down the rapacious growth, I could only imagine death by plant entanglement. I took to asking the rare person I met how it was, and one patronisingly said, "Well, you will find it very difficult, but it was fine for me," but most agreed the vegetation was collaborating to shove walkers off the mountain. Progress was likely to be something like half a mile an hour if that. Calling it a creek was also misleading: from the notes I gleaned it was a torrid white-water river, and likely to be raging from the recent rains. Made milky from churning up the riverbed chalk, it would require extra filtering, and threatened to clog up our Sawyers. Jeff's already barely flowed now so we had taken to sharing mine. We were cautioned against trying to get to water there due to its ferocity and the difficulty getting down the steep sides to the water. On the plus, there was an intact bridge so we wouldn't be forced to ford it.

The night prior, we'd camped up at a campsite that I awarded four-stars. It had copious flat surfaces spread far and wide, logs for sitting on, a brimming river for water and best of all, an en-suite toilet. It would have five stars, but alas it lacked any substantial view. Planning the next day's adventure, we were alarmed to discover that we would have to choose between a sixteen-mile day or a twenty-four mile one, the latter including the hell of the ascent after

Milk Creek. Neither Jeff nor I were fans of night-hiking, but sixteen miles seemed pathetic. Back in 2019, there were unconfirmed rumours of a camping spot barely off trail, so we opted to risk it. The trained eye will spot tiny little flattened informal paths, like the traces of deer tracks, and if followed they can reveal refuges of clearings not marked on Guthook.

The following day we battered our way through the demoralising downhill switchbacks sapping our dwindling reserves of energy. Drenched with a combination of sweat and drizzle, Jeff had gone ahead and found the spot rumoured to be suitable for a tent or two. It was up a small hillock and had clearly been used by horses in recent times but sleeping amongst manure was far preferable to facing the two-thousand-foot horror awaiting us. I squeezed the Castle into a snarly root-bound spot then settled into my lumpy toboggan. Outside my tent, I'd blocked two large holes, possibly fox, but hopefully marmot. I prayed fervently they'd not be nimby about my presence. Overnight the rain hammered down ensuring our five-mile upward hike would be the most miserable it could possibly be.

As with all things Washington, this was one long switchback after another, zig-zagging our way up the hill, but it wasn't the leg burner I'd dreaded. Jeff and I climbed in tandem, chatting throughout: something that wouldn't ordinarily happen if it was a particularly steep hill. Within two hours of our ascent, we had sorted out the American electoral system, all the major religions and ended world poverty. Unfortunately, I failed to note exactly how in my diary so I can't be more forthcoming now.

The higher we climbed, the more the temperature dropped. My hands tingled, fingers cold or numb. My gloves were disintegrating in any case and I wondered if they'd make it to the border at all. They were my fifth pair. Unlike Jeff, I'd opted not to bother with wet weather trousers, just an anorak, following my fall at Vasquez Rocks back in the desert. We paused halfway up to put back on previously discarded layers, my lower half already wringing wet. "I'm as dry as a bone under all this," Jeff announced. "Pleased for you, Jeff. I'm really pleased for you," I half-laughed between tapping teeth. He took a snapshot of my sodden being for posterity.

It was a relief to summit as the clouds started to dissipate and weak rays bore through. We walked along the ridge and found a wide-brimmed tree to nestle under, spreading our tents to dry out on low brush. All too soon, we commenced the long, slow amble down. It had taken us five and a half hours to do the five-mile ascent, pretty nifty. I certainly wouldn't claim it to be hell. Oddly, we'd changed leadership roles: Jeff had led the way uphill although I was the faster of the two, and I led the way downhill, although I was most definitely the slug. We were both baffled when we still managed to outdo our day's expectations with a twenty-miler.

The following day's twenty-two-mile hike perplexed us still further. We'd taken to walking together for much of the day and to fill the time we began to debate mileage endlessly. I always included the thirty-mile return to Hart's Pass, whereas he didn't. We discussed themes from books we had listened to. He'd just finished one about a hermit living in the wilderness who ended up in prison and was now enamored with a novel about trees. As if going up, over, down or around them wasn't enough! To be fair, he'd hated the book to begin with, but it was growing on him. I was switching between two audiobooks: one a long drunkalogue, as most recovery books are wont to be, giving grisly details of a life on booze; and the other a biography of a hell-raising Hollywood type. Both seemed odd choices in such a place, but they reduced the tedium of crushing miles when our inane conversations petered out.

We staged a 'race'. I took a road route that ran adjacent to the PCT, and Jeff remained on the trail. I won by a mile. Well, that was not exactly true, I won by about ten minutes. When we reunited, I told Jeff I was mildly indignant to discover that campsites off the PCT were far superior to what we were giving five stars to. This one had come with two pit toilets despite being a single campsite. Even better than that, these latrines had the nicest toilet paper I'd used in the US since I arrived - including that found in sumptuous hotels. I still have no idea why Americans stock their restrooms with single-ply toilet paper. Jeff explained it was because it was lower priced, but I maintained that it was a false economy, one simply uses twice as much. The toilet paper in the pit latrine had been double-ply and quilted. Even I don't opt for that plush back home. The site itself was made even more deluxe by having two bear-proof trash bins. I gladly removed about a litre of rubbish from my backpack. I sensed Jeff's envy. Best of all, the toilets had hand sanitiser. I was able to clean my glasses properly for the first time in a week. The views in the afternoon remained largely uninspiring, but oh-so-much sharper!

****

The awakenings

"I now know why dogs rotate around and around before collapsing onto their beds," I remarked to Jeff as I watched him circle the bare earth deciding which way to put his funnel-shaped tent. It was a ritual he conducted every night and he laughed at my observation of his idiosyncrasies. His tent has one entrance point from the front. Making sure his head is higher than his feet is imperative to avoid waking up with a headache. My tent has two openings either side, giving me a bit more flexibility, and I can easily change direction inside my own tent. Still, I sniggered at his careful mutt-like contemplation each night.

"Do you have a gazillion flies between your fly sheet and your inner?" I enquired of Jeff through the tent walls as we cooked dinner. "Yeah, everywhere." The swarm was rammed up against the netting that protected me from the outside world. I wondered if the density of fly population was directly proportional to the number of days since my last shower, now numbering eleven.

Jeff and I anticipated we would be finishing on the seventh of September as he'd initially wanted, and I had previously thought was too exigent. Winter could strike at any time, a sudden snowfall could white out the mountains, making the ridges impassable. The further one wanders into September, the greater the odds of this happening, potentially thwarting the year's hiking.

That evening Jeff did a stocktake of his supplies for getting to the end. Since we'd left Steven's Pass, he'd been consuming seventy-five percent of his usual intake as he'd mismanaged his rations. This might have explained why I was able to keep up with him in recent days. I gave him my spare Mexican Rice meal for dinner, but for the first time ever, I was going into a resupply with absolutely no excess foodstuffs. I was even waking up hungry in the middle of the night and struggling to get back off to sleep. I contemplated raiding the next day's snacks but then I couldn't bear the thought of being starving on top of ravenous.

By the time we got to Rainy Pass, just shy of the two thousand, six-hundred-mile mark, we now could agree there was less than one hundred miles of walking no matter how we calculated things. After that, I'd never need to hike a day in my life again. As for sleeping in a tent, although it had become the norm, it was becoming noticeably cooler once more, and the condensation was likely to sprinkle a small shower as I sat upright first thing.. Drying it out was a chore to be done every afternoon.

We had started to prattle about 'after'. I had grand plans of owning a coffee percolator like they had in American hotel rooms so I could have it on tap all day, every day. They say alcoholics stop drinking, but they never lose the thirst. Before I hiked, I had to have a drink on the go all the time - coffee or tea. Rarely anything cold. This trip had weaned me off the stimulant for the most part, but I fantasized about it continuously. I was just grateful I no longer craved alcohol. In the future, if I wanted a coffee, I could drown myself in a vat of it once life returned to 'normal'. No more drinking from a tiny two-glug blue plastic cup. I could also cook properly once again: large meals with vegetables, smothered in real, gooey, decent yellow cheddar cheese. I'd never really been that keen on fruit, aside from melon, but now I could visualise a trolley full of tropical delights. I certainly never wanted to taste another insipid Knorr packet meal nor three-minute ramen noodle. Weeks previously, I had pledged to never eat another cereal bar for the rest of my days. Alas, all of this reality was still five very long days away, all going well.

At Rainy Pass we had yet another respite from trail food. Laura, her sister, Ray, Leslie and Joe were all there, yet again with hot coffee, ice-cream, fruit, cold pizza and tortilla chips. In the pit latrine, a trail angel had left trail magic: a bag of granola bars, clearly indicating it was for PCT hikers only. I left them for those more unfortunate than I.

Ray offered Jeff and I the only two proper chairs from his campervan. Sitting with something to cradle one's back is an understated luxury. Picnic tables were as welcomed as Washington's wooden toilet boxes for a reprieve but incomparable to leaning back to have one's entire body supported. Everyone else was left to stand around as we demolished the picnic - a rudeness, given they were all my senior by several years. Laura had brought my shopping, and a brand-new battery pack to replace the spare I'd asked her to charge. It had spontaneously broken. It absolutely wasn't her fault, but she wouldn't take a cent for the new one, which was considerably more expensive than the one it replaced.

When we departed, I left behind the heavier items I possessed. My laptop cable and my second battery pack, now nearly deplete, in Joe's vehicle. Ray, Leslie and Joe were about to head further north in Joe's car to Hart's Pass, the last intersection between the PCT and a road to civilisation. From there they would be hiking south back to their campervan, so we'd cross paths with them as we continued our quest north. When we connected, Joe would turn around to join Jeff and I, coming to the monument with us, and then he'd be our ride back to Seattle. It was all mapped out and all so very slick. I couldn't believe I'd spent all of Oregon worrying about Washington. Once again, the trail had provided, or God, or the universe or whatever; it had all been taken care of, and I just had to do the bloody hiking. Sometimes I even managed to do that without whinging, proving, if nothing else, miracles never cease.

Later that day, as we bumbled along a gravelly and very exposed ridgeline, the temperature roared back into the nineties. I was glad to spy Jeff chatting amiably to another hiker: I'd made the cardinal sin of not carrying enough water for the conditions. All that experience, all those hundreds of miles in the desert, and I was still making rookie mistakes. Jeff had excess and off-loaded a half-litre, making the day more bearable than it would otherwise have been, and so the miles dallied on. I'd also realised I'd underbought chocolate bars. I was one day, and four bars short, of a decent picnic.

That night we crashed into a campsite not noted on Guthook high up the hill. Both of us knackered, the fight to stop early was a limp one. We'd already passed a glorious spot with astonishing views over the canyon, but it would have left a twenty-two mile hike the following day. Neither of us were sure we could manage the longer stints anymore. My feet were shot to pieces and Jeff was struggling with a pinched hip. I figured fatigue was incremental and we were both labouring now. We squeezed our two tents into levelled ground and chewed the fat until long after dark, which was rare. I mentioned how much I loved it when we popped up out of the tree line to gaze at the tops of mountains with nothing but sharp ridges projecting far into the sky, their tips ferociously spiky. Some of the mountains had patches of snow clinging on to their walls, whereas others held full glaciers. "Snow fields," Jeff corrected me.

Glaciers are made of ice packed over centuries I learnt, and they crawl slowly downhill whereas a snowfield is considerably younger and fluffier, lying stock still, but no less permanent. It was great talking with someone who knew the geology of the area as, after the Sierra, I was still inclined to call it 'that white bastard stuff.' He also told me how larch trees are the only conifers which shed their needles in winter, after turning a golden yellow. They only grow amongst the bedrock, happiest above six thousand feet, and they hate competition from other trees.

"Bear activity is really high around here," Jeff mumbled, "there's even grizzlies thought to be knocking around." Before I could formulate a reply, I could hear him gently snoring. It was pitch black. With my glasses on, I could spot the stars twinkling away but they offered little by way of lighting, as I contemplated death, this time by grizzly bear mauling.

An hour or so later, we were disturbed by the searching beams of two headlights, although we were high up from the trail, I could hear the voices of two women. Jeff roused himself so I bawled 'hello?' loudly several times and in response the lamps searched far and wide, but not up.

In the morning Jeff departed first. Just metres below us in a small nook beside the trail, he disturbed two women tucked tightly in their bivouacs - tiny little shelters. Amazingly, he knew them. They were ultramarathon runners in training. One of them had pulled an injury which truncated their plans, and they were returning to Rainy Pass a day earlier than expected. They gave Jeff their excess supplies, and he in turn gave me an extra chocolate bar. I ambled off, leaving Jeff to talk the ludicrous language that is marathon running. With extra supplies he soon caught up.

By nine o'clock in the morning we ran into Joe, Ray and Leslie looking thrilled to be out camping and hiking, high on an adventure of their own. Leslie unwrapped two chocolate flapjacks she'd been sneakily carrying to delight Jeff and me. All my ability to make conversation ceased. I collapsed onto a log and decimated it in three bites. She then handed me a bag of peanut butter sweets, or candies, as she called them. I crushed through them within two minutes flat. Her jaw-dropped at my voracity. "Just you wait 'til this time next year!" I smiled at her again. "Just you wait!" Shortly after, I said my goodbyes for the last time, and we headed up a three-thousand foot, six-mile-long path up yet another jeffing mountain, now with Joe for company. Joe, by his own admission, is one of life's talkers. Jeff, in contrast, is quite an exceptional listener and question-asker. The pair of them are a comedy act and thus provided some entertainment for this otherwise bloody knackered, and half-starved, Englishwoman.

We arrived at Hart's Pass where all the campsites were already taken so we jumped in Joe's truck and went off to a nearby formal campsite off the PCT. It was stony and horrid, and bizarrely, one had to pay ten dollars for the use of it. In buying a permit, Joe was informed spots were limited to two tents. Joe wouldn't take a penny in compensation and opted to sleep in his long-wheel based vehicle. He was struggling with a painful hip and I witnessed him wincing here and there. He had planned on coming with us to the monument, but admitted he was worried he'd be a liability so he booked himself into the campsite for the next three nights and would wait there for us. He'd brought with him Quorn Burgers; I didn't even know these things had made it across the pond! And biscuits and crisps. I gorged and gorged the entire time, so that by the time the Quorn burger had been barbecued I was, for the first time in months, too full to eat it. I kept half of it for breakfast.

Karma retaliated Jeff for the bear remarks of the previous night: when each passing car interrupted his slumber, made fragile by a coffee with dinner. It had kept his mind wandering all over the shop for most of the night. I, on the other hand, slept for the both of us, conking out before the sun had fallen behind the mountains, right up until Jeff hollered at me it was time to get moving and commence the final thirty miles there, and then the bastard thirty miles back.

****

The result of these steps

I sit here on a weak Spring day and now know why women often opt to have two children, if not more. The brain is hardwired to forget exquisite pain. Over there, in a place currently banned to the UK traveller, Ray and Leslie are about to embark on what may be a six-month odyssey. Perhaps, perhaps not. Late in the day, the PCTA, and only at the behest of the US Forestry Service, began issuing thru-hiking permits for 2021. The pandemic is on-going, but we know more now than we did before. I am jealous of Ray and Leslie, and all the others embarking on this monumental act of idiocy. I miss it enormously. I'd do it again at the drop of a hat, but I still remain clueless as to why I did it in the first place.

I flew home, learning I had to go and stuff myself off into a remote cottage for two weeks' quarantine seeing no one. I picked up my car from my friend's house, paid off the hideously large MOT bill, and as is always the case for me, found myself with no working SatNav - neither in my car, nor on my phone. I then had to drive at sixty miles an hour along a motorway to a remote farm I'd never been to before. It was the most terrifying experience I had had in the last six months.

I had grandiose plans of writing at least three chapters of this book during those two weeks of confinement. What actually happened was I slept for fourteen days solid: a combination of jet lag, and physical depletion. I could barely limp from the bedroom to the adjacent bathroom. They call hikers' numbed feet 'Christmas toes'. It's now nearly Lent and one remains quite dead, but I can now massage my calves again. My feet have shrunk back down a size but remain a half-size bigger than they used to be. Alas, the rest of my body has grown back several sizes. My ankles can still gripe, especially in the mornings. I have just one scar on my leg from the log at Idyllwild. I have clean fingernails for the most part. I wear deodorant religiously.

I had to find a place to live and after some stop-starting I found the quaintest little Cotswold cottage in a tiny village in Warwickshire. I picked up my cat, who to my amazement, remembered me. That said, he probably just wanted feeding. If novels are to be believed, I'd now find a job nearly instantly in a nearby vintage bookstore and meet a man I'd go on to marry. Of course, we'd need some quirky misfortune to bring us together. In this neck of the woods, it would most likely be a murder in the *midsummer* months. Then we'd live happily ever after, cat and all. So far, the cat has rewarded me with two near-death experiences, and the average age of single men in my village is, well, there aren't any.

I went for a job interview, having applied for hundreds, if not thousands. The first thing I was asked was what I'd be doing with my children whilst I worked. I told them that Jacinta and Horace would be quite fine in the cupboard under the stairs with some dry bread and water to sustain them whilst I enjoyed the privilege of a paid job. At another job I was asked how I felt about going into people's houses - being a woman and all. He only asked because he knew Suzy Lamplugh's family's old neighbour. I am a particularly good friend of an aunt of a famous murder victim, but I stopped myself short from playing serial killer top trumps. "I've slept with grizzly bears," I told him. I didn't get the job.

I'm a life-long sufferer of anxiety, but these days, I don't really struggle with it. It wasn't just the PCT that changed that, but more from knowing that I'm also a raging alcoholic who is learning how to live life on life's terms. It was never about the drink, I learnt. I cling on to my faith, deeper than it has ever been, that in its own way, in the way it's supposed to, this will all work out just fine. When I doubt that, I can tell myself I once walked across America. It's the second-best thing I have ever done. And all because of everything you ever taught me.

I used to be terrified of the thought of not drinking. It began by just not picking up a drink one day at a time as well as doing it all one step at a time. Annoyingly, it would take six months for it to occur to me there are only twelve steps to the AA programme, and not the bazillion I'd walked. AA's twelve steps are truly an easier, softer way.

My story doesn't finish at the forty-ninth parallel, but I detoured there in this on-going quest for sobriety, sanity and serenity. My favourite section of the PCT was indeed the final thirty miles. I staggered up Rock's Pass, a small woodland devoid of rocks, and then Woody Pass, which was full of rocks but lacked a single tree. On the penultimate night thru-hiking, I pitched my tent up at four-thirty in the afternoon, something I'd not done since my first month on trail. We'd found a very sheltered spot, high up on the mountain. Somewhat predictably, I'd arrived at the wrong spot from what we'd planned. It left us with an extra eight-tenths of a mile to walk the following day to the northern terminus, and then back again, making it a twenty-three-mile return trip. Around us the marmots whistled back and forth, and a small patch of snow clung on to the mountain opposite. A small rocky landslide distracted us momentarily. Then dusk announced itself, ribbons of red and orange slowly petering out to let in a crystal-clear night. The temperature plunged but not quite

288

to zero. I slept well except when I didn't. And when I didn't, I got up and sat on a small log, gazing up to wonder at the galaxy above me.

My feet were no less excruciatingly painful than any other day as I hauled my way upright the following morning. I retrieved my hiking poles from my tent but left everything underneath the canvas to await my return. We'd only need to carry our daily food and water in our packs. I'd even leave the laptop hidden in my putrid sleeping bag, safe in the knowledge that no one expects a thru-hiker to have one.

The nicest part of the day was the 'school reunion' type meetings I had as I made my way to the border. First up was a flip-flopping, thru-hiking thirty-year-old Southbounder I'd previously given my excess coffee to. She had another three months of walking left to complete further south. Next came two men, whose names I didn't catch, but they were clearly thru-hikers: their scrawniness, the beards, the haggard faces and the thousand-mile stare gave them away. They were emotional and beaten-looking. It was early in the morning, and although they'd already had a night to process what they'd accomplished, they looked utterly shell-shocked and struggled to articulate how they felt.

Jeff and I plodded on and by mid-morning I met a Czech woman who was now returning to Hart's Pass. "I'm happy and sad," she said when I congratulated her on her achievement. "Goblin is still going," she told me. "He's very injured but I think he will do it." I stopped for a rest and a pee, when suddenly bounding down the hill came Crocs of all people, wearing yet another pair of Crocs. I congratulated him, he congratulated me before realising I was going in the same direction and it was all a little bit too previous. He too planned to return to the PCT before he could truly consider himself a PCT thru-hiker. He will start again in the Sierra going towards Campo in the summer of 2021.

Soon enough, I could finally acknowledge it was all downhill to Canada. All the usual grousing remained - my sore feet, aching back, my stodgy descending pace, plus the laborious chore of slowly filtering yet more drinking water. Then, finally, after a series of switchbacks, Jeff and I came upon a clearing. A deliberate one. The forty-ninth parallel is gouged out of the forest in a straight and very obvious line. A small walk along that, and there before me was the wooden monument, proudly standing in the centre of very bare, worn ground. I'd have climbed it, but quite frankly, I still didn't trust my feet to keep me stable.

There was already a small gathering of people. I'd imagined it would just be me and Jeff. Crocs arrived shortly after. There were no high-fives or yee-haws. No cracking of champagne. A young man came along right after and lit up a spliff and stunk the place out. It had taken him two years to finish because he'd had too much of a good time the year before. There was a rescue dog too, shy and insecure, with its new family. Another group dribbled in. Section hikers. I ate my dry, squashed cheese-filled burger buns before pulling out a few poses for the camera. My favourite was me collapsed face-down at the foot of the monument, exhausted.

"What made you decide to thru-hike?" someone asked for the final time. "Not a bloody clue," I replied. I retrieved the trail register to sign. Bird had finished two days before. I had already glimpsed him at Hart's Pass hitch-hiking. He left thoughts for his deceased son. He had killed himself earlier in the year. Dr. Doolittle and Photo were also in it, as were the Belgium father and son duo. Skyscraper too. Another couple from the UK I'd met in the first week. I didn't see French Guy's name, which saddened me. Later I learnt he had just forgotten to sign the register. There was also the gorgeous Australian hiker's name from the first day. He had acquired a trail name of "Dried Fruit", and referenced Trevor "Microsoft" Laher, whose demise he'd witnessed. Amsterdam and Scraggy were there too, each one adding something thoughtful about their hike in the year 2020 when the world went to hell in a handbag. Others, whom I didn't know, hoped their lives would be forever changed by the adventure. There were probably about thirty-five names in all, but not all had completed the entire trip. It had been a helluva year for the thru-hiker. The PCTA does not recognise us, and that's okay with me.

My name is Person Irresponsible, and I am an anonymous thru-hiker. I signed the final trail register and added: "The only philosophical insight I have gained from this experience is that I have no philosophical insight whatsoever."

I was glad it was over. I was sad it was over. But mostly, I was bloody starving and my feet jeffin' hurt.

****

Final thoughts...

You, the reader, are the light of my life. Quite literally, you buying this book helps me pay the electric bill. If you'd be so kind as to leave a review too – I'd be even more grateful.

Acknowledgements

I told the mountains all about how grateful I was for you. I can't name you because doing so would infringe on AA's tradition of anonymity - but to the women and men who helped me pack up my house, who looked after my car, my cat, and my containers. You made this adventure possible. Thank you, thank you, thank you.

Thank you to those people who sent little messages spurring me on. Words are powerful things, and I was always glad of them.

Thank you to the editors, the proof-readers, the motivational-speech makers. Writing this book has been yet another epic adventure, with more than one "Oregon" moment to counter.

Thank you to the women and men of the *Pacific Group*, amongst other AAs, who recorded podcast after podcast, publishing them for free on-line, so people like me never forget what we were like, what happened and what we are like now. Your thoughts taught me so much.

Names have been changed to protect the innocent, the guilty and those of us who hover in between, but especially I should thank Jeff and his partner, and their circle of friends - you were true angels.

Thank you to every single person who transported me from the trail to a motel and back again.

Thank you to the cache-attenders, the secretive trail magicians, the hostel-runners and to the unpaid labourers keeping the trail sustainable.

Thank you to my fellow renegade thru-hikers, I'm sorry I couldn't mention you all, but you were just great! Thank you to the ones who wrote notes on Guthook or Facebook keeping the rest of us informed. Thank you to everyone who walked or talked with me. Without you, there is no story.

Thank you Cheryl Strayed for writing the book *Wild* and Reece Witherspoon for producing the film. *What do I do now?*

Thank you Bex. I miss you terribly. I know you're proud.

Most importantly, thank you to the Higher Power working within my life, helping me stay sober one day at a time, one step at a time, one crisis at a time.

Printed in Great Britain
by Amazon

23725487R00169